Patty - a blessed
christmas!

Don da

# MODERN MORAL PROBLEMS

Monsignor William Smith

# MODERN MORAL PROBLEMS

Trustworthy Answers to Your Tough Questions

Edited by Father Donald Haggerty

IGNATIUS PRESS    SAN FRANCISCO

Nihil obstat: Monsignor J. Warren Holleran
Imprimatur: † Most Reverend George Niederauer
Apostolic Administrator
Archdioceses of San Francisco
Spetember 29, 2012

These questions and answers originally appeared in *Homiletic and Pastoral Review*. Reprinted with permission.

Cover design by John Herreid

# CONTENTS

# ABBREVIATIONS

| | |
|---|---|
| *AAS* | *Acta Apostolicae Sedis* (Acts of the Apostolic See) |
| *AOC* | NCCB, *Always Our Children* (October 1, 1997) |
| *CCC* | *Catechism of the Catholic Church* |
| CDF | Congregation for the Doctrine of the Faith |
| DS | Denzinger-Schönmetzer, eds., *Enchiridion Symbolorum* |
| *DV* | CDF, *Donum Vitae* (February 22, 1987) |
| *ERDs* | NCCB, *Ethical and Religious Directives for Catholic Health Care Services* (1971, 1994, 2001) |
| *EV* | Pope John Paul II, *Evangelium Vitae* (March 25, 1995) |
| *FC* | Pope John Paul II, *Familiaris Consortio* (November 22, 1981) |
| *GS* | Vatican Council II, *Gaudium et Spes* (1965) |
| *HPR* | *Homiletic and Pastoral Review* |
| *HV* | Pope Paul VI, *Humanae Vitae* (July 25, 1968) |
| IVF | *in vitro* fertilization |
| NCCB | National Conference of Catholic Bishops |
| *PCHP* | CDF, *On the Pastoral Care of Homosexual Persons* (October 1, 1986) |
| *ST* | *Summa Theologiae* |
| USCC | United States Catholic Conference |
| USCCB | United States Conference of Catholic Bishops |
| *VS* | Pope John Paul II, *Veritatis Splendor* (August 6, 1993) |

# INTRODUCTION

*Father Donald Haggerty*

Monsignor William B. Smith (1939–2009) was a well-known and highly regarded moral theologian in the United States during the difficult decades of theological struggle in the Church following the Second Vatican Council. Ordained for the Archdiocese of New York in 1966, he was sent after a brief stint in parish work to the Catholic University of America, where he attended graduate classes taught by Father Charles Curran. By that time, Father Curran had achieved notoriety as a zealous organizer of public dissent against Pope Paul VI's encyclical *Humanae Vitae* condemning artificial birth control. Later, after a Vatican investigation in the 1980s, Curran lost his license to teach theology at any Catholic institution. Monsignor Smith liked to mention on occasion that Father Curran was a significant influence on his own thought—precisely to counter and refute aberrant positions in moral theology. After completing his doctoral studies, Monsignor Smith began a long career of thirty-seven years teaching at New York's major seminary until his untimely death in 2009. He taught continually there until the last weeks before his final illness.

During those years, he became a founding member of the Fellowship of Catholic Scholars, which was established in the 1970s for the mutual support and collaboration of scholars faithful to the Pope and the Magisterium. He worked extensively for the pro-life movement in the United States, giving countless talks all over the country and keeping the protection of human life a first-priority moral issue. He was a consultant to the Congregation for the Doctrine of the Faith (CDF) as well as a primary advisor on moral matters to Cardinals Cooke, O'Connor, and Egan in New York. He served on ethics committees in a number of New York Catholic hospitals. He was a steady presence in a Westchester County parish on weekends, but he was also very close to Mother Teresa of Calcutta's Missionaries of Charity and to the Sisters of Life. He served as a weekly confessor and spiritual guide to the Missionaries of Charity for twenty-eight years; and at the personal request of Cardinal John O'Connor, he gave weekly conferences in moral theology to the Sisters of Life for two decades.

While never writing a book, he published numerous articles in theological journals and established himself in the 1970s and '80s as a premier voice of Catholic faithfulness in the gritty arena of moral theology. His strong suit was an uncompromising fidelity to the Magisterium and to the Catholic moral tradition. His articles show a particular ability to measure the weight of tradition against more questionable, recent approaches to morality. In areas of medical ethics, for instance, he displayed expertise and great care, consistently basing his arguments on authoritative sources. His appeal as a writer, however, went beyond the clarity of his moral arguments. He wrote with verve and wit; he was neither timid nor tentative in exposing the foolishness of error. One might surmise that his writings were motivated by a profound sense of the harm done to lives when evil choices are rationalized.

The collection contained here is a selection of questions and answers submitted to Monsignor Smith and published in the monthly *Homiletic and Pastoral Review* between October 1992 and July 2005. The variety of questions and responses spreads far and wide over the course of these years. For the most part, the selections for this collection concentrate on questions of moral matters, with occasional items of sacramental interest. In many cases, the issues and responses are examples of what has been called in the moral tradition the exercise of casuistry. The term *casuistry* refers to the study of cases involving particular moral dilemmas that require resolution. At times, such matters are without a current clear teaching in the Church. The answers of Monsignor Smith are presented with careful awareness of distinctions and possible ambiguities. They display as well his zest and vigor for a lively rejoinder. These concise responses to still relevant moral questions are accessible to any informed Catholic today; undoubtedly, they will continue to interest new generations of priests. Even knowing an answer, one may find oneself enjoying Monsignor Smith's broad range of references and his pungent prose.

The encyclical *Veritatis Splendor* was issued on August 6, 1993, less than a year after Monsignor Smith began to write his monthly contributions to *Homiletic and Pastoral Review*. It was among the most notable writings in the pontificate of Pope John Paul II. Addressing fundamental principles of moral theology and the incompatibility of some contemporary moral approaches with Catholic theology, it applied a broadside blow to the dissenting moral theology that had gained much ground in the previous twenty-five years. The collection of these questions and answers can be read now as an expression of a more confident turn in moral theology that ensued in the years following *Veritatis Splendor*. Monsignor Smith and like-minded theologians found in the encyclical a vindication for a sound Thomistic foundation in the Catholic moral tradition. Many of the responses contained here make explicit use of principles found in the encyclical. The title of the encyclical, moreover, *The Splendor of Truth*, evokes the attractive radiance that truth offers to those who seek it with honesty. One can sense throughout the answers in this collection a profound respect for truth as an ultimate value.

Monsignor Smith's honesty and love for truth was a characteristic mark of his personality. I remember as a seminarian in his classroom that we used to joke that he was unable to give his oral true-and-false quizzes properly. Anytime he read a false statement he managed to give it away with a cough or some stumbling over a syllable or word. This attachment to truth was a deeply rooted commitment in him. On the other hand, what he really disliked in the various expressions of dissent in the Church was an inherent dishonesty. In his view, dissent from authentic Catholic teaching always combined some poisonous chemistry of dissimulation and personal pride. His own approach to teaching and public talks was to represent the Church's teaching with clarity, never to minimalize it or make excuses for it, never to allow distortions of it. He was not one to posture with contrived sincerity or assume the correctness of a conviction simply because it was convenient or offered a chance for some victory in debate. As is evident in many answers here, he often turned with deference to a greater authority than his own intelligence in seeking his final resolution of a moral matter.

Sometimes we mistake being faithful with mere submission to obligations in the Church. But of course faithfulness is not simply obedience in itself, except superficially. Faithfulness is an expression of love, a fruit of personal love for God. The intellectual apostolate of Monsignor William Smith is inseparable, I believe, from his spiritual life. His convictions paralleled his sense of vocation.

My initial contact with him was to observe him offering Mass at a Missionaries of Charity chapel in the Bronx, and in a sense, my view of him never changed from that time. In the twenty-five years I knew him, he was first of all a spiritual man, a prayerful man, whose daily presence in prayer at the seminary or at Mass radiated a love for these actions, a man whose soul had long been given to God. His thought when dealing with serious matters of theological controversy followed in a very spontaneous manner from this fidelity to his Lord. He was a man of God first, and then a theologian and teacher. May the Church continue to produce priests of this quality and character.

# I

# Life and Death

# I

# The Respect for Life

*Positive Prescriptions of the Fifth Commandment*

Question: Almost always, the Fifth Commandment is stated negatively: "Thou shall not kill." It is rare to hear or to read of positive prescriptions of the same commandment. Can you recommend some references apart from generalities on the environment?

Answer: The *Catechism of the Catholic Church* (*CCC*) summarizes neatly and pertinently the positive prescriptions of the Fifth Commandment (nos. 2288–91).

First, the *Catechism* teaches that life and health are precious gifts of which we must take reasonable care, not in splendid isolation, but taking account of the needs of others and the common good. Concern for life and health requires that society help its members to attain living conditions that allow them to grow and mature: including such necessities as food and clothing, housing, and health care, as well as basic education, employment, and social assistance (no. 2288).

It is typical of the *Catechism* to consider the social dimensions and principles as fundamental to the correct understanding of the human person. This aspect of the new *Catechism* has received little attention, but it is true. Concern for the person's place in society (nos. 1877–96), his participation in social life (nos. 1897–927), and social justice (nos. 1928–48) are now part of the fundamental moral theology of the Catholic Church. This concern now informs all specific moral teaching, including that on the Fifth Commandment.

To return to your question, the balanced treatment of the *Catechism* speaks for itself. Positive respect for the life of the body does not make it an absolute. The Church rejects the neopagan promotion of the "cult of the body", in which everything is sacrificed for the body's sake, physical performance and appearance are idolized, and the strong are preferred over the weak (no. 2289).

The *Catechism* exalts the virtue of temperance as that which helps us "to avoid every kind of excess" (no. 2290), such as the abuse of food, alcohol, tobacco, or drugs. We are neither Muslims nor Manicheans. The Church does not condemn the use of alcohol, but she properly condemns its abuse; very little adult experience is needed to appreciate the immense human damage that flows from resisting this truth.

Driving while intoxicated is given as an example of intemperate behavior that places oneself and others in harm's way (no. 2290). When the *Catechism* was first published, some secular journalists zeroed in on the condemnation of drunk driving and even poked fun at what they described as a "new" sin. But what the *Catechism* teaches is true, and as any pastor or parent can tell you, about half the family and pastoral grief in this country is caused by alcohol abuse.

The *Catechism* also condemns the production, sale, and use of non-therapeutic drugs as a direct cooperation in evil, because these encourage and facilitate behavior gravely opposing the moral law (no. 2291).

—February 1995

## The Seamless Garment and Formal Church Teaching

Question: Is the "seamless garment" or "consistent ethic of life" the formal, authoritative teaching of the Catholic Church?

Answer: I find the question difficult to answer in that precise form. I say that not to duck the question but to answer it as best I can because I don't think the terms *seamless garment* and *consistent ethic* are exactly the same.

If you can bear the distinction, I find it more helpful to distinguish matters of certain moral principle from chosen frameworks that reflect more pragmatic or policy (how-to) judgments that embrace principles of different kinds and degrees of certitude.

Some twenty years ago, it became common in some circles to propose a so-called seamless-garment approach, meaning that the fabric or garment of life was a seamless one and that committed Catholics should oppose killing of every kind. This is transparently true when it comes to the killing of a moral innocent, e.g., direct abortion, direct infanticide, and direct euthanasia.

What was neither transparent nor morally true to many was whether killing in a just war, by capital punishment, or in self-defense belonged under the same garment or blanket condemnation. If the motive, especially vis-à-vis capital punishment, was the hope, that by opposing capital punishment, pro-life Catholics would win over more citizens and advocates to oppose abortion and euthanasia, the motive was understandable, but the moral principle was muddled. That is, the direct killing of the innocent is not the same as the direct execution of the presumably non-innocent. For me, it is simply a mistake to link the two as moral equivalents for the straightforward reason that they are not morally the same.

By this, I do not mean to say that there are not reasons to oppose capital punishment or its necessity. Indeed, there are reasons, powerful reasons, to oppose capital punishment or its necessity—but the direct killing of the innocent is not one of them because that is not a morally accurate description of what capital punishment is.

To my knowledge, no formal Vatican teaching document nor any formal teaching document by the bishops of the United States has ever employed the term *seamless garment*. Indeed, the promise some saw in the seamless-garment approach does not seem too promising today. If the hope then was that by opposing capital punishment pro-lifers would gain more friends and advocates to oppose abortion and euthanasia, Europe seems to be going in the opposite direction.

Every member state of the European Union forbids capital punishment. In fact, no candidate state can be admitted to that union unless it forbids capital punishment. However, first Holland and now Belgium have legalized euthanasia. To legalize the killing of the innocent while forbidding the killing of the guilty does not strike me as consistent or pro-life. It looks like a garment unraveling.

In our country, at least two states (California and New Jersey) have legalized "therapeutic cloning" while banning what they call "reproductive cloning". The former initiates human life only to destroy it and harvest the embryonic stem cells for what some hope might benefit others. I have no way of knowing whether cloning advocates are opposed to capital punishment, but my hunch is that they oppose it strongly. Yet, they see no inconsistency in initiating embryonic life with the sole purpose of destroying it. No doubt, they see this destruction done for a good purpose, but the little ones destroyed are never asked for their consent in their own destruction.

As above, linkages that do not rest on shared moral principles are often neither consistent nor persuasive. On the other hand, approaches or frameworks to address multiple issues need not, to my mind, be inconsistent. Many statements, formal and informal, of the United States Conference of Catholic Bishops (USCCB) have been presented in the framework of what they call a "consistent ethic of life" approach.

One of the most comprehensive and concrete statements of the U.S. bishops is *Living the Gospel of Life* (1998). Quite correctly, it states that "abortion and euthanasia have become preeminent threats to human dignity because they directly attack life itself, the most fundamental human good and the condition for all others" (no. 5).

Referring to their own prior 1995 statement *Political Responsibility*, they demonstrate a consistent ethic of life, explaining that the Catholic Church sees in a broad spectrum of issues the need to protect human life and human dignity from inception to natural death. But appealing to Catholic lawmakers, they add that "being 'right' in such matters can never excuse a wrong choice regarding direct attacks on innocent human life" (no. 23).

Every four years for the last twenty-eight years, the bishops have issued *Forming Consciences for Faithful Citizenship*. Here too, the stated moral framework is that of a consistent ethic of life, in which the preeminent threats to human life (abortion and euthanasia), "because they directly attack life itself", are distinguished from some others that can threaten or relate negatively to life, dignity, or justice.

Some people read these quadrennial statements as "seamless garment" statements, which I do not. I read them as collective statements addressing many issues: some are statements of normative moral principle; others are prudential best judgments. While all of them are relevant to the formation of my Catholic conscience, I do not read them as equally normative.

I may be mistaken about this, but I do not believe that such statements are meant or offered as some kind of one-size-fits-all moral equivalency but rather as a framework presenting principles of different kinds and different degrees of moral certitude.

—February 2004

# 2

# Abortion

## Thomas Aquinas on Abortion

Question: Our congressman justifies pro-abortion votes by appealing to Saint Thomas Aquinas. His enclosed letter, after thanking me for sharing my concerns, states: "One of the great theologians of the Catholic Church, St. Thomas Aquinas, held that abortion was not always a mortal sin." What about this?

Answer: I have no idea what your congressman knows about the U.S. Constitution or about your district, nor do I know where he got this point from Saint Thomas—it is certainly not from anything Aquinas wrote. Perhaps this can be found in the Cuomo-Kennedy school of "I am personally opposed but . . ."; however, it cannot be found in the teachings of Aquinas.

Indeed, Saint Thomas Aquinas taught the opposite. In his *Commentary on Sentences of Peter Lombard*, Aquinas taught that all abortions are a "grave sin" (*peccatum grave*), "among evil deeds" (*inter maleficia*), and "against nature" (*contra naturam*) (bk. 4, d. 31).

Medieval understandings of gradual animation (ensoulment) could allow for different and increasing grades of penalty (civil and canonical), but the grave immorality of all direct abortions was the same in every case.

On November 18, 1974, the Congregation for the Doctrine of the Faith issued its *Declaration on Abortion*. This most authoritative teaching of the Catholic Church on the subject of abortion is, I find, both underread and underappreciated. The declaration makes the very point at issue: it is true that in the Middle Ages the pastors and doctors of the Church made a distinction between the evaluation of the sin (immoral) and the gravity of penalties (punished as homicide after ensoulment; punished, but not with the same penalty as homicide, if before ensoulment). Noting that distinction regarding penalties, the declaration then teaches: "But it was never denied at that time that procured abortion, even during the first days, was objectively a grave fault. This condemnation was in fact unanimous.... St. Thomas, the Common Doctor of the Church, teaches that abortion is a grave sin against the natural law" (no. 7). The documentation for this teaching of Aquinas is in the declaration's footnote 11, which cites his *Commentary on the Sentences* mentioned above.

Usually, unsubstantiated remarks about Saint Thomas Aquinas, or a canonical decision of Pope Innocent III, or changed canonical penalties of Pope Gregory XIV, turn up misleading and unexplained in the literature of the self-proclaimed Catholics for a Free Choice. Their agenda is known and not friendly to the truth—moral or historical.

Your congressman's letter to you states that he appreciates "the dialogue". If that is honest, and he has any genuine interest or reverence for the saint, who is the Common Doctor of the Church, perhaps in the interest of dialogue and truth, he would be willing to correct or at least omit his misstatement of the teaching of Saint Thomas Aquinas.

—October 1992

## Abortion and Probabilism

Question: What is Probabilism, and how does it apply to abortion? Whenever bishops make a public statement on abortion, some academic takes to print to announce the doctrine of Probabilism, stating, "Where there is doubt, there is freedom."

Answer: Probabilism is not a doctrine of faith but rather a technical term of moral theology that describes a moral system. A moral system is not an entire system of morality, but rather a method of casuistry for solving practical cases of doubtful obligation.

If one is uncertain about the existence or cessation of some law (obligation), and if he must act, the best approach for a reasonable person is to seek direct practical certitude, i.e., an act of prudence, the perfected ability for making right decisions. That means use the brains God gave you to think it through and do the right thing.

If direct certitude is not possible or available, one is free to use "reflex principles", including Probabilism, which holds that one may follow an opinion for liberty even though the opinion for law is more probable. The fundamental insight of this approach is that "a doubtful law does not bind" (*lex dubia non obligat*). The better exponents of Probabilism explain that the opinion for liberty must be a truly solid and probable opinion; after all, this kind of casuistry is a method of solving hard cases; it is not meant to be a way of life.

Now all of the above has nothing really to do with the immorality of direct abortion. The letter you sent me was that of Daniel C. Maguire, a professor at Marquette University, published in the *New York Times*.[1] It is Maguire who opines that "where there is doubt, there is freedom", and he seems to believe that Catholic teaching against direct abortion is somehow in doubt.

Actually, apart from Maguire and his tight circle at Catholics for a Free Choice (Francis Kissling, Mary Hunt, Giles Milhaven, and Rosemary Ruether), I truly wonder whether there are any believing Catholics who really think that the law or commandment against direct abortion is a doubtful law.

Recall that doubtful law is the only basis for a correct usage of Probabilism: *lex dubia non obligat*. As a method for trying to solve doubtful obligations, a sincere searcher for truth should have practical certitude before he acts, in order to fulfill the maxim: one can always act on a *certain* conscience, while one should not act on a *doubtful* conscience.

All of these distinctions, principles, and maxims are part of the serious effort to form and inform a correct conscience within the framework of Catholic moral theology. However, when the Church has formally taught, recently and relevantly, on some moral doctrinal teaching, no serious Catholic author can claim or insist that the formal teaching is uncertain or that the law (obligation) is doubtful.

Indeed, here is an example of the most formal, and I would think infallible, teaching—that of Pope John Paul II in *Evangelium Vitae* (March 25, 1995), which is an exercise of the teaching authority of the Petrine office in communion with the bishops of the world: "I declare

[1] Daniel Maguire, letter to the editor ("On Abortion, Church Teaching Isn't Absolute"), *New York Times*, Nov. 20, 1998, A-32.

that direct abortion, i.e., abortion willed as an end or a means, always constitutes a grave moral disorder, since it is the deliberate killing of an innocent human being" (no. 62). This doctrine, the Pope writes, is based upon the natural law, the written Word of God, and the Church's Tradition, and it is taught by the ordinary and universal Magisterium of the Church.

Again, I don't see how any serious Catholic could maintain that the moral law against direct abortion is somehow in doubt: the universal *Catechism* teaches the same truth (nos. 2270–75; even wrongful cooperation, no. 2272), as does the universal *Code of Canon Law* (cann. 1398; 1329–32).

Sadly, the Maguire group likely has e-mail letters all set to go before or whenever the Pope or our bishops teach Catholic doctrine on this moral truth. It may be that Maguire et al. have personal doubts and denials about every Catholic moral teaching (I can't say for sure; someone would have to interview them). But for media effect, it is usually their pro-abortion advocacy that finds its way into print. I suppose it's the man-bites-dog news angle, but this tired piece of journalistic street theater has been chanting the same rehearsed lines in certain publications since January 22, 1973.

What you have in these programmed print bites is not a probable opinion but a distortion—a confused and erroneous conscience trying to form more erroneous consciences.

In his other great moral encyclical, *Veritatis Splendor* (August 1993), Pope John Paul II reminds us:

> In any event, it is always from the truth that the dignity of conscience derives.... It is never acceptable to confuse a "subjective" error about moral good with the "objective" truth rationally proposed to man in virtue of his end. Evil done as the result of invincible ignorance or a non-culpable error, may not be imputable; but it does not cease to be an evil, a disorder in relation to the truth about the good. (no. 63)

The length of this Maguire distortion is long enough. Much better reading would be the bishops' document that Maguire tried to undermine and undercut: *Live the Gospel of Life: A Challenge to American Catholics.*

—April 1999

## Drugs That Cause Direct Abortion

Question: News reports highlight off-label drugs that when used in combination cause abortion. Does this amount to direct abortion as the Church uses the term?

Answer: I believe, yes, it is direct abortion that is morally prohibited (*CCC*, no. 2271) and penalized by Church law (can. 1398).

The headlines reflect a report published in the *New England Journal of Medicine* by Dr. Richard U. Hausknecht, a New York City gynecologist affiliated with the Mount Sinai School of Medicine.[2] Dr. Hausknecht reported that 96 percent of 178 women have successfully aborted after the drug treatment. This finding extends the results of some prior, smaller studies toward the same end.

The method uses in succession two inexpensive medications: methotrexate, which interferes with cell growth and division; then misoprostol, an ulcer drug that causes uterine contractions. Used together they produce an abortion within the first nine weeks of pregnancy. The technique is most successful during the first five weeks of pregnancy, calculated from the first day of a woman's last menstrual period.

In most cases, it takes seven to ten days from first administration to abortion completion. Unlike surgical abortion, best done after six weeks of pregnancy, this drug regimen can be begun as soon as a woman knows she is pregnant. It is seen as an alternative both to surgical abortion and to RU-486, not yet approved for use in this country.

Drugs already approved by the Food and Drug Administration, like methotrexate and misoprostol, can be used by any licensed physician for any purpose, although the doctor who prescribes medications for off-label use may lack insurance coverage for malpractice in that use.

The combination is the following: first an injection of methotrexate, widely used in higher doses for some cancers and lower doses for psoriasis and rheumatoid arthritis. Methotrexate interferes (even stops) the growth of the embryo and the placenta by blocking the B vitamin folic acid. Five or six days after the methotrexate injection, the woman returns to the doctor for the insertion of a suppository containing

[2] Dr. Richard U. Hausknecht, "Methotrexate and Misoprostol to Terminate Early Pregnancy". *New England Journal of Medicine* 333, no. 9 (Aug. 31, 1995): 537–40.

misoprostol. Both drugs in generic form are in local pharmacies for
less than $10.00. Usually, within two days of the suppository insert,
cramping and bleeding occur, resulting in an abortion that resembles
an early miscarriage. A third visit to the doctor is needed to confirm
that the pregnancy has in fact been terminated. Even the advocates of
this lethal combo do not recommend general use until (numerically)
larger studies are done in several centers to clarify what to do and
how to do it effectively.

For a comprehensive and up-to-date treatment of the immoral use
of methotrexate in ectopic pregnancies, see William May's "The Management of Ectopic Pregnancies".[3]

My focus is not medical; I'm not a doctor. My focus is moral, both
on this present drug combo and possible future ones. Chemical abortions in the next century may well replace the gross surgical destruc-
tions now common in our society. They will be harder to oppose
morally and legally because the general public will have a harder and
harder time fashioning a correct picture (even a mental image) of what
is really going on.

An excellent one-page summary by Lawrence Roberge, "Abortion
Vaccines", recently appeared in *Crisis* magazine (June 1995). This
research scientist outlines two pregnancy vaccines: HCG and TBA.
HCG (human chorionic gonadotropin) trains the woman's immune
system to attack and cleanse the bloodstream of HBC, an embryo-
produced hormone. Without HBC, the embryo dies as the uterine
lining breaks down, resulting in menstruation. TBA (trophoblastic anti-
gen) trains the woman's immune system to attack directly and destroy
the developing embryo in its earliest days, usually prior to day fourteen.

Both vaccines are being designated for long-term use of two to five
years; both require infrequent booster shots; both are touted as a form
of birth control, which they are *not*—they are clearly abortifacients.
Various international agencies, including the World Health Organization, have funded this research over many years—HCG trials now sur-
face from Mexico, the Philippines, and Tanzania. To get as far as possible
*away from* informed consent laws, poor and remote regions are purposely selected for trials and experiments. Human guinea pigs are more
available where researchers are rich and recipients are poor.

---

[3] William E. May, "The Management of Ectopic Pregnancies: A Moral Analysis" in *The Fetal Tissue Issue* (Braintree, Mass.: Pope John Center, 1994).

Eloquent and prophetic is the description of this aspect of the "culture of death" in Pope John Paul II's *Evangelium Vitae*. He notes the preoccupation of science with and the "enormous sums of money" that have gone into producing "ever more simple and effective" pharmaceutical means of abortion without the assistance of a doctor, "which at the same time are capable of removing abortion from any kind of control or social responsibility" (no. 13).

Similarly, in 1988, the Pontifical Council for the Interpretation of Legislative Texts issued a ruling clarifying that canon 1398 in the *Code of Canon Law* applies to any killing of a fetus "in whatever way or at whatever time from the moment of conception it may be procured".[4] Thus, the canonical penalty for abortion can apply to these early chemical abortions where the effect follows.

—January 1996

## Management of Ectopic Pregnancy

Question: I read of a shelling-out procedure for ectopic pregnancy. This leaves the fallopian tube in place and intact, and some argue that it is the more pro-life and pro-fertility procedure. Is this a direct abortion?

Answer: I believe it is a morally direct abortion and that it is not a legitimate application of the principle of double effect as some have argued.[5]

Factually, according to the Centers for Disease Control (CDC), there has been a very large increase in ectopic pregnancies in this country: from a rate of 4.5 per 1,000 in 1970 to 19.7 per 1,000 in 1992. The CDC attributes major increases to chlamydia and other sexually transmitted diseases that can and do scar fallopian tubes. A number of pelvic inflammatory diseases cause serious infections in fallopian tubes and ovaries—especially affecting the sensitive lining of the tubes known as the endosalpinx. It is almost impossible for ectopic tubal pregnancy

[4] Cf. *Acta Apostolicae Sedis (AAS)* 80 (1988) 1818.

[5] For a summary of opinions, see John E. Foran, M.D., "Ectopic Pregnancy: Current Treatment Options, déjà vu *Humanae Vitae*", *Linacre Quarterly* 66, no. 1 (Feb. 1999): 21–28.

to happen without some preexisting disease or irregularity of the endosalpinx.

Over the past decades, two Catholic moralists have engaged in a nuanced and pointed debate about what is and is not permissible in the moral management of ectopic pregnancies. William E. May discussed the question in his chapter in *The Fetal Tissue Issue* as well as in *Ethics & Medics*.[6] Albert S. Moraczewski has published on the subject in *Ethics & Medics* three times as a response, one in the same volume as May.[7]

Some estimate that about half of ectopic pregnancies spontaneously resolve, but our present concern is deliberate intervention (surgical or chemical) to resolve the tubal pregnancy. In the past, the vast majority of tubal pregnancies were discovered because of the rupture of the tube, at which point it was too late to do anything except to remove the now-damaged and ruptured tube with the death of the unborn a concomitant and unavoidable fact.

Currently, the diagnosis of unruptured ectopic pregnancy is possible by ultrasound or laparoscopic techniques, and this earlier (i.e., pre-rupture) information raises questions of the appropriate management of intact ectopic pregnancy.

All Catholic authors agree that salpingectomy is a licit application of the principle of double effect. In full salpingectomy, the entire fallopian tube (together with the ectopic pregnancy) is surgically removed; in partial salpingectomy only the damaged segment of the tube enveloping the ectopic pregnancy is removed, and then the severed ends of the tube are brought together and sutured.

Clearly, the surgery here is on the tube, a portion of which is pathological and poses a significant threat to the health and life of the mother. The death of the unborn is foreseen but not directly intended. The improvement in mother's health and life is not precisely caused by the death of the unborn but comes through (is caused by) the removal of pathological tissue. Thus, this procedure involves an indirect abortion and is a legitimate application of double effect.

[6] May, "Management of Ectopic Pregnancies"; William E. May, "Methotrexate and Ectopic Pregnancy", *Ethics & Medics* 23, no. 3 (Mar. 1998): 1–3.

[7] Albert S. Moraczewski, O.P., "Managing Tubal Pregnancies: Part I," *Ethics & Medics* 21, no. 6 (June 1996): 1–4; "Managing Tubal Pregnancies: Part II", *Ethics & Medics* 21, no. 8 (Aug. 1996): 3–4; and "Ectopic Pregnancy Revisited", *Ethics & Medics* 23, no. 3 (Mar. 1998): 3–4.

But, different from salpingectomy is salpingostomy, in which the tube is sliced longitudinally directly over the embryo who is extracted with forceps or gentle suction. The unborn is thus detached from the tubal wall and removed (which is death-dealing if the embryo is alive).

Similar to salpingostomy, but nonsurgical, is the chemical administration (systemically or injected at the site) of methotrexate, a folic acid antagonist developed over forty years ago as a chemotherapy for certain types of cancer. Methotrexate inhibits DNA synthesis so that normal implantation enzymatic activity ceases. Its primary effect is on the trophoblast (the precursor of the placenta). Clearly, this is not a cancer case; the point and purpose of methotrexate here is to shut down the life support system of the developing child (doing so is death-dealing).

It seems to me that salpingostomy and this administration of methotrexate are direct abortions and that May's analysis is correct while Moraczewski's is mistaken.

Moraczewski prefers to examine the classical *fontes moralitatis* and ask specifically: What is the *moral object* of salpingostomy? He argues that the specific object and good of that act is "the stopping of the enzymatic activity of the trophoblast". That enzymatic action would be proper and normal in the uterus but is here causing damage in an abnormal site, the tubal lining. Thus, contra May, he says his conclusion is not based on the distinction between removing the embryo from the site and destroying it in situ. "It is based on stopping the destructive activity of the trophoblast by removing trophoblastic cells along with the damaged tubal tissue." [8]

However, when you directly remove the embryo from the site, what you do (*finis operis*) is destroy it in situ. Neither trophoblast nor its activity is in any sense "diseased", and thus the salpingostomy or methotrexate is in no sense therapeutic for or to the embryo; it is, rather, a death-dealing procedure meant to improve mother's health and life. This violates the double effect condition (regarding causality): that the good effect not be caused by, not come through, the evil effect. As mentioned above, tubal pregnancies don't happen because tiny embryos do what they naturally do; almost always there is a preexisting problem in the endosalpinx from whatever cause.

Thus, I believe May is correct when he states that salpingectomy is a medical intervention performed on the *mother*, whereas salpingostomy

---

[8] Moraczewski, "Ectopic Pregnancy Revisited", p. 4.

and methotrexate are interventions performed on the *unborn child*. More-over, the procedures are undertaken *"not* for the benefit of the unborn child, who is killed as a result of their use, but for the benefit of another, the mother".[9] Since the procedures performed on the embryo are not necessary to protect the mother's life (salpingectomy can pre-serve that) but are used in order to preserve future fertility, I would judge that the final condition of double effect, proportion, is also not verified here. Thus these procedures upon the embryo are not legit-imate applications of double effect and are direct abortions.

—July 1999

[9] May, "Methotrexate and Ectopic Pregnancy", p. 2.

# 3

# Exploitation of Human Embryos

## Vaccines from Aborted Embryos

Question: Some pro-life literature warns against vaccinations for rubella and chicken pox because the vaccines were originally cultivated from human cells taken from aborted humans. One states bluntly: "Don't infect your child with the culture of death!" What is the morality of this?

Answer: I find myself in substantial agreement with Edward J. Furton in "Vaccines Originating in Abortion".[1] Since Furton has more space to respond there than I do here, that issue of *Ethics & Medics* is worth careful reading and close study. (As an aside, *Ethics & Medics* is a monthly journal published by the National Catholic Bioethics Center. It is a great contemporary resource: scientifically up-to-date and always providing a reliable Catholic perspective on current biomedical questions.)

Back to your question—vaccines begin with the growth of a weakened strain of a known virus in a culture. Two human cell lines (MRC-5 and WI-38) that were used by Merck and Company to grow weakened virus strains had their origin in cells taken originally from the lung tissue of two aborted fetuses in the 1960s. Human cell lines could have been taken from other sources—avoiding the moral question entirely—but they were not, as their manufacturer admits.

Thus, Merck's Meruvax, the widely used vaccine for rubella (German measles) uses the WI-38 cell line, while its chicken pox vaccine, Varivax, uses both MRC-5 and WI-38.

---

[1] Edward J. Furton, "Vaccines Originating in Abortion", *Ethics & Medics* 24, no. 3 (Mar. 1999): 3–4.

Thus the question arises: Does immunization with these vaccines involve the Catholic parent in some kind of cooperation with evil? In moral theology, *cooperation* means assistance, help, aid, facilitation, and complicity. (Of course, cooperation in good is recommended; however, cooperation in evil raises difficult moral questions.)

Assessing cooperation in evil involves at least two factors: intention and causality. Thus, *formal* cooperation occurs when one helps some evil and agrees with it; formal cooperation in evil is always wrong. However, it often happens that the cooperator does not agree with or concur in some evil, yet some good or neutral work or act of his is connected with the performance of or completion of some evil. This is what the textbooks call *material* cooperation.

In the case of material cooperation, the closeness, proximity, or immediacy of that causal (helping) connection must be examined and assessed morally to determine its permissibility. *Immediate* material cooperation occurs when without one's help the evil can't be done. This is considered the same as formal cooperation and is wrong (apart from some justice applications where life takes precedence over property).

*Mediate* material cooperation can be further distinguished as *proximate* or *remote, free* or *necessary*. These determinations are made according to the actual, factual circumstances in a given case. I think there is widely shared general agreement among reliable moralists in these areas, but some prudential assessments of highly circumstantial cases may not generate unanimous agreement. Perhaps, this is the case with these vaccines.

In my judgment, the use of vaccines derived from an originally aborted source so long ago (1965) does not qualify as true cooperation. I would not approve, nor, I presume, would any faithful Catholic parent approve, of any direct abortion. However, this connection is so long ago in time and so remote in causality, that I do not see how this is properly called true cooperation.

The British bishops (1994) properly described some current medical research as "parasitic" toward abortion, but they also noted a considerable separation between the abortion act (1965) and the (then) current production of vaccine (1994). Indeed, the original tissue was removed after the aborted fetus was clinically dead, and the individuals involved in the vaccine production were not involved at all in the abortion act. Where there is and remains no support for abortion, it seems to me permissible for individuals to use the vaccine.

Some will argue that while there is no direct cooperation here, there is, nonetheless, some ambiguous, even contradictory witness as well as questions about scandal either given or taken. For some, profiting or benefiting from the results of some distant evil sounds like a good end will justify or camouflage a bad means to that good end (result).

There is a serious *present* concern. Rather than a time-strained retroactive application of direct cooperation to a wrongful act over thirty years ago, it seems to me Catholic witness does require opposition to the development of new vaccines, therapies, and studies from aborted fetal tissue today.

Most commercial firms are tone deaf to ethical protests and have developed public-relations techniques that specialize in disinformation and computerized letters that rarely go beyond saying, "Thank you for sharing." Nevertheless, well-targeted protests are not a waste of time. According to a report in *Our Sunday Visitor*, a single Catholic parish in Olney, Maryland, called the American Cancer Society to caution against human embryo research and met with positive results.[2]

—January 2000

## Previous Vaccine Column Challenged

Question: A column of yours is cited as contributing to the culture of death by favoring vaccination with products that originated from induced abortion. How do you respond?

Answer: It is true, a prior column of mine (January 2000) did address the question, but not quite that way. The question then posed concerned Meruvax, the widely used vaccine for rubella (German measles) that uses the WI-38 cell line, and the chicken pox vaccine Varivax that uses MRC-5 and WI-38.

Vaccines begin with the growth of a weakened strain of a known virus in a culture. The two human cell lines (MRC-5 and WI-38) did have their origin in cells taken originally from the lung tissue of two aborted fetuses in Japan in the 1960s. Human cell lines could have

<hr />

[2] *Our Sunday Visitor*, Aug. 8, 1999, pp. 8–9.

been taken from other sources, but they were not, as their manufacturer, Merck and Company, admits.

I wrote in January 2000 that I was in substantial agreement with Edward J. Furton in his article "Vaccines Originating in Abortion". Furton argued there that this was not a case of impermissible cooperation, i.e., it was not wrong for parents today to have their children vaccinated against rubella or chicken pox.

More recently, the same author has published a further and fuller article, "Vaccines and the Right to Conscience".[3] In this more recent effort, Furton raised further and fuller questions not only about the wisdom of preventing vaccination but also about the conscience claims of parents who refuse to have their children vaccinated.

Neither is Furton nor am I in any hurry to trample the rights of parents, especially their right and obligation to provide for the education of their children and their duty to protect the life and health of their children.

Parents and all Christians are free to make strong statements against the evil of abortion. However, on this precise question of moral or immoral cooperation in abortion, I know of no formal magisterial teaching that binds the Catholic conscience as *certain* Catholic teaching. There are, of course, a number and variety of published opinions by authors and moralists worthy of respect and study. But again, to my knowledge, there is no definitive Catholic teaching on this matter.

In brief, cooperation involves both subjective *intention* and objective *causality*. Furton correctly asked what kind of cooperation is it when a parent decides to immunize a child against rubella. Surely that parent has no intention of participating in abortion in the present and has no causal connection at all with two abortions performed thirty years ago in Japan. Further, it is not the actual cells taken from the aborted fetus that are being used by these parents, but the vaccine that was grown in descendant cells.

Clearly, this is not formal cooperation, wherein the parent agrees with or approves of the evil of abortion. At most, this is material cooperation of a very remote kind. If parents have no choice but to use these products in order to protect their children and society from serious diseases, and the good they seek to secure through vaccination

---

[3] Edward J. Furton, "Vaccines and the Right to Conscience", *National Catholic Bioethics Quarterly* 4, no. 1 (Spring 2004): 53–62.

exceeds any harm that might be caused by that use, then I think Furton is correct: it is excessively harsh that children should undergo the risk of serious disease so that someone else might make a strong statement against abortion.

I believe my prior column is very similar to Furton's conclusion, that is, the use of vaccines derived from a tainted source so long ago (1965) does not register as true cooperation. Again, I would not approve, nor, I presume, would any faithful Catholic parent approve, of any direct abortion. However, this case is so remote in time and so remote in causality that I do not see how this is properly called true cooperation in evil.

There are and remain true concerns. But instead of a time-strained retroactive application of the most remote kind of possible material cooperation, it seems to me that Catholic witness should focus on preventing and protesting new vaccines and projects from aborted fetal tissues so that this mistake is not repeated anew.

—January 2005

## Fetal Tissue

Question: On the "fetal tissue" issue, is there any way to argue for correct principles without sounding like you favor the continued suffering of the sick?

Answer: There may be no happy answer to this question, and surely there is no easy one. First, some initial caution, even scientific skepticism, is called for.

This is especially true of "claims" made for the use of fetal brain tissue and all embryonic tissue. Thus far, all the "claims" are, at best, "promises"—hoped-for results that have not been achieved. Yet, the journalistic promises continue to overestimate and over-publicize "claims" and "promises" that fetal brain tissue can alleviate Parkinson's disease, Alzheimer's, or diabetes. A single chapter in Dr. Bernard Nathanson's book, The Hand of God,[4] is a welcome dose of reality: the "claims" are many; the scientific results are none!

[4] Chapter 10, "Vector of Life", in Dr. Bernard Nathanson, The Hand of God (Washington, D.C.: Regnery Publishing, 1996), pp. 163–81.

More recently, a reasoned exchange in the letter-to-the-editor section of *Commonweal* magazine highlights the question you pose. Robert J. White, M.D., a professor of neurological surgery at the Medical School of Case Western in Cleveland, wrote to critique a point in a prior article of Daniel Callahan.[5]

I will let Dr. White speak for himself, but recall the caution above on getting the scientific facts straight. Dr. White writes:

> I have significant disagreement with him [Callahan] having to do with fetal brain cellular implantation when he says a particular treatment for Parkinson's disease shows a "fair promise of working." Nothing could be further from the truth. He is referring to a formal brain operation requiring the stereotaxic introduction and depositing of a small fetal brain graft in a precise location in the depths of the patient's brain. As a neurosurgeon, I am totally unimpressed by the clinical results from this invasive surgical methodology. What little symptomatic improvement has been reported in a very small group of patients is simply the result of an injury artifact caused by the instrument, a thin cannula used for placing the transplant, causing damage to the brain tissue. (This is the exact region where a destructive legion is created to reduce symptoms of this tragic neuro-degenerative disease.)

White lists two reasons why this procedure is immoral: (1) it requires living fetal brain tissue from six to eight fetuses, and (2) the procedure itself is "simply a bad operation". He goes on to point out another problem—namely, "a NRH protocol" calling for a control group of patients to receive burr holes (small openings) in their skulls but not the actual brain grafting, at least not until the future. White characterizes this as "not totally safe" and as a "sham or placebo surgery; one more serious moral dilemma".

White does agree, however, with Callahan's "overall critique of contemporary medical research in this country": "He is perfectly right that we overestimate and over-publicize this work and often promise miracles that will never come to pass." But what is more significant, White says, is that biotechnology "has lost its moral compass in its attempt to redesign the human existence".[6]

---

[5] Daniel Callahan, "Scientific Research: Skepticism Is in Order", *Commonweal*, May 21, 1999.

[6] Robert J. White, M.D., letter to the editor, *Commonweal* 126 (Aug. 13, 1999): 4.

Daniel Callahan replies that Dr. White is correct about this particular procedure. But he also notes that if any significant results did turn up, further research would escalate to improve outcomes. Callahan is correct that the public, scientists, and the media would be thrilled with a way to deal with this terrible disease.

Callahan then asks and answers your question: Is Dr. White prepared to say that even if it works it would be wrong—to allow continued suffering rather than an immoral use of fetal tissue?

> I think I might now and then be prepared to say that, but I doubt most people in our society would, and surely not most of those with the disease. I am troubled to be saying that, but it seems to me reasonably accurate. The trouble with the research imperative is that it makes skeptics like myself look cold and indifferent; we uphold high principle while our fellow creatures suffer. I can't feel too good about that, even if that is the way I think I must go.[7]

The "high principle" to be defended of course is no direct lethal assault on any moral innocent! Pope John Paul II has already focused on this problem in *Evangelium Vitae*:

> Furthermore, the number of embryos produced is often greater than that needed for implantation in the woman's womb, and these so-called "spare embryos" are then destroyed or used for research which, under the pretext of scientific or medical progress, in fact reduces human life to the level of simple "biological material" to be freely disposed of. (no. 14)

Already the British have approved of some forms and uses of what they call "therapeutic cloning". The National Institutes of Health have announced (August 2000) new "Guidelines" for the Clinton Administration to use human embryos in cell research. The editors of *The New York Times* have already dismissed "Congressional opponents who consider the clumps of embryonic cells a form of life that must be protected".[8]

The Church is not the enemy of medicine or true science. But, science must be at the service of the human person not *vice versa*. Even little human beings, indeed the tiniest human beings, must not be converted into mere means or "stuff", even for the benefit of other human beings, even suffering human beings.

---

[7] Daniel Callahan, Author's Reply, *Commonweal* 126 (Aug. 13, 1999): 29.
[8] "Sensible Rules for Stem Cell Research", *New York Times*, Aug. 25, 2000, p. A-24.

Again, there may be no easy way to state that, and I suspect others can state it better, and I suspect we will see more challenges here rather than less. Nonetheless, it's still important to get the facts straight first, then do the best we can to respond in a principled way. It's not just the nature of science at issue here but another difference between a culture of life and the culture of death.

—November 2000

## Embryonic Stem Cell Research

Question: I was somewhat surprised by the intensity of religious criticism of President George W. Bush's stem cell decision last August [2001]. Did he get it all wrong?

Answer: No! I think the President got it almost entirely right except for one problematic dimension. I too was surprised at the intensity of some criticism. My guess is that some had statements and reactions ready for broadcast before the announcement was made and did not wait to see or to read what he actually said.[9]

In large part, President Bush is to be congratulated for what he did say, e.g., that here we confront "the beginnings of life and the ends of science"; "I also believe human life is a sacred gift from our creator"; "I strongly oppose human cloning and recoil at the idea of growing human beings for spare body parts." "Even the most noble ends do not justify any means."

Indeed! The end does not justify the means (Rom 3:8). To me, this is a most welcome statement from the White House, whose prior eight-year occupant sent and lived a different message—that any personal end justifies any means to get it.

Quite correctly, President Bush decided not to fund (via tax money) *further* or *future* embryo destruction, but he did allow federal funds to be used for research on those existing (sixty-plus) stem cells from previously destroyed embryos where the life–death decision was already made and done in private research.

---

[9] For the President's text, cf. *Origins* 31, no. 12 (Aug. 30, 2001): 213–15. [Or see "President Discusses Stem-Cell Research", White House Archives website, August 9, 2001, http://georgewbush-whitehouse.archives.gov/news/releases/2001/08/20010809-2.html.—*Ed.*]

It's this last dimension that *is* morally tainted since it is a federal first—i.e., a government-funded choice to use results of what was wrongfully destroyed. What the government funds can be reasonably understood to be what the government favors, and this is the first time we have given public sanction (through public funding) to the use of parts and products of deliberately destroyed human embryos.

It is a moral plus that the public treasury does not directly fund human destruction, but the conscious use and funding of what was immorally destroyed does raise serious scandal and potential problems in cooperation. If human life is a sacred gift from God, deliberate destruction is no way to treat a gift of God; if the end does not justify the means, some hoped-for end of curing something does not justify destroying tiny humans to get there.

Again, I applaud the President's decision not to fund (tax money) further and future embryonic destruction. However, how long will that ban last? I don't know. How strong is the norm forward only with those cell lines of those already cloned in? I don't know. Just how slanted is this slippery slope? Again, I do not know.

Against profound media bias and selective non-reporting, the average reader would hardly guess that there are workable and even fruitful alternatives. There are other sources for human stem cells: bone marrow, bloodstream, brain, spinal cord, dental pulp, cornea, liver, and pancreas. A rich source is blood within umbilical cords and placental materials no longer needed by newborn babies; some research indicates that human fat contains stem cells. All these cells can be removed by means that do not hurt the patient.

It is, however, the stem cells taken ("harvested") from within human embryos that are *the* focus of the media crusade. They "harvest" these by extracting the inner mass (the thirty to thirty-four cells) that is developing into the baby's organs and tissues. They are taken from the center of the human embryo in the first week of *life*, and removing these cells destroys that embryo. The most available source for these is frozen embryos from fertility clinics carelessly called "leftover", "surplus", "spare", or "excess" conceived *in vitro* but not implanted.

The media mantra is "People Will Die" unless the government funds embryonic stem cell research! That is not an accurate statement. Thus far, no disease has been successfully treated by human embryonic stem cells. The truth is, hoped-for therapies are still hypothetical and highly experimental. The current effort is trying to figure out how to induce cells into particular types of cells that theoretically could be transplanted. Media hype would have you think that if the country poured millions into this, we could have a few "cures" by Labor Day weekend. The truth is that basic research is many years away from any practical application.

It is also true that the red warning flags of safety are up all over the place: embryonic stem cells have a tendency to form tumors; fetal brain tissue transfers have caused problems; and in animals, all clones have run into problems. On the other hand, doctors already use adult stem cells to cure a host of human diseases. The reporting of the popular media is so unbalanced, I must conclude, it is designed to mislead.

Ours is a pragmatic society, not a philosophical one! Most often our first question is "Does it work?" "Is it effective?" or "What does it cost?" Just as often our last question is "Is this the right thing to do?"

What is the real problem here? It is another entrée on the expanding menu of the culture of death. True, the smallest human embryo differs from us, but it differs from us only in *degree* not in kind. True, just as an embryo differs from a fetus, so do both (embryo and fetus) differ from a newborn, and all three differ from a teenager and again from an adult; but they differ in degree. They differ in age and size and function—but it is our human sameness that is essential and lasting, while age and size and function differ throughout our life.

Some say that ten-day-old embryos don't look like us! That is true, they don't look like us, but they do look like what ten-day-old humans look like at that tender age—as you did at day 10, and I also.

The first rule of all medical ethics is *Primum non nocere*! "First, do not harm!" That first rule applies to humans on their first day, born or unborn.

The International Helsinki Code on human research forbids all "nontherapeutic research on any unconsenting subject". The human embryo (as human subject) *cannot* give consent, that is simply impossible in any country or any religion. No other human can give valid consent that deliberately and directly destroys another human. Why break an international code? Surely, this is nontherapeutic research on an unconsenting subject.

The few remaining and inadequate AMA restrictions[10] on fetal research will simply collapse when and if the embryo that precedes it

[10] Council on Ethical and Judicial Affairs, *Code of Medical Ethics: Current Opinions, 2000–2001* (Chicago: AMA Press, 2000), no. 2.10.

can be destroyed at will. Deliberate embryo destruction would simply obliterate the formal teaching of the Church on this subject (cf. *Donum Vitae* [February 22, 1987], pt. 1, nos. 4–6).

If the smallest among us are reduced to mere chemical status, *mere* "chemical stuff" to be patented and processed, like other raw materials, then any alleged "advances" on that basis are really "retreats". Deliberately to quash a *tiny* human to benefit a bigger human is not a step forward but a step backward, because it steps on someone to get there. That end does not and never will justify means to get there.

Is this really medicine or is it high-tech cannibalism? Automobile "Body Shops" routinely chop up wrecks and abandoned cars for their parts—either to salvage usable parts piece by piece or transplant remaining good parts to make sick or worn cars better.

If we fund and finance Bio-Labs (next to body shops) and there chop up human embryos for their parts or their cells and cell lines, is that not medical cannibalism, since the subjects who are the objects are never volunteers?

Principles, of course, do seem abstract, while diseases of any kind are terribly concrete. But sound principles are our only defense against the culture of death and our only way to distinguish ourselves from it. Principles like "First, do no harm!"

No nontherapeutic research on any unconsenting subject. And the principled *advice* of the late Paul Ramsey—that the good we do will only be made concrete by some of the things we refuse to do. One thing we should refuse to do is to destroy some humans to try to benefit other humans.

—March 2002


## Reproductive Human Cloning

Question: Is there an official Church teaching on human cloning?

Answer: The instruction *Donum Vitae* (*DV*) of the Congregation for the Doctrine of the Faith explicitly addresses cloning. Part 1 addresses manipulating embryos and "techniques of human reproduction". The instruction says, in part: "Also, attempts or hypotheses for obtaining a human being without any connection with sexuality through 'twin fission,' cloning or parthenogenesis are to be considered contrary to the moral law, since they are in opposition to the dignity both of human procreation and of the conjugal union" (no. 6).

*Human* cloning is a deep invasion of *human parenthood*. A "clone" technically has no human parents, not by accident but by design. This does disrespect both to the dignity of human procreation and to the dignity of conjugal union (marriage). Contrary to the right of every person to be conceived and born within marriage and from marriage (*DV*, pt. 1, no. 6), the clone is reduced to the level of a *product* made, rather than a *person* begotten.

Biblical anthropology respects the divine design of life-giving love: the two "become one flesh" (Gen 2:24; Mk 10:8; Eph 5:31). In the case of cloning, this personal, unitive, two-in-one-flesh dimension of life-giving marital love is rejected and replaced by technological replication. Thus, cloning contradicts the creative plan of God. As Pope John Paul II teaches in *Evangelium Vitae*, begetting is the continuation of creation (no. 43). Manufacturing is proper to and productive of *things*, but not of *persons*.

To reduce human procreation to no more than plant or animal replication (without human parenthood) is to remove the *humanum* from human parents and the human child. The psychological consequences, proximate and remote, for both "clone" and "cloner" are simply unknown. With humans, it is not enough not to know we do harm; with humans, we must know that we cause no harm. The first canon of medical ethics remains *Primum non nocere!* (First, do no harm!)

Twenty-five years ago, the late Professor Paul Ramsey of Princeton wrote the book *Fabricated Man*,[11] which detailed many objections to the manufacture of humans from the Christian point of view. His well-argued objections very much pertain here.

Take a look at our external environment and the manmade damage to the environment, some foreseen, much unforeseen, and ask a question of human wisdom: Is anyone so sanguine about the state of our external environment that he is now anxious to "engineer" our internal evolution?

—July 1997

---

[11] Paul Ramsey, *Fabricated Man: The Ethics of Genetic Control* (New Haven, Conn.: Yale University Press, 1970).

## Therapeutic Human Cloning

Question: Is there any moral difference between "therapeutic cloning" and "reproductive cloning"?

Answer: Frankly, no. The *noun* (cloning) tells us *what* is done; the *adjective* (therapeutic or reproductive) *suggests* the hopes or motives of the doer or advocate. Although the terminology sounds different, I am convinced that these descriptions are employed only to deflect criticism and confuse public discussion.

Verbal warfare is a media essential to defang the culture of life and promote the culture of death. Words are tactics in the pro-life challenge—either for it or against it, and this has been true since *Roe v. Wade* (1973).

For that many years, I have promoted the maxim: "All *social* engineering is preceded by *verbal* engineering." By that I mean that no social movement begins with the bold call: "Let's kill the unborn!" or "Let's kill the old folks!" The first thing to change is always the words, the terms of reference, since whoever frames the question helps to shape the answer—verbal engineering.

It seems to me that this verbal engineering is at work again in the media's current use of "reproductive" and so-called "therapeutic" cloning. *Reproductive* cloning would be the classic cause of asexual reproduction—to create (Xerox) another you by initiating another human life with your exact, unique genetic inheritance (same 46 chromosomes). The purpose, I suppose, would be to produce another you for possible transplantable parts of advanced narcissism. This is clearly contrary to the moral law since it contradicts both the dignity of human procreation and of conjugal union (*Donum Vitae*, pt. 1, no. 6).

Thus far, almost all voices condemn this drastic misuse of technological reproduction. Even elected officials say they oppose this kind of cloning, i.e., so-called *reproductive* cloning. However, while in 2001 the U.S. House of Representatives passed a bill to ban *all* human cloning (reproductive or research), the U.S. Senate demurs, pretending to distinguish reproductive cloning from so-called therapeutic or research cloning. They say they oppose the former (reproductive) while wanting to protect/preserve the latter (research).

In truth, they do not oppose human cloning but only one kind of cloning (reproductive). In a near rerun of the human embryonic stem cell debate, they want to preserve and protect the possibility that human life be cloned and not allowed to come to term. That means, artificially initiated human life only for the purpose to destroy it for its early parts and cells.

It is this that the verbal engineers call "therapeutic". Clearly, this cannot be "therapeutic" for the clone who is initiated only to be destroyed for some other purpose or use. In a sense, the whole project is intrinsically lethal—you initiate only to terminate, begin a new life only to end that life! This is not Western medicine; this is pure active research without moral boundaries.

On April 10, 2002, President George W. Bush gave a fine talk urging the U.S. Senate to ban *all* cloning as the U.S. House did the year before[12]—this was news the *New York Times* did not see fit to print.

Some contest, as the *New York Times* often does, that this is *not* human life but only "cell clusters" or a "tiny clusters of cells".[13] Verbal engineering at its normal speed and volume—so that the general public do not get the idea that we are killing someone but just research cells getting moved around.

I avoid as well the expression "fertilized egg"; it is both misleading and not scientifically accurate. When the 23 chromosomes from a human ovum completely link up with the 23 chromosomes from a human spermatozoa, the scientific result is not an egg but is properly called a zygote. A new human life (with 46 chromosomes) has begun—distinct in itself and distinguishable from others.

Words here are important too—the unaided naked eye will never see a living zygote, thus what we call it (him or her) matters greatly. The mention of egg or eggs prompts most Americans to think in forms: scrambled, boiled, fried, poached, etc. No one mourns the loss, manipulation, or even the destruction of an egg. But, the deliberate destruction of a living human zygote or morula is no inanimate thing—it is as all of us alive once were; it is the destruction of human life.

---

[12] Cf. "President Bush Calls on Senate to Back Human Cloning Ban", *National Right to Life News* 29, no. 4 (Apr. 2002): 12–13.

[13] "The President's Narrow Morality", *New York Times*, Apr. 11, 2002 [http://www.nytimes.com/2002/04/11/opinion/the-president-s-narrow-morality.html]; "The Pro-Life Case for Cloning", *New York Times*, May 2, 2002 [http://www.nytimes.com/2002/05/02/opinion/the-pro-life-case-for-cloning.html].

As above, watch your words. Words are tactics in the culture of life or death, and in our country, if you are really good with words, you can get away with murder.

—August/September 2002

# 4

## Catholic Medical Ethics

### Burden to the Community

Question: In the new *Ethical and Religious Directives* (1994) for Catholic Health Services, the description of ordinary/extraordinary means speaks of benefit/burden to the patient, to the family, and to the community. Is this the traditional distinction?

Answer: In my judgment, the addition of burden and/or expense to the community is not traditional, and its addition is puzzling, perhaps misleading, and a potential trapdoor.

The conventional distinction of "ordinary/extraordinary" means is calculated on a case-by-case basis to actual patient circumstances, i.e., positively what offers a reasonable hope of benefit (to the patient), without negatively imposing excessive hardship, serious danger of death, excessive pain, excessive expense (on the patient, and, by extension, the patient's family).

Traditionally, if a treatment, operation, or procedure offers the reasonable hope of benefit, in a given case, without the excessive negatives, that treatment for that patient is morally ordinary (and obligatory). If, however, in a given case, the small or no benefit is outweighed or overwhelmed by the excessive burdens, hardships, or expenses, then that treatment for that patient is considered morally extraordinary (and non-obligatory or ethically optional).

Your question is correct that, unlike the old *Directives* (1971), the 1994 *Directives* repeatedly employ the terminology of burdens on the patient or excessive expense to family or community (directive 32; cf. also directives 56 and 57).

In all three such directives, all three footnotes (cf. footnotes 18, 40, 41) cite the same source—part 4 of the Congregation for the Doctrine of the Faith (CDF) document *Declaration on Euthanasia* (May 5, 1980). Surely, that CDF declaration is the authentic teaching source, but part 4 of that declaration nowhere mentions "expense to the community" nor does the word *"community"* even appear.

Further, Pope John Paul II's recent encyclical, *Evangelium Vitae*, speaks directly to this ordinary/extraordinary distinction only in terms of what would "impose an excessive burden on the patient and his family" (no. 65). Again here, there is no mention of "expense to the community".

There is in this some reason for caution and concern. Obviously, costs and expense are not irrelevant to a proper moral estimation. However, in the traditional analysis and application, the benefit-and-burden is a first-person standard, i.e., benefit or burden to the patient (by personal extension, the patient's family). On the other hand, "expense to (or on) the community" strikes me as a third-person standard, e.g., third-party payer, Medicare, Medicaid, community funds, or social services resources.

The cost factor is and remains a factor, but, it seems to me, this novel addition introduces a somewhat different standard of measurement. If civic virtues were as robust as the profits of insurance companies, or, as driven as the "bottom-line" thrusts of managed care or merging providers, I would not worry.

However, in a cost/benefit society, I would be concerned that this wording is not only open to misinterpretation but begging for misinterpretation. In my judgment, the present wording of those directives clearly does not reflect accurately the authorities cited for it, and it is quite unclear how often or how widely the new language can be misapplied.

—January 1996

## Cooperation with Evil in Catholic Health Care

Question: Can a Catholic hospital properly be the sponsor or part owner of a joint venture that governs and delivers "services" that Catholic moral teaching prohibits (e.g., direct abortion, direct sterilization, assisted suicide)?

**Answer:** My short answer is no; however, the reasons for saying no are not short.

The principles of cooperation are admittedly a subtle and very nuanced part of moral theology. Nonetheless, what we once called "approved authors",[1] all published explanations and applications of the "principles of cooperation" with ecclesiastical approbation. To complicate things further, while all these "approved authors" agree in concept, their chosen terminology is not always in agreement.

In short, *moral cooperation* means participation (assistance, help, contribution, aiding-and-abetting, the civil law notion of "complicity"). Cooperation in good is no problem; it is always welcome. Cooperation in moral evil raises all sorts of problems—problems of kind and problems of degree.

Traditionally, "cooperation" is of two kinds: *formal* cooperation and *material* cooperation. *Formal* cooperation means that the cooperator agrees (approves, concurs) with and participates in some evil. All Catholic authors agree that *formal* cooperation is wrong; e.g., *Evangelium Vitae* condemns it absolutely: "[I]t is never licit to cooperate formally in evil" (no. 75).

*Material* cooperation means that the cooperator does not agree (does not approve, nor concur) in the order of *intention*, but the pivotal question here is one of *causality*: What kind of cooperation or participation is involved? How proximate or remote is this material cooperation? Is it free or necessary cooperation?

It is here that all authors speak to the same concept, but not always in the same terms. For clarity, I find it easier to ask the intentionality question first: Does one agree with what (evil) is going on (*formal*)? Or, does one not agree with what is going on (*material*)?

Since the first, "formal cooperation", is never permissible, one must then ask about the second: What *kind* of cooperation (participation) are you placing? Is it such *immediate* material cooperation (i.e., without your assistance the wrong cannot be done, cf. can. 1329, §2), or, such *mediate* material cooperation (accessory) that your participation is helpful but not crucial?

---

[1] Joseph Aertnys, Cornelius Damen, and Jan Visser, C.Ss.R., *Theologia Moralis*, 4 vols (Rome: Marietti, 1967–1969); H. Noldin, A. Schmitt, and G. Heinzel, *Summa Theologiae Moralis* (Rauch, 1961); Marcellino Zalba, *Theologiae Moralis Compendium* (Madrid, 1958); Henry Davis, S.J., *Moral and Pastoral Theology* (London, New York: Sheed and Ward, 1949); even A. Vermeersch, S.J., *Theologia Moralis* (Rome: Universita Gregoriana, 1928).

Again, I believe, all Catholic authors consider *immediate* material cooperation as impermissible, i.e., illicit cooperation—except for some cases involving the Seventh Commandment. Take the example of the manager of the 7-11 who is the only employee present who knows the combination to the safe. The thief says, quite seriously, "Open the safe or I'll blow your brains out." Given an ordered hierarchy of virtues, the true nature of life and property, and that morally "stealing" is a taking against the reasonable will of the owner, I must reasonably presume the owner of the store prefers the life of the manager to the contents of the safe. This immediate cooperation is not impermissible *in se*, but I would not label that simply as "duress" without qualification (more below).

It is certainly worth nothing that the "approved authors"— mentioned above—all speak to the cooperation of *individuals*, NOT the cooperation of *institutions*.[2]

Quite recently, the National Conference of Catholic Bishops (NCCB) revised the *Ethical and Religious Directives for Catholic Health Care Services* (hereafter *ERDs*). This 1994 revision included and inserted a new part 6, "Forming New Partnerships with Health Care Organizations and Providers", with its own introduction, directives (67–70), and a final appendix on "The Principles Governing Cooperation".

I'm not sure how to say this politely or correctly, but this clarifying appendix on moral cooperation is not the clearest explanation of Catholic moral teaching I have read. In ways, it can confuse as much as it clarifies.

Some commentators see easy and automatic transfer of the principles of cooperation from individuals to institutions (e.g., Kaveny and Keenan who equate and then collapse cooperation *in* evil into the toleration of evil).[3]

Other commentators, notably Russell Smith, make more nuanced distinctions, outline the basic principles, and apply them to various joint ventures in health care, much of which I could agree with.[4]

---

[2] Aertnys-Damen-Visser., *Theologia Moralis*, vol. 1, no. 356; Noldin-Schmitt-Heinzel, *Summa Theologiae Moralis*, vol. 2, no. 119, n. 4; Zalba, *Theologiae Moralis Compendium*, vol. 2, no. 253, n. 1; Davis, *Moral and Pastoral Theology*, vol. 1, p. 342.

[3] M. Cathleen Kaveny and James F. Keenan, "Ethical Issues in Health-Care Restructuring", *Theological Studies* 56, no. 1 (1995): 145–46.

[4] Cf. chapter 15 in *The Splendor of Truth and Health Care: Proceedings of the Fourteenth Workshop for Bishops, Dallas, Texas*, ed. Russell Smith (Braintree, Mass.: The Pope John Center, 1995), pp. 217–31.

Recently, Germain Grisez proposed and responded to a difficult moral question: "How Far May Catholic Hospitals Cooperate with Non-Catholic Providers?"[5] Like Smith (above) Grisez considers simple contractual arrangements, integrated networks, co-sponsored HMOs, and purchased practices of groups of physicians (or providers) who remain free to provide services to some which a Catholic organization can't provide without violating the ERDs.

In Grisez's analysis, "formal cooperation" is likely to occur not only in carrying out a cooperative agreement "but also, and even especially, in setting it up". Material cooperation can also be wrong and a Catholic hospital's material cooperation with the provision of morally unacceptable services (called "proscribed services") is likely to be wrong.[6]

I think Grisez is closer to the truth, although the consequences are sobering. I cannot overemphasize the radical difference between cases of cooperation involving *individuals* and those involving *institutions*. Conventional teaching and teachers consider the individual doctor or nurse or social worker whose good or neutral work (service) is somehow connected with some evil practice or procedure there. When those individuals do not agree or approve, they are not formal cooperators. And depending how immediate or mediate, how proximate or remote, their material cooperation will be permissible or not depending on the presence or absence of these actual factors in a given case.

Clearly, in this conventional understanding of cooperation, the individual employee does not set the policy for the institution. However, in a joint institutional venture, a full merger, a limited co-sponsor, co-owner, or limited partner, from the viewpoint of corporate governance, the religious order or Catholic group that formally and freely establishes such a joint venture cannot pretend they do not set policy. They do; that's what governance is. Unlike the employee who does not set policy, surely the employer (owner, sponsor, partner) does set policy. Thus, Grisez's telling point: "but also, and even especially, in setting it up".

—July 1996

[5] Germain Grisez, "How Far May Catholic Hospitals Cooperate with Non-Catholic Providers?" *Linacre Quarterly* 62, no. 4 (Nov. 1995): 67–72.
[6] Ibid., pp. 68–69.

## Previous Opinion on Cooperation with Evil Challenged

Question: Your July 1996 Q/A on cooperation with evil in Catholic health care seems to be at odds with the *Ethical and Religious Directives* on cooperation. Are you with the Church on this or not?

Answer: I certainly hope I am with the Church; if not, I would just as certainly retract my opinion as mistaken if it were truly against Church teaching.

The real question here is what precisely does the Church teach. Regarding the *Ethical and Religious Directives for Catholic Health Care Services* (1994), you seem to be referring to the one-page appendix: "The Principles Governing Cooperation" (p. 29). I do not believe that that appendix is either well stated or well reasoned. In fact, I think it's a bit misleading.

One reason for saying that is some history of questionable citation. Concerning hospital partnerships, joint ventures, mergers, co-sponsors, etc., we are all in debt to Father Russell Smith for his printed contributions to this difficult area; e.g., his article in *Linacre Quarterly* and his prior efforts at the Workshop for Bishops, Dallas, Texas.[7]

As Father Smith has correctly pointed out, not all that much has been written about institutional cooperation. While that is true in part, it is not all that's true.

By some curious twist of fate, much confusion can be traced back to great clarity. Back in the early 1970s, the bishops of the U.S. posed some moral and practical questions to Rome concerning sterilization in Catholic hospitals. Technically, the question then posed was whether directive 20 (in the 1971 *Directives*) was correct as it read in view of the fact that some theologians don't accept it or teach it, and that it could raise serious practical problems like closing hospitals, conflicts with personnel, possible polarization, etc.

On March 13, 1975, the Congregation for the Doctrine of the Faith issued an authoritative response: *Quaecumque Sterilizatio* (*Responses to*

---

[7] Russell E. Smith, "Ethical Quandary Forming Hospital Partnerships", *Linacre Quarterly* 63, no. 2 (May 1996): 87–96; *Faith and Challenges to the Family: Proceedings of the Thirteenth Workshop for Bishops, Dallas, Texas*, ed. Russell E. Smith (Braintree, Mass.: Pope John Center, 1994), pp. 81–92; *Splendor of Truth and Health Care*, pp. 217–31.

*Questions concerning* "Sterilization in Catholic Hospitals").[8] To my mind, this official response is a pearl of theological precision and doctrinal clarity. Since it is only six or seven paragraphs in length, it is easily read and should be read since it clearly answers the questions posed. It is so clear it needs no commentary.

In those pre–*Veritatis Splendor* days, it was my opinion[9] that the CDF was clearly correct and that competing and counter voices[10] were clearly wrong about cooperation in sterilization.

As mentioned above, the CDF response ("Sterilization in Catholic Hospitals") was exceptionally clear and to the point. To my personal amazement, after unusual delay, a subcommittee of the United States Catholic Conference (USCC) on Health Affairs with the approval (35–3) of the Administrative Board of the NCCB published a "Commentary" (September 15, 1977) on the CDF response.[11]

As clear as the 1975 CDF response is, so unclear are parts of the 1977 USCC commentary. For example, prominent and crucial mention is given to "duress" in the understanding of the principles of cooperation in the 1994 *ERDs* (p. 29). However, the term *duress* never appears in "Sterilization in Catholic Hospitals"; that term first emerges in the USCC Commentary (no. 2).

Next, the overly simple distinction regarding cooperation that the object of the cooperator must be distinguishable from that of the wrongdoer (*ERDs*, p. 29) is a distinction that does not appear in "Sterilization in Catholic Hospitals", but again emerges first in the USCC commentary in the distinction between the reason for the sterilization and the reason for the cooperation (no. 4). This reduces the moral question largely to a matter of intentionality only, the justification being: will it do more harm than good? ("Commentary", no. 2).

---

[8] Cf. *Origins* 6 (June 10, 1976): 33; 35; also in *Vatican Council II: More Post-Conciliar Documents*, vol. 2, ed. Austin Flannery, O.P. (Boston: St. Paul, 1982), pp. 454–55.

[9] Cf. Msgr. William Smith, "Catholic Hospitals and Sterilizations", *Linacre Quarterly* 44 (May 1977): 107–18.

[10] Charles E. Curran, *Ongoing Revision in Moral Theology* (Notre Dame, Ind.: Fides/Claretian Publishers, 1975), pp. 210–48; Richard A. McCormick, "Sterilization and Theological Method", *Theological Studies* 37, no. 3 (1976): 471–77; and Kevin O'Rourke, O.P., "An Analysis of the Church's Teaching on Sterilization", *Hospital Progress* 57, no. 5 (1976): 68–75, 80.

[11] NCCB, "Commentary on the Reply of the Sacred Congregation for the Doctrine of the Faith on Sterilization in Catholic Hospitals", *Origins* 7, no. 25 (Dec. 25, 1977): 399–400.

This more-harm-than-good calculus cries out for clarification. What kind of goods (or evils) are being calculated? Closing a service or a hospital? Loss of revenue or patients? Are these financial and functioning "goods" to be measured and calculated against moral goods or moral evils? The commentary does not say, but it surely opens the way for a "proportionalist" reading and calculation in those pre–*Veritatis Splendor* (1993) days. The USCC commentary seemed more intent on not offending the McCormick school of "proportionalism" than in faithfully rendering the clear teaching of the CDF response.

While I still value the several printed contributions of Father Russell Smith, it is here that I differ with him and from him. He writes that both the USCC commentary and "Sterilization in Catholic Hospitals" address "duress" and then tries to discern the nature of the "duress" both documents have in mind.[12] The CDF response never mentioned "duress", let alone spelled out its nature.

Unfortunately, the recent *Ethical and Religious Directives*, in their appendix on "The Principles Governing Cooperation", relies more heavily on the USCC commentary than on "Sterilization in Catholic Hospitals". To me, that is the basic misstep that is no small part of the confusion here.

The traditional doctrine on "cooperation" was articulated for, developed in, and applied to individuals *not* institutions, especially Catholic institutions! The transfer of these principles *from* individuals to institutions is not easy and rarely legitimate.

Indeed, while the placement of the appendix on cooperation in the 1994 *ERDs* was aimed at the current situation of institutional mergers, joint ventures, co-sponsors, etc., the principles as they read there (even misstated) are examples of individual cooperation rather than institutional cooperation. When a Catholic institution ends up owning, sponsoring, or otherwise merging their Catholic mission with the delivery or sponsorship of what the Catholic Church forbids, the reality of positive scandal also demands a correct statement of principles rather than a misleading one.

No one can deny the very difficult problems that do arise in these areas today—great challenges both to the viability and identity of Catholic health care institutions. But faulty explanations of "material

---

[12] Smith, "Ethical Quandary", p. 93.

cooperation" will only preserve viability for a while; then in time, both viability and identity will be compromised.

—January 1997

## Cooperation with Evil in 2001 Directives

Question: Do the USCCB's 2001 *Ethical and Religious Directives* differ at all from the prior *Directives* (1994)?

Answer: Yes, they do differ in small part with a significant correction and a small drawback as well. First, the full title: USCCB, *Ethical and Religious Directives for Catholic Health Care Services* (4th ed.) approved at a general meeting of the U.S. bishops (June 2001).

In effect, these *ERDs* serve as an ethical code for Catholic hospitals and Catholic nursing homes in this country. The 2001 *ERDs* consist of six parts and seventy-two directives. This preserves the same basic framework of the 1994 *ERDs* (3rd ed.), also of six parts but only seventy directives.

The 1994 *ERDs* had an appendix, "The Principles of Cooperation" (p. 29) that has been removed from the current *ERDs*. Also, there is an explanatory footnote (n. 44) to the present directive 70 that "supercedes" previous commentary published by the NCCB in September 1997.

Some background and history might clarify just what is at issue here. The first *Ethical and Religious Directives* were jointly approved by the U.S. and Canadian bishops in 1955. In the post–*Humanae Vitae* (1968) era, the Canadian bishops decided to go their own way with their own medical-moral guide, while the NCCB approved revised and updated *Directives* in 1971 just for the United States.

At that time, questions about participation or cooperation in "prohibited services" (direct abortion, sterilization, and euthanasia) simply were not raised in hospitals under Catholic auspices (i.e., under Catholic ownership, governance, or management). Since these immoral procedures were not performed in Catholic hospitals, there were no cases of "prohibited services" to cooperate with or in under Catholic auspices. Nonetheless, back in the early 1970s, a committee of the U.S.

bishops' conference posed some moral and practical questions to Rome concerning sterilization in Catholic hospitals. Technically, the question then posed was whether directive 20 (in the 1971 *ERDs*) was correct as it read in view of the fact that some theologians did not accept it or teach it and that prohibiting nontherapeutic sterilizations might have serious consequences, like closing hospitals, conflicts with personnel, possible polarization, etc.

On March 13, 1975, the Congregation for the Doctrine of the Faith issued an authoritative response: "Sterilization in Catholic Hospitals".

To my mind, the official CDF response was and is so clear, I thought it needed no commentary. Yet, all the usual dissenting subjects (Charles Curran, Richard A. McCormick, Kevin O'Rourke) registered their non-acceptance of this formal teaching, but the teaching of the Church was clearly stated and reaffirmed by the CDF.

In September 1977, a subcommittee of the USCC on Health Affairs published a two-page "Commentary" on the CDF response of 1975.[13] Parts of this commentary were unclear and potentially misleading, as I explained in an earlier *HPR* Q/A column (January 1997).

As mentioned above, the early *ERDs* (1955 and 1971) did not accept or accommodate this contradictory witness in Catholic institutions. However, in the late 1980s and early 1990s some Catholic hospitals began to enter formal mergers, joint ventures, and co-sponsorships with non-Catholic institutions wherein the "prohibited services" were available and performed.

This, we take it, was the presenting reason for introducing an entirely new section to the 1994 *ERDs*, Part Six—"Forming New Partnerships with Health Care Organizations and Providers"—along with some new directives (67–70), and a new appendix, "on cooperation".

Unfortunately, the new appendix was not a resume of the clear teaching of the 1975 CDF Reply but rather a resume of the confused reasoning and novelties of the 1977 USCC commentary: heavy emphasis on "duress"; different and differing intentions; and while pretending to solve questions of institutional cooperation gave examples only of individual cooperation which, of course, are not exactly the same.

Thus, when the present *ERDs* simply removed the poorly stated appendix of 1994, that was a clarifying step forward. The 2001 directive 70 is rather straightforward: "Catholic health care organizations

---

[13] See footnote 11 on page 50 above.

are not permitted to engage in immediate material cooperation in actions that are intrinsically immoral, such as abortion, euthanasia, assisted suicide and direct sterilization." It is footnote 44 of this current directive 70 that explains: "This Directive [70] supersedes the 'Commentary' on the CDF Reply published by the NCCB on Sept. 15, 1977."

At the start of this answer I did mention one drawback. The drawback is this—that the introduction to part 6 of the current *Directives* states: "Reliable theological experts should be consulted in interpreting and applying the principles governing cooperation" (p. 36). It is just possible that this brings us back to the situation prior to the 1994 *Directives*. Of course, we should all attend to "reliable theological experts", but we can hardly forget that pre-1994 it was theological experts who provided the bishops' conference with the most unreliable advice.

The same is still true of some today. In a most recent issue of the *Linacre Quarterly*, the Reverend Thomas Kopfensteiner published an article: "The Meaning and Role of Duress in Cooperation in Wrongdoing".[14] It is widely rumored that Father Kopfensteiner played a major role in contributing to the *ERDs* revision of 1994 and the confusion therein, especially the confused explanation of "cooperation". In his recent article, he often quotes the 1977 commentary as the normative interpretation, including the it-will-do-more-harm-than-good rubric (p. 153) so dear and central to proportionalist thinking. Surely, Father Kopfensteiner is aware that the USCCB teaches that the prior commentary is not normative; indeed, it is now superseded, but given his strategic placement, this confusion will not disappear overnight.

—December 2003

## Killing One Twin to Save the Other

**Question:** I read of Siamese twins (sharing one heart and part of a liver) who were separated surgically to save one while the other dies. Many moralists were quoted—some contradicting each other. Do you have an opinion?

---

[14] Rev. Thomas Kopfensteiner, "The Meaning and Role of Duress in Cooperation in Wrongdoing", *Linacre Quarterly* 70, no. 2 (May 2003): 150–58.

Answer: The twins, Amy and Angela Lakeberg, were born June 29, 1993, at Loyola University Medical Center near Chicago. Joined from chest to navel, they shared a malformed, six-chamber heart. Their life expectancy together was relatively short—six to seven weeks.

The doctors at Loyola recommended ending medical life support and allowing the twins, already near death, to die naturally. Doctors at Philadelphia's Children's Hospital offered to operate, but the procedure involved separation surgery in which one twin would certainly die, while the other had a 1 percent chance (or less) to survive. (In the five previous attempts to separate twins sharing a single heart, no child has survived beyond three and a half months.)

As you note, some theologians were quoted with wide (even contradictory) variation. Most presumed, and some pronounced, that this surgical separation was an unusual example of the usual principle of double effect. Some saw the surgery as unjustifiable simply because of the excessive expense—at or over one million dollars. Others highlighted the very strong parental interest in saving the life of at least one of the twins.

First, we should consider what all do agree on. All agree that the surgery is an ethically extraordinary means and therefore not obligatory. Besides the gigantic expense, one would have to question the qualifier *reasonable* in the positive criterion of offering a *reasonable* hope of benefit. Any operation that does not offer even a sure outcome of 1 percent probably deserves the title *experimentation* instead of *procedure*.

As you note, several theologians presumed that this surgical separation was a legitimate application of the principle of double effect. I am not so convinced. Surely, the intention was to save one twin; the good effect did not come precisely through the bad effect (death of other twin); and the proportion question seems satisfied. However, I find it difficult to describe the primary act (the cause that has two effects) as "good" or "neutral". The required surgery (as I understand it) separates the twins physically so that the heart and connected vessels are apportioned to the one with the better chance of survival. Yet, that one malformed heart is a heart they both share and on which both are dependent for life; the causal act does deprive the other twin of her rightful share of the single heart, and the same act does cause her death.

The death of the latter twin is certainly foreseen and surely caused—albeit for the good purpose of trying to benefit her sister. That death is perhaps not directly intended as an "end", but it is surely foreseen and intended as a "means", as a necessary and causative condition of the hoped-for outcome.

Emotionally, one can surely understand the tragic plight and pressure on the parents, but one can also question what kind of reasonable hope is offered here by medical authorities. It is almost certain that the surviving child will not leave the hospital without life support; she might not even leave the hospital alive.

On this basis, I would agree with the reasoned opinion of Albert Moraczweski: "It is better morally, even if not emotionally, for both twins to die of natural causes, in this case, from a defective heart which is inadequate to support the lives of both twins than by human intervention to deliberately remove the heart from one twin (thereby terminating her life) and give it to the other." [15]

—March 1994

## Doctors as Executioners

Question: Is it true that the American Medical Association forbids its members to participate in capital punishment?

Answer: Yes. The Code of Medical Ethics of the American Medical Association is published by the Council on Ethical and Judicial Affairs of the AMA in Chicago. The 1998–1999 edition of this Code states the following regarding "capital punishment": "An individual's opinion on capital punishment is the personal moral decision of the individual. A physician, as a member of a profession dedicated to preserving life when there is hope of doing so, should not be a participant in a legally authorized execution" (no. 2.06; p. 13).

This is a noble statement, especially the self-description of medicine as a "profession dedicated to preserving life when there is hope of doing so". This is a standard with which I agree and salute. It is my personal

---

[15] Albert S. Moraczweski, O.P., "What Nature Has Misjoined Together", Ethics & Medics 18, no. 11 (Nov. 1993): 2. A similar opinion is given toward the same case by Thomas J. O'Donnell, S.J., Medical-Moral Newsletter 29, no. 5 (May 1992): 18.

conviction that direct killing is no part of true medicine and should have no legitimate place in it.

Unfortunately, a few pages prior in the same *Code of Medical Ethics* a very different standard begins the section on "Social and Policy Issues". It reads: "Abortion. The Principles of Medical Ethics of the A.M.A. do not prohibit a physician from performing an abortion in accordance with good medical practice and under circumstances that do not violate the law" (n. 2.01; p. 3).

What is puzzling here is what happened to the noble profession "dedicated to preserving life when there is hope of doing so"? Why no declared space for the "personal moral decision of the individual" physician? Is it not even worthy of mention? What is direct abortion if not a "legally authorized execution", albeit without any hearing, trial, or any due process of law?

As above, I believe "direct killing" is not and should not be any part of the practice of ethical medicine. After all, the purpose of medicine is to cure when possible, or when not possible, at least to provide care. If there is a "consistent" ethic here, why not extend the noble profession of dedication "to preserving life when there is hope of doing so" to the millions unborn that is extended to the hundreds convicted of capital crimes?

—December 2000

# 5

# Euthanasia

## Living Wills and Advance Directives

Question: I am often asked about living wills and advance directives. Is there any reliable publication that would explain the dangers and pitfalls of these things without being book length or a law review article?

Answer: As you correctly mention, there has been a proliferation, indeed, an explosion of "documents" that confuse and cloud an already confusing area. In terms of shaping public attitudes and directions, perhaps none has been more successful than the living will, first promoted by the Euthanasia Education Council in 1967, then promoted by the Society for the Right to Die, Concern for Dying, Inc., and now Choice in Dying, Inc. The Hemlock Society is now joined to the latter as is Americans against Human Suffering.

The living will itself is as dangerous as it is attractive both in its simplicity and ambiguity. While compatible with the received Christian teaching that no one is obliged to use "extraordinary" means or treatment to prolong life, it is broad and vague enough to expand and include the alleged "right" to refuse or decline *all* means or treatment, which would include "ordinary" means that are morally obligatory and not ethically optional.

From this germinal confusion—linking and lumping, by design, the permissible with the impermissible—all advance directives flow. Once wrapped in the noble language of "rights", painted with a few coats of "choice", fueled by some winning slogans—"Whose life is it, anyway?"—a social trend has advanced very far in the wrong direction.

Given the legal currency of absolute, unqualified (and therefore un-Christian) autonomy, given our societal obsession with control—birth control, life control—the final piece of absolute individualism logically has to be "death control". Of course, "death control" by choice and as a new legal "right".

Whether the living will is an expansion or an erosion of a patient's rights is both a practical and important question. There is a fine pamphlet in understandable English by Mary Senander, entitled *The Living Will*, published by the Leaflet Missal Company (St. Paul, Minn.). It is forty-four pages, but in rather large print and an easy read. A single copy is $2, but bulk orders can greatly reduce that (e.g., 25 copies are 80 cents each).

The pamphlet is a faithful explanation of genuine Catholic sources on this subject and would serve as an excellent, readable resource for parishioners who might ask about the subject or would like to read up on the subject.

There are two other formal and authentic teaching documents in this general area but not specifically focused on the living will.

For the general framework and authoritative Catholic teaching on the immorality of direct euthanasia, see the fourteen-page *Declaration on Euthanasia* released by the Congregation for the Doctrine of the Faith. This *Declaration* concisely covers: (1) value of human life; (2) euthanasia; (3) meaning of suffering for Christians and the use of pain-killers; and (4) due proportion in the use of (ordinary-extraordinary) remedies. As the footnotes attest, this definitive teaching of the Holy See is heavily indebted to and explanatory of the teaching of Pope Pius XII.

In the highly specific and nuanced technical questions concerning assisted nutrition and hydration, the Administrative Board of the NCCB approved of the statement of their Committee for Pro-Life Activities: "*Nutrition and Hydration: Moral and Pastoral Reflections*" (April 2, 1992).

This last document requires but rewards very careful reading: an introduction and statement of eight moral principles is followed by seven specific questions, with a conclusion and appendix. This document does not attempt to answer all cases, but it is an excellent statement of correct principles and presumptions that are pertinent and helpful in resolving all cases in this area. A suicide is a crime in most jurisdictions; and it should be kept a crime for that is what it is—the direct killing of another albeit (supposedly) at the request of the victim.

This is not hysteria nor guesswork about how the slippery slope slips or slopes. We are grateful to the good citizens of Washington

State (November 1991) and California (November 1992) for defeating statewide propositions to legalize direct killing. Advocates of legalized killing no longer debate the merits or demerits of their advocacy, rather they presume voluntary euthanasia is accepted and now argue only what conditions or cautions should be in place to contain this plague.

The *New England Journal of Medicine* is surely the most prestigious medical journal in this country, perhaps in the world. I suspect that the editors of the *NEJM* guessed wrong on the outcome of California Proposition 161. Guessing that the California voters would approve assisted suicide on November 3, 1992, the *Journal* published a "Sounding Board" article timed for the same week.[1] Note well! The ethical case *for* assisted suicide is not argued at all; it is simply assumed, taken for granted that we have passed that barrier, all that remains to discuss is conditions ("criteria") to control this new "medicine". This is not what's next; this is where we *are* in the most prestigious medical publication in the country.

—October 1993

## Caring for Those with Dementia

**Question:** Is it obligatory to use assisted nutrition and hydration for an Alzheimer's patient who is otherwise healthy but whose dementia only increases?

**Answer:** This question does not seem to get the attention it deserves, and, often enough, is linked or lumped with very different cases.

First, the Alzheimer's patient is *not* a *dying* patient. The disease is chronic and usually progressive, but as your question notes, the person is otherwise healthy. Thus, he is a *non-dying* patient with increasing dementia, whose moral status is no different from a physically healthy person with mental retardation or senility.

More printed attention has been given to the permanently unconscious (PVS = persistent vegetative state) patient and medically assisted

[1] Timothy Quill, Christine Cassel, Diane Meier, "Proposed Clinical Criteria for Physician-Assisted Suicide", *New England Journal of Medicine* 327, no. 19 (Nov. 5, 1992): 1380–84.

nutrition and hydration. Thus, e.g., Benedict M. Ashley and Kevin D. O'Rourke argue that "if the cognitive-affective function cannot be restored, the artificial nutrition and hydration may be withheld or withdrawn".[2] Whereas Germain Grisez, in one of the longest case studies in his *Difficult Moral Questions*, argues the opposite with other and nuanced proposals.[3] It seems to me that Grisez has the correct answer because of his more careful philosophical presuppositions and an equally careful argument of virtue ethics.

As mentioned above, the case you present is not as extreme as the permanently unconscious and thus is free from the uncertainties of how permanent is "permanent", what is the true pathology, and how clinically tight is the definition and diagnosis of PVS.

Surely, Grisez, and perhaps Ashley and O'Rourke, would give an affirmative answer to your question, as I would, but in fairness, I cannot quote these authors for an opinion they did not explicitly formulate.

The NCCB Board–approved statement *Nutrition and Hydration: Moral and Pastoral Reflections* remains, I believe, the best resource document on this area. The bishops wisely do not attempt to answer every possible case antecedently, but they do provide principles and presuppositions that are highly useful in addressing any case.

At one point, the bishops say: "The area of legitimate controversy does not concern patients with conditions like mental retardation, senility, dementia or even temporary unconsciousness" (no. 6). As stated above, the patient with Alzheimer's is *not a dying* patient, but rather a patient with increased or increasing dementia.

On this particular case, I consulted with my special "experts": the Little Sisters of the Poor and the Carmelite Sisters, who administer several large nursing homes in my area. The Little Sisters (LSP) exercise great effort to avoid tube-feeding, a principle which in practice sometimes involves great amounts of time in the oral feeding of advanced Alzheimer's—forty-five minutes to more than one hour in feeding. Only in exceptional cases are they forced to go the route of tube-feeding. The Carmelite Sisters have a similar policy that, apart from dementia, with no big disease or fatal pathology, they always provide feeding, even medically assisted feeding when necessary.

---

[2] Cf. Benedict M. Ashley, O.P., and Kevin D. O'Rourke, O.P., *Health Care Ethics: A Theological Analysis* (Washington, D.C.: Georgetown University Press, 1997), pp. 426–48.

[3] Germain Grisez, *Difficult Moral Questions*, vol. 3 of *Way of the Lord Jesus* (Quincy, Ill.: Franciscan Press, 1997), pp. 218–25, q. 47.

One factor, often not mentioned but institutionally operative, is that the tube-feeding decision is sometimes motivated more by economic reasons than by clinical reasons. The bishops in their statement make the same point that helpless patients sometimes "receive tube feedings not because they cannot swallow food at all but because tube feeding is less costly and [less] difficult for healthcare personnel" (no. 4).

In some jurisdictions, administrators see a double efficiency advantage: personnel spend eight minutes instead of forty-five feeding someone, and "tube-fed" patients are considered sicker in some jurisdictions and reimbursed at higher rates.

In view of the above, it seems to me, that Alzheimer patients, without any fatal pathology, are *not dying* patients and should be fed, even with assisted nutrition and hydration when necessary.

—June 1998

## When to Withdraw Nutrition and Hydration

Question: There was a "right-to-die" case in Virginia with Catholic clerics and commentators on all sides. Is it legitimate to withdraw assisted nutrition and hydration from someone in a persistent vegetative state?

Answer: I cannot deny the controversy; see John J. Paris who argues "yes" and William E. May who argues "no" in this case.[4]

The case at issue here was that of Hugh Finn, a Catholic from Louisville, who ruptured his aorta in an auto accident that left him brain damaged. A feeding tube was inserted for assisted nutrition and hydration (N&H).

I was not and am not privy to the medical chart in this case, but almost every aspect of it was contradicted by someone. News reports have his wife arguing to remove the tube feeding, while his own parents and some siblings argued against that. The case was even brought

[4] John J. Paris, "Hugh Finn's 'Right to Die'", *America* 179, no. 13 (Oct. 31, 1998): 13–15; William E. May et al., "Tube Feeding and the 'Vegetative' State, Part One", *Ethics & Medics* 23, no. 12 (Dec. 1998):1–2; May et al., "Tube Feeding and the 'Vegetative' State, Part Two", *Ethics & Medics* 24, no. 1 (Jan. 1999): 3–4.

to the Virginia Supreme Court by the governor of that same state. The governor's appeal not to remove the feeding was rejected by that court, the assisted N&H was removed, and Hugh Finn died eight days later.

To complicate things further, some visitors and family members insisted that Mr. Finn was not in a persistent vegetative state (PVS). Some of these contentions were anecdotal, but they were statements of personal eyewitnesses. The actual medical chart and record would surely be of large importance here.

I doubt that there is a simple, single answer for all cases, such as, always yes or always no. Sound principles and presuppositions must be applied to the clinical, individual facts of a given case on a case-by-case basis.

In some prior columns, I have often referred to the U.S. Bishops' Pro-Life Committee statement *Nutrition and Hydration: Moral and Pastoral Reflections*. This is an excellent teaching document and a reliable reference that wisely, to my mind, does not try to answer all possible cases antecedently, but does provide moral principles and presuppositions necessary for resolving individual cases.

One specific question of the bishops' statement directly concerns this case: "Do persistently unconscious patients represent a special case?" (no. 6). Without repeating here their full response—which full response rewards close reading and study—two quick points can help all discussions.

First, terminology! The label *"vegetative"* in "persistent vegetative state" carries a somewhat pejorative connotation that might lead some to forget we are talking about *someone*, an unconscious patient, not about *something*, a subhuman vegetable. Thus, the bishops use the more humanly sensitive terminology "persistently unconscious patients".

Second is the bishops' well-reasoned presumption: "In light of these concerns, it is our considered judgment that while legitimate Catholic moral debate continues, decisions about these patients should be guided by a presumption in favor of medically assisted nutrition and hydration" (no. 6).

A presumption, of course, is just that, a presumption. The bishops continue to explain that this presumption can yield to facts, when there is "no reasonable hope of sustaining life" (e.g., when inevitable death is imminent from some other cause) or pose such excessive risks or excessive burdens as to render such treatments morally "extraordinary".

Further, the bishops are clear: "Such measures [assisted N&H] must not be withdrawn in order to cause death" (no. 6). Thus, all cases are not answered antecedently, but a sound presupposition is in place antecedently for considering all cases.

The Vatican *Charter for Health Care Workers* (1995) repeats the same presumption when explaining the principle of due proportion in treatment: "The administration of food and liquids, even artificially, is part of the normal treatment always due to the patient when this is not burdensome for him; their undue suspension could be real and properly so-called euthanasia" (no. 120).

The NCCB's *Ethical and Religious Directives* (1994) are also explicit: "'There should be a presumption in favor of providing nutrition and hydration to all patients, including patients who require medically assisted nutrition and hydration, as long as this is of sufficient benefit to outweigh the burdens involved to the patient" (no. 58).

On October 2, 1998, in an *ad limina* address, Pope John Paul II made explicit reference to this principled presumption and to the U.S. bishops' 1992 statement:

> The Statement of the U.S. Bishops' pro-life committee, "Nutrition and Hydration", rightly emphasizes that the omission of nutrition and hydration intended to cause a patient's death must be rejected and that, while giving careful consideration to all factors involved, the presumption should be in favor of providing medically assisted nutrition and hydration to all patients who need them. To blur this distinction is to introduce a source of countless injustices and much additional anguish, affecting those already suffering from ill health or the deterioration which comes with age, and their loved ones.[5]

Thus, from both universal and particular authorities, there is a well-founded presumption to provide assisted N&H unless there is no reasonable hope of sustaining life or the provision of this means itself places such excessive risks and burdens to be considered ethically extraordinary in a given case.

The U.S. bishops' statement takes note of some in-house Catholic debate on this point. That sounds like all Catholic authors agree on basic principles, but differ somewhat on their proper application to fact situations. From what I have read, some debates are not about applications

---

[5] Pope John Paul II, "Address to the Bishops of the Episcopal Conference of the United States of America [California, Nevada and Hawaii]", no. 4.

only but are real disagreements in principle. Thus, it is sometimes not a debate about a "reasonable hope of sustaining life", nor a debate that the "risks and burdens" are so excessive as to be ethically extraordinary and therefore non-obligatory in a specific case. Rather, some basic definitions and principles are truly at issue here, and they are crucial for framing the question properly. There is high potential for begging the question regarding N&H, depending on how you define it.

It was, I think, Daniel Callahan who first reported the term "biologically tenacious individuals", and who are they except those folks who are not dying fast enough. Father Richard McCormick has written of "merely physiological existence", which is, I take it, a breathing body but not a talking one. Twenty years ago, McCormick wrote that a good preserved independent of any capacity for conscious experience is "vitalism", and to continue mere physical life in that offers no human benefit.[6] Father Kevin O'Rourke writes: "If cognitive-affective function cannot be restored, then artificial nutrition and hydration can be withheld or withdrawn."[7] Father Paris in the *America* article above also speaks of restoration to a functioning cognitive existence.[8]

All of these definitions strike me as "dualism", which radically separates the body-soul composite so that mere "physical" existence is not considered truly *personal* or *human* existence. Once defined that way, the N&H question is already answered.

"What's the point?" some will ask. What's the point of feeding and hydrating mere physicality when it provides no *human* benefit? This seems to me at odds with the anthropology of Pope John Paul II concisely presented in the Vatican *Charter for Health Care Workers*: "What is and what happens biologically is not neutral. On the contrary, it has ethical relevance; it is the indicative-imperative for action. The body is a properly personal reality, the sign and place of relations with others, with God and with the world" (no. 41).

The body is a properly *personal reality*! Human bodily life is a good *of* the person, not just a good *for* other purposes. Bodily life is an intrinsic good *of* the person, not just an instrumental good *for* other plans. In sound Catholic doctrine, you are as much the soul of your

---

[6] Fr. Richard A. McCormick, "The Quality of Life, the Sanctity of Life", *Hastings Center Report* 8 (Feb. 1978): 30–36.

[7] Kevin O'Rourke, O.P., in "Suffering and Death", *Health Care Ethics*, 4th ed. (Washington, D.C.: Georgetown University Press, 1997), p. 426.

[8] Paris, "Hugh Finn's 'Right to Die'", p. 14.

body as you are the body of your soul. The two are not separated unless you are dead.

A brother may be diminished in "cognitive-affective" function; he may be profoundly short-changed in rational or relational "capacity"; even from birth, his I.Q. may be lessened, lowered, or flat, but his soul is no less, nor lowered, nor flat. He is one of us, no matter how little or poorly he functions. To frame it otherwise is to define him *out* of the human circle *into* some-less-than-human limbo. Such verbal engineering begs this and almost any other question in medical ethics.

In the Catholic understanding, we must distinguish between the dying patient and the *non-dying* patient. Thus, "when inevitable death is imminent" almost all treatments can become optional so long as the normal care due to the sick person is not interrupted (CDF, *Declaration on Euthanasia*, no. 4).

It seems to me—from what I have read—that Hugh Finn was not a dying patient, and surely not a patient for whom inevitable death was imminent. Of course, once assisted food and fluids were withdrawn, he then became a dying patient, since what was set in motion was a chain of events known to be death-dealing.

As above, medical, clinical factors could nuance the judgment, but what I would reject is a "cognitive-affective" criterion that effectively begs the question for PVS patients and almost any chronically ill who are also cognitively impaired. This, I believe, is not just a difference in application but a difference in principle.

Human life is a good of the person—an intrinsic personal good, not an instrumental one. This truth is repeated endlessly in *Evangelium Vitae*. This is not a "vitalism" to preserve or extend life by every possible means in every medical instance. No Western religion requires that, including Catholicism. But, the challenge on a case-by-case basis is to consider actual clinical and personal factors that make a means "extraordinary", not to collapse the whole question into cognitive-affective function or relational capacity where, by definition, the mentally impaired are doomed to lose.

The challenge of the case-by-case assessment is taxing and, at times, difficult, but the challenge must be met lest the chronically ill who are mentally impaired be dealt out and done in not by clinical facts but by fluid definitions.

—March 1999

## Persistent Vegetative State

Question: Press reports of a recent papal address claim the Pope has changed Church teaching regarding patients in a persistent vegetative state. Is that so?

Answer: Unlike many prior statements and studies, the recent (March 20, 2004) Vatican conference was highly specific and completely *ad rem*: "Life-Sustaining Treatments and Vegetative State: Scientific Advances and Ethical Dilemmas".[9]

No doubt, all agree with the papal reminder and caution that the adjective "*vegetative*" (in the term "vegetative state") must not cast doubt on the "human quality" of the patient—"vegetative" describes a clinical state and should not be used to demean the value or personal dignity of the patient. The intrinsic value and personal dignity of any human being does not change because of circumstances. A man—even if disabled or impaired in the exercise of his highest functions—is and always will be a man while alive, never a "vegetable", nor an "animal" (no. 3).

It is, however, number 4 of that papal address that has gathered the most attention and some varied and variant reactions. Here too, the introductory remark is accepted by all: "The sick person in a vegetative state, awaiting recovery or a natural end, still has the right to basic health care (nutrition, hydration, cleanliness, warmth, etc.) and to the prevention of complications related to his confinement to bed." It is, rather, the following specific that some contest or do not understand:

> I should like particularly to underline how the administration of water and food, even when provided by artificial means, always represents a natural means of preserving life, not a medical act. Its use, furthermore, should be considered in *principle* ordinary and proportionate, and as such morally obligatory insofar as and until it is seen to have attained its proper finality, which in the present case consists in providing nourishment to the patient and alleviation of his suffering. (no. 4, emphasis added)

It is here some assert that the Pope has opted for an excessively restrictive interpretation, that somehow departs from what they claim

[9] Cf. *Origins* 33, no. 43 (Apr. 8, 2004) papal address, pp. 739–40; other papers, pp. 742–52.

is the Church's sound moral tradition. In particular, some accuse the Pope of restrictively moving away from the normative standard of the CDF's *Declaration on Euthanasia.*[10]

Since John Paul II himself approved of and ordered the publication of that CDF *Declaration*, I find it unlikely that this Pope departs from or misunderstands his own formal teaching. It is true, that the Pope does not endorse the post-1980 interpretations of John J. Paris and the late Richard A. McCormick, but to disagree with Paris and McCormick hardly establishes a departure from Catholic tradition.

The conventional distinction between "ordinary", and "extraordinary" means remains what it is: (1) what offers a reasonable hope of benefit; (2) without a serious danger of death; and (3) without excessive pain, burden, or hardship. If it offers the positive (reasonable benefit) without the negative (excessive burden) it is "ordinary" for that patient and morally obligatory. If not, it is "extraordinary" and is ethically optional.

In this, we are committed to a case-by-case analysis, always attentive to the clinical facts and actual circumstances of the individual patient in a given case.

I see nothing in the Pope's March 2004 address that departs from this traditional analysis concerning assisted nutrition and hydration for patients in a persistent vegetative state. What the Pope specifies is a presumption—a presumption to provide food and water, even assisted food and water. This is considered "ordinary", "in principle", and "insofar as and until"—thus, a positive presumption that can, by exception, yield to extraordinary clinical facts.

The very same positive presumption about "assisted nutrition and hydration" is formally stated in the USCCB's *Ethical and Religious Directives* (1994 and 2001) in directive 58. The same presumption is found in number 120 of the Vatican *Charter for Health Care Workers.* Thus, there is no novel departure in the papal address, but a rather carefully stated consistency in papal and hierarchical teaching from which perhaps other sources have departed.

In particular, we must attend with great care to the doctrinal *Declaration on Euthanasia*. In the dispositive part of that declaration ("Due Proportion in the Use of Remedies"), there is this key teaching: "When

---

[10] E.g., cf. the somewhat tendentious article by Ronald Hamel and Michael Panicola, "Must We Preserve Life?" *America* 190, no. 14 (Apr. 19–26, 2004): 6–13.

*inevitable death is imminent* in spite of the means used, it is permitted in conscience to take the decision to refuse forms of treatment that would only secure a precarious and burdensome prolongation of life, so long as the normal care due to the sick person in similar cases is *not interrupted*" (no. 4, emphasis added).

Both the beginning and the end of that sentence are crucially important. "When inevitable death is imminent . . ." Clearly, there is a great moral difference between the case of the dying patient and that of the *non-dying* patient. When imminent (hours or days) death is inevitable, all sorts of means can become "extraordinary". But, that is clinically and morally different from the case of the non-dying patient.

Many simply assume that the cognitively impaired or unconscious patient is dying, and that, quite often, is simply not true. If, of course, we do withhold food and fluids from the cognitively impaired or unconscious patient, then we do set in motion another chain of events known to be death-dealing (dehydration and starvation). And this last omission cannot be confined merely or only to those in a persistent vegetative state.

Here too, the end of the above sentence is highly relevant: "normal care . . . is not interrupted". The Pope correctly identifies food, water, bed rest, room temperature, and personal hygiene as "normal care". Their deliberate or judicial omission is lethal; their deliberate omission to the non-dying is abandonment and not medical practice at all!

It has been almost customary for the past decade to say that all Catholic theologians surely agree on the same first principles, while some do not agree on some few applications of the same principles. Frankly, I do not think all theologians agree on all first principles.

Back in April of 1992, the U.S. bishops' Committee for Pro-Life Activities published a careful and detailed teaching document: *Nutrition and Hydration: Moral and Pastoral Reflections*. This is an excellent document that does not try to answer antecedently all possible cases but does present principles and presuppositions that are helpful in answering all questions.

While specifically commenting on the persistently unconscious patient, the bishops noted that some moralists hold the position that the chief criterion to determine the benefit of a procedure "cannot be merely that it prolongs physical life", but they assert "that the spiritual good of the person is union with God, which can be advanced only by human acts, i.e., conscious free acts". Since the PVS patient seems now or in the future incapable of conscious, free human acts, they argue it is not obligatory to prolong life by assisted nutrition and hydration. While admitting that this is the opinion of some, the bishops did not endorse that opinion; rather, indeed, they reject it: "While this rationale is convincing to some, it is not theologically conclusive and we are not persuaded by it. In fact, other theologians argue cogently that theological inquiry could lead one to a more carefully limited conclusion" (no. 6).

In 1992, this judgment of the NCCB was confirmed by the CDF, and clearly, the same is the confirmed judgment of John Paul II, i.e., a more "carefully limited conclusion".[11]

Of late, these theological positions have come to be called "the May position" and "the O'Rourke position".[12] In my judgment, the O'Rourke position is not a Catholic variant but is in fact mistaken. For O'Rourke, feeding is not a human benefit for those who lack (or seem to lack) "cognitive-affective functioning". In that analysis, it is not so much the clinical facts of the case that determine ordinary/extraordinary judgment, but rather one type of functioning includes or excludes a person from the human community. Human life is not seen as an intrinsic good of the person but more an instrumental good for other, albeit higher, purposes. In my judgment, the emphatic teaching of *Evangelium Vitae* repeats over and over that human life is an intrinsic good of the person, not merely an instrumental good.

For this reason, I do not believe all theologians agree on all first principles with some disagreements on the application of some. The difference in principle here is fundamental and can result in contradictory practice.

Unfortunately, the legal landscape today is both bleak and pervasive. Every court case that I know of and have read of has been settled in one direction, i.e., legal sanction for the omission of all means, including food and water, assisted or not. This is not the result of theological *uncertainty* but the uncritical legal exaltation of "absolute individual autonomy". While we should respect patient autonomy, that autonomy must be understood in a non-suicidal way—i.e., any action

---

[11] CDF, PN #230/74, (Mar. 17, 1992): 3.

[12] Cf. Msgr. Kevin McMahon, "Should Nutrition and Hydration Be Considered Medical Therapy?", *Origins* 33, no. 43 (Apr. 8, 2004): 746, referring to Prof. William E. May et al. and Rev. Kevin O'Rourke et al.

or omission that of itself or by intention causes death should not be given legal sanction.

I think the Pope's address does contribute carefully limited conclusions to this present discussion. My fear is that other careless or unlimited positions, especially within the Catholic community, will confuse rather than clarify present discussions.

—June 2004

## The Case of Terri Schiavo

Question: Given the massive media coverage of the Schiavo case, do you think that there may be some pro-life benefits in this tragic situation?

Answer: I would like to think that there may be some pro-life benefits, but my fear is that much of the fallout may well be negative.

In terms of media exposure and Congressional action, some aspects of the Terri Schiavo case are surely unique. That the U.S. Congress should meet in emergency session to pass legislation to cover the case of just one patient is unique. The President of the United States encouraged and signed the same legislation—all to no avail.

I am not a lawyer, but my hunch is that the legal dimension here was improperly canonized some fifteen years ago in the Nancy Cruzan case (Missouri) by the U.S. Supreme Court on June 25, 1990. While completely at odds on the moral assessment of the Schiavo case, two good legal minds have published clear and convincing legal analyses of it: George J. Annas and Robert T. Miller.[13]

Annas bemoans and belittles what he calls the "interference" of elected officials in this case, whereas Miller correctly points out that our laws already authorize a guardian to starve to death a ward and the only extraordinary thing about the Schiavo case is the amount of process and publicity it received compared to the others to whom the same thing has happened in almost every state, but quietly.

[13] See George J. Annas, "'Culture of Life' Politics at the Bedside", *New England Journal of Medicine* 352, no. 16 (Apr. 21, 2005): 1710–15; and Robert T. Miller, "The Legal Death of Terri Schiavo", *First Things*, no. 153 (May 2005): 14–16.

Thus, the first big fallout from the Schiavo case is surely a negative blow against the culture of life. It is now assumed by almost everyone that being fed is a "medical treatment". It is further assumed that there exists a court-approved legal "right" of *absolute individual autonomy*! So absolute is this personal autonomy that I now have a "legal right" to starve myself to death if that's what I really want and this is what I choose. And if I am unable to express that lethal choice, the "substituted judgment" of someone else (guardian, agent) can put the final word in for me.

Now, that is a dangerously unqualified principle. But, it is, I submit, an unprincipled principle that has no place in the culture of life but has legal standing and control in every court in the land.

This is the complete triumph of procedural ethics over substantive ethics. The substantive question about withholding or withdrawing assisted food or fluids is this: "Is this the right thing to do or not?" Factual, clinical circumstances matter greatly in correctly answering the substantive questions: Is the patient dying? Is the patient terminal? Is this procedure hurting far more than helping the patient? These must be answered on a case-by-case basis by the actual, factual circumstance of a given clinical case.

However, the substantive question of right-or-wrong does not get answered directly. Instead, and in its place, the substantive question is replaced by key legal questions of process and procedure—all procedural questions: Did the patient say so? By what evidence? Oral or written? Was it witnessed?

Judges, lawyers, and jurists love procedural questions because in answering them it does not sound like you are making value judgments (e.g., right/wrong; moral/immoral; ethical/unethical), but every time the substantive question of right or wrong is swallowed by a procedural question, a value judgment is certainly made; it is just not expressed directly.

As to the case in point: Was Terri Schiavo a dying patient? Surely not. Was she terminal? No. I have no access to her medical record and just about every aspect of it was contradicted by someone in print. Nonetheless, someone who is cognitively impaired, gravely damaged, even in a persistent vegetative state is not necessarily a dying patient. However, the withdrawal of assisted nutrition and hydration from an impaired person sets in motion a chain of causative events that we know is death-dealing (dehydration).

In Catholic teaching, assisted nutrition and hydration enjoy presumption of clinical use unless and until that presumption is contradicted by clinical facts—and that judgment rests and turns on medical facts not legal maxims.[14]

Again, this is a presumption of substantive ethics, and a presumption can yield to different and differing facts in a given case. However, since the Cruzan case of 1990, every court case I have read of simply runs over the substantive question of right-or-wrong and replaces it with the announcement of absolute autonomy—whatever the patient asked for, or whatever their agent said they said.

Another possible negative factor from the Schiavo case may be that it will be the occasion, if not the cause, of a rush or stampede to make out and sign carelessly worded or hastily drawn "living wills". "Living wills" are not legal documents in my state (New York), but they do and can serve as evidence in disputes.

We have, instead, a proxy document whereby a competent adult designates who can make decisions for you when you can't. That's fine. But, so-called "living wills" with simple checklists of sound bites—"no tubes for me", "no antibiotics" either—these misleading simplicities only foster the illusion that some checklist you sign today will somehow answer a case-specific choice in the future, and it will not.

Also, I don't know that I would call it a campaign, but the culture of death did a lot better in Hollywood this year than did the gospel of life. While Mel Gibson's *The Passion of the Christ* grossed over 600 million dollars, you might think that the movie Academy might have come up with some notable award for such a commercial success. Not so! The Oscar winner was *Million Dollar Baby*, kind of a female version of *Rocky*, full of struggle and despair along with the message that once you lose the ability to pulverize another woman in the boxing ring, life is not worth living. The Oscar for the best foreign-language film went to *Sea Inside*—a film about a Spanish quadriplegic who persuaded eleven friends to assist his suicide in a way whereby no one of them was technically guilty of homicide.

[14] Cf. USCCB, *Ethical and Religious Directive* (2001), no. 58; Vatican, *Charter for Health Care Workers* (1995), no. 120; Pope John Paul II, "Address to the Participants in the International Congress on 'Life-Sustaining Treatments and Vegetative State'" (Mar. 20, 2004).

Away from Hollywood and back to medicine, on March 10, 2005, the *New England Journal of Medicine*, the most prestigious medical journal in the world, published an article by two Dutch physicians about euthanasia for "severely ill newborns". These two doctors did not apologize nor deny that they have deliberately killed some medically compromised (but non-dying) newborns, but rather they went into print to show how their approach suits, what they call, "our legal and social culture" in the Netherlands.[15]

The late Pope John Paul II was correct when he spoke of the culture of life and the culture of death. It's not just one bad judge or one bad case, nor one bad movie or one bad article in a prestigious publication. It's the culture—the ethos, character, lived virtue, and morality—that need witness and support across the board.

For anyone who was created (which is all of us), there is no such thing as absolute individual autonomy. We must witness that truth in positive affirmation and negative avoidance through every means available to every one of us.

—July 2005

## Brain Death Criteria

Question: Does the Church accept "brain-death criteria" as a proper definition of death?

Answer: Yes, but the potential for answering the wrong question here is high, so we must be as precise as we can.

In our country, the NCCB's 1994 *Ethical and Religious Directives* correctly states: "The determination of death should be made by the physician or competent medical authority in accordance with responsible and commonly accepted scientific criteria" (no. 62). "Brain-death" is not explicitly mentioned in that directive, nor is it specifically excluded. Indeed, "brain-death" criteria are "commonly accepted scientific criteria" and those criteria are "canonized"—if you will.

[15] Eduard Verhagen, M.D., J.D., and Pieter J.J. Sauer, M.D., Ph.D., "The Groningen Protocol—Euthanasia in Severely Ill Newborns", *New England Journal of Medicine* 352, no. 10 (Mar. 10, 2005): 962.

It is not the function or the competence of the Church to establish scientific criteria as such, whereas it is the function and competence of the Church to judge the compatibility (or lack thereof) of such criteria with true teaching and certain moral principles.

The Vatican *Charter for Health Care Workers* states the same position: the moment of death is not directly perceptible, and the problem is to identify the signs: "To ascertain and interpret these signs is not a matter for faith and morals but for medical science" (no. 128).

The same *Charter* notes that the Pontifical Academy of Science offers this definition: "A person is dead when he has irreversibly lost all ability to integrate and coordinate the physical and mental functions of the body" (no. 129). As to the precise moment of death: "Death comes when (a) the spontaneous functions of heart and breathing have definitively ceased, or, (b) the irreversible arrest of all brain activity. In reality 'brain death' is the true criterion of death, although the definitive arrest of cardio-respiratory activity very quickly leads to brain death" (no. 129).

Faith and morals accept these findings of science, but they also demand the most accurate use of the various clinical and instrumental methods for a *certain* diagnosis of death.

The traditional criteria for the clinical determination of death were (and are) lack of spontaneous respiration and heartbeat. The development of the stethoscope in the nineteenth century greatly enhanced accurate determination of respiration, just as the development of the electrocardiogram in the twentieth century enhanced diagnosis of heartbeat (or its absence).

Later in the twentieth century, several generations of improved ventilators were able to support respiration artificially, as cardiac pacemakers were able to support heartbeat artificially. Thus, the traditional "signs" of no spontaneous respiration and heartbeat could be "clouded" when surrounded by artificial interventions.

Nonetheless, it is still true from the viewpoint of physiology that natural control of respiration is centered in the brain stem. And so, the modern focus on the *interrelationship* of cardiac, respiratory, and central nervous system functions. Correctly and perceptively, the Linacre Institute Position Paper of the Catholic Medical Association pointed out that "brain-death" *criteria* do not invent a new kind of death but "rather they reinforce the concept of death as the phenomenon in which there is disintegration of the human organism as an integrated whole". Thus, "the brain-death standards are merely supplementary to the existing cardiopulmonary standards which will continue to be adequate in the overwhelming majority of cases." [16]

Quite recently, Pope John Paul II in an address to a transplant congress in Rome taught directly on this subject, clarifying authoritatively what the Church does teach and what she does not teach on this matter. Since the Pope's words and distinctions are so carefully chosen, it is best to quote him at length:

> When can a person be considered dead with complete certainty?
>
> In this regard it is helpful to recall that the *death of the person* is a single event, consisting in the total disintegration of that unitary and integrated whole that is the personal self. It results from the separation of the life-principle (or soul) from the corporal reality of the person. The death of the person, understood in this primary sense, is an event which *no scientific technique or empirical method can identify directly*.
>
> Yet human experience shows that once death occurs *certain biological signs inevitably follow*, which medicine has learnt to recognize with increasing precision. In this sense, the "criteria" for ascertaining death used by medicine today should not be understood as the technical-scientific determination of the *exact moment* of a person's death, but as scientifically secure means of identifying *the biological signs that a person has indeed died*.
>
> ... [S]cientific approaches to ascertaining death have shifted the emphasis from the traditional cardio-respiratory signs to the so-called *"neurological"* criterion. Specifically, this consists in establishing, according to clearly determined parameters, ... the complete and irreversible cessation of all brain activity (in the cerebrum, cerebellum and brain stem). This is then considered the sign that the individual organism has lost its integrative capacity.
>
> With regard to the parameters used today for ascertaining death ... the Church does not make technical decisions. She limits herself to the Gospel duty of comparing the data offered by medical science with the Christian understanding of the unity of the person, bringing out the similarities and the possible conflicts capable of endangering respect for human dignity.
>
> Here it can be said that the criterion adopted ..., namely, the *complete* and *irreversible* cessation of all brain activity, if rigorously applied, does not seem to conflict with the essential elements of a sound anthropology. Therefore a health-worker professionally responsible for

---

[16] Eugene F. Diamond, M.D., "Determination of Death", Linacre Institute Position Paper, *Linacre Quarterly*, 57, no. 4 (Nov. 1990): 49, 50.

ascertaining death can use these criteria in each individual case as the basis for arriving at that degree of assurance in ethical judgment which moral teaching describes as "moral certainty". This moral certainty is considered the necessary and sufficient basis for an ethically correct course of action. Only where such certainty exists, and where informed consent has already been given by the donor or the donor's legitimate representatives, is it morally right to initiate the technical procedures required for the removal of organs for transplant.[17]

## Addendum

While accepting the evidence or "signs" of "brain death" (i.e., the whole brain together with the brain stem), the rules of prudence still apply in this area. For example, the 1994 *Ethical and Religious Directives* require that we avoid what could be an obvious conflict of interest: "Such organs should not be removed until it has been medically determined that the patient has died. In order to prevent any conflict of interest, the physician who determines death should not be a member of the transplant team" (directive 64).

The Linacre Institute Position Paper on "Determination of Death" properly insisted that the determination of death by brain-based criteria must be clearly distinguished from other controversies:

(1) The *Persistent Vegetative State* (PVS): where brain-stem function remains but major components of cerebral function are irreversibly destroyed, that patient is *not* "brain-dead." These patients may exhibit sleep-wake cycles, yawning, involuntary movements and independent respiration— they are not "brain-dead."

(2) *Do Not Resuscitate* (DNR) orders: This is a decision that cardiopulmonary resuscitation and other extraordinary measures are contraindicated because of the hopelessness of the patient's prognosis. A declaration of death is not required before ceasing such aggressive treatment. Indeed, to call an aggressive full "code" on a dead person is not only useless but obscene.

(3) *Anencephalic organ donation*: The anencephalic infant is born with brain-stem function and therefore does not qualify for the "dead-donor" rule. Precisely because the anencephalic is not demonstrating whole brain loss of function it would be immoral to use him as an

---

[17] "Address of the Holy Father John Paul II to the 18th International Congress of the Transplantation Society" (Aug. 29, 2000), nos. 4, 5, emphasis in original.

organ donor. The anencephalic newborn is close to death, even dying, but is not dead!

(4) *Ordinary and extraordinary* distinction: This traditional formulation of differing obligations to use or accept certain forms of therapy is not relevant to the patient who is brain dead. That patient is beyond benefit or burden; all means—ordinary or extraordinary—are now irrelevant, what was a patient is now a corpse and is due the respect we owe to that state.[18]

---

[18] Diamond, "Determination of Death", p. 48.

# 6

# Organ Transplants

## Organ Donation

Question: Does the Church recommend organ donation for purposes of transplant?

Answer: Traditionally, the question is posed in terms of permissibility, rather than recommendation: Does the Church prohibit organ donation? The answer since the time of Pope Pius XII is no—the Church does *not* prohibit this (cf. *CCC*, no. 2296 for a clear and concise statement).

There are, of course, different kinds of transplants. First, among the living (*inter vivos*), i.e., the transplant of a non-vital organ, which does not cause the death of the donor. One well-publicized example is the transplant of a single kidney from a healthy person to another in grave medical need (cf. NCCB's 1994 *ERDs*, directive 30, which prescribes informed consent and proscribes commercial advantage).

There are, as well, *post mortem* (cadaver) transplants (e.g., heart, lungs, liver, both kidneys). In the traditional analysis, this can be justified on the principle of fraternal charity, provided the following conditions are met: (1) proper prior consent is given by the patient, or, with the deceased, consent of nearest of kin; and (2) that the remains of a human being be treated with the respect consonant with what was, until death, a temple of the Holy Spirit.

The 1994 NCCB *Ethical and Religious Directives* state: "Catholic health care institutions should encourage and provide the means whereby those who wish to do so may arrange for the donation of their organs and bodily tissue, for ethically legitimate purposes, so that they may be used for donation and research after death" (no. 63).

Directive 62 addresses the question of the determination of death, and directive 64 states, in order to avoid any obvious conflict of interest "the physician who determines death should not be a member of the transplant team."

Now, in chapter 4 ("For a New Culture of Human Life"), Pope John Paul II writes in his encyclical *Evangelium Vitae* (*EV*):

> Over and above such outstanding moments, there is an everyday heroism, made up of gestures of sharing, big or small, which build up an authentic culture of life. A particularly *praiseworthy* example of such gestures is the *donation of organs*, performed in an ethically acceptable manner, with a view to offering a chance of health and even life itself to the sick who sometimes have no other hope. (no. 86, emphasis added)

To my knowledge, this is the first time papal teaching has moved from simple justification in this area to something that is called "praiseworthy". This both accords with and supports the NCCB wording of directive 63 above.

In all of the above, however, consent is not simply presumed but rather must be truly informed consent. Further, there is a necessary qualification in this endorsement: "performed in an ethically acceptable manner" (*EV*, no. 86).

One reason for some caution is stated earlier in the same encyclical: "Nor can we remain silent in the face of other more furtive, but no less serious and real, forms of euthanasia. These could occur for example when, in order to increase the availability of organs for transplants, organs are removed without respecting objective and adequate criteria which verify the death of the donor" (*EV*, no. 15).

—November 1995

## Catechism Changes on Organ Transplants

**Question:** I read that the *Catechism* changed its explanation of transplants. If so, where do you find these corrections?

**Answer:** The *Catechism* treats the subject of transplants in number 2296. As to your second question first, the Latin (definitive) edition of the *Catechism* is now in print.[1]

---

[1] *Catechismus Catholicae Ecclesiae* (Vatican City: Libreria Editrice Vaticana, 1997).

While some few corrections are significant, most are not so important as to warrant a new translation. A complete list of the changes in the *Catechism* was published in *Origins*[2] (the English translation was released by the Vatican). I have found that the tiny or editorial corrections can be easily inserted with a ballpoint pen; longer ones, if xeroxed, can be simply attached or inserted at the proper page.

As to your first question, the *Catechism* regarding transplants now reads:

> *Organ transplants* are in conformity with the moral law if the physical and psychological dangers and risks to the donor are proportionate to the good that is sought for the recipient. Organ donation after death is a noble and meritorious act and is to be encouraged as an expression of generous solidarity. It is not morally acceptable if the donor or his proxy has not given explicit consent. Moreover, it is not morally admissible directly to bring about the disabling mutilation or death of a human being, even in order to delay the death of other persons. (no. 2296)

If you compare this official version (1997) with your original English translation (1994), there is a slightly different editorial arrangement and a conditioned encouragement not present in the original French *Catechism*.[3] The last sentence is the same in both versions—to cause death or disabling mutilation to help someone else is immoral.

The original treatment began with the requirement for informed consent and then proportionality without explicitly distinguishing *inter vivos* transplants from cadaver transplants. The Latin edition now places the proportionality requirement first, and then calls *post mortem* (cadaver) transplants "a noble and meritorious act and is to be encouraged as an expression of generous solidarity". To be morally acceptable, this cadaver transplant requires the *explicit* consent of the donor or his proxy. The original *Catechism* said only that transplants "can be meritorious", whereas the corrected *Catechism* goes further, regarding cadaver transplants, calling it a noble and meritorious act "to be encouraged".

To my knowledge, no prior document of the Holy See ever "encouraged" cadaver transplants, but left it strictly as an elective and ethically extraordinary procedure—one is free to consent to this if the moral

[2] "Vatican List of Catechism Changes", *Origins* 27, no. 15 (Sept. 25, 1997): 257–62.

[3] Papal approval was first given to the *Catechism*, originally written in French, in December 1992. The English translation of that first edition was not released until 1994. Some changes were made to the final, official Latin version published in 1997.

requirements are fulfilled, or free to forgo the same. That *explicit* consent remains a moral requirement, and it still remains an ethically optional (extraordinary) procedure.

Perhaps, the added nuance of qualified "encouragement" reflects the positive teaching of Pope John Paul II in *Evangelium Vitae*, where he wrote: "A particularly praiseworthy example of such gestures is the donation of organs, performed in an ethically acceptable manner, with a view to offering a chance of health and even life itself to the sick who sometimes have no other hope" (no. 86). The corrected 1997 *Catechism* now also adds a cross-reference to this passage (no. 2296), referring to number 2301.

—March 1998


## Anencephalic Donors

Question: What about the use of anencephalic neonates as organ donors?

Answer: I report with profound sadness and genuine alarm that the Council on Ethical and Judicial Affairs of the American Medical Association (AMA) published a Council Report on this very topic in the *Journal of American Medical Association*.[4]

As recently as 1988, the same Council had examined the same issues and concluded that it is "ethically acceptable" to use organs from anencephalic neonates *only after they have died.*[5]

Then, in June 1994, the same Council "revised" its position and issued a new opinion: that it is ethically acceptable to transplant the organs of anencephalic neonates *even before the neonates die*, as long as there is parental consent and certain other safeguards are followed.[6] This, of course, is no small "revision" but a complete "reversal" and a profound ethical collapse.

---

[4] Council on Ethical and Judicial Affairs of the AMA, "The Use of Anencephalic Neonates as Organ Donors", *Journal of American Medical Association* 273, no. 20 (May 24/31, 1995): 1614–18.

[5] AMA, "Reports", vol. 1 (1992), pp. 49–52.

[6] AMA, *Code of Medical Ethics* (Southern Illinois University, 1994), p. 162, n. 2.

The most recent Report published in May 1995 presents the rationale for this reversal while noting, somewhat drolly, that what they advocate is illegal in most jurisdictions. The presenting reasons are as follows: (1) a shortage of organs for transplant in infants and young children; (2) anencephalic neonates lack functioning cerebral hemispheres and never experience any degree of consciousness; (3) the benefits of such transplants will be saving other young from death, and many others will realize a substantial improvement in their quality of life, arguing that parents too might benefit since faced with a tragedy with no solution their distress might be alleviated by the good results that can benefit others (CEJA, "Use of Anencephalic Neonates", pp. 1614–15).

The Council Report lists five objections to parental donation of organs from anencephalic neonates: (1) it violates the prohibition of removing life-necessary organs from living persons; (2) false diagnosis of anencephaly may result in the death of neonates who could achieve consciousness; (3) it may open the door to organ removal from patients in a persistent vegetative state or other severely disabling conditions; (4) anencephalic neonates are rarely the source of organs for transplant; (5) it might undermine public confidence in the organ transplantation system (p. 1615).

All of these objections have merit but the first is so transparently important that it is an ethical Rubicon that should never be crossed and never sanctioned. Both sound law and sound ethics require that persons be dead before their life-necessary, nonrenewable organs be taken. In the literature, this is called the "dead donor" rule. A good rule!

As the AMA Council admits, this critical principle ensures that one person's life will not be sacrificed for the benefit of another person, even to preserve the life of that other person. And while the Council argues that this principle must be "vigorously maintained", they argue further it must not be applied without regard for the purpose of its application. After considering the purposes of the prohibition, they argue it would not be compromised by parental donation of organs from anencephalic neonates.

Here, their reasoning and rhetoric become truly Orwellian: "Protecting the Interests of Persons from Whom Organs Are Taken". Ordinarily, the "dead-donor rule" protects the fundamental interest in life of persons from whom organs are taken. "However, it does not make sense to speak of an interest of anencephalic neonates in staying alive." Why? "Because they have never experienced consciousness and will never experience consciousness, *anencephalic neonates cannot have interests of any kind*" (p. 1615, emphasis added).

If their lives are shortened, they lose days of life, but have no awareness of that loss. "If there is a loss, it is a loss for others, whether for their parents or for society generally. Similarly, the value in the life of an anencephalic neonate is a value only for others" (p. 1615).

There it is as boldly as one can state it—true twentieth-century gnosticism in its crudest form: bodily life is not seen as a good of the person; no, it is only an instrumental "good" for others, perhaps "society generally". Nothing could be more profoundly at odds with a basic theme of *Evangelium Vitae*—that life is *always* a good (nos. 29–41).

The AMA Council Report nowhere informs us how or why doctors of medicine are best able to determine who has "no interest" in living. Is it even a question of medicine to ask, much less answer, which life (or lives) have *no* value in themselves but only for others? Were not doctors of another continent but this century put on trial at Nuremberg for acting out such "value" shifts?

Anencephaly is a tragedy, but why compound the tragedy with killing? "If their lives are shortened, . . ." the Report reads. That, of course, is shorthand for: if their lives are "taken", that is, if they are *killed*. Doctors must not kill. As *Evangelium Vitae* argues so consistently, the Fifth Commandment of God applies to everyone—"Thou shalt not kill!" It applies to doctors of theology, doctors of law, and doctors of medicine too.

—November 1995

## Organ Sales

Question: I enclose an article from the *New York Times Magazine* (May 27, 2001) on the sale and marketing of kidneys from live donors for transplant. My impression was that the sale of organs from live donors was both illegal and immoral. Does the Church have a teaching on this?

Answer: I would agree that the commercial sale of human organs is both illegal and immoral; however, popular and professional opposition to this commerce may be weakening.

The *New York Times Magazine* article, "This Little Kidney Went to Market" by Michael Finkel is a good example. While some pros and cons are duly noted, the basic utilitarian shift and drift in the wrong direction is pretty obvious. (Indeed, a prior ethics column in the British medical journal, *The Lancet*, "The Case for Allowing Kidney Sales" [7] went pretty much unnoticed in our country.)

The *New York Times Magazine* reports that the sale of human organs is against the law in virtually every country, with perhaps the exception of Iraq. It has been condemned by all of the world's medical associations. Yet, in Israel, and a few other nations, including India, Turkey, China, Russia, and Iraq, organ sales take place without excessive secrecy. China apparently sells cadaver organs from dead prisoners. Some insurance providers see a quiet benefit here—while the short-term cost of kidney surgery is high, the long-term cost of dialysis may be more.

Very few transplants (legal or illegal) take place in Israel, but they can take place as an arranged package deal (trip-surgery-recovery-return) in Istanbul, Turkey, and in Iraq. An American entrepreneur, Jim Cohan of Los Angeles—who does not like to be called an "organ broker" since he prefers the title "international transplant coordinator"—used to accompany clients on their transplant trips until he was arrested in Italy in March of 1999. The Italian courts ultimately let him go since they concluded that he had broken no laws.

*The Lancet* and some other advocates of organ sales duly register some cautions about "potential abuse", but almost all of the *Times* article's examples document *actual* abuse. There is the tragic case of a forty-four-year-old Turk who sold a kidney to help pay for some corrective surgery for his youngest child that he could never possibly afford. He received half ($10,000) of the promised price, and his child never did get the needed surgery for a degenerative bone disease. Turning one's poverty into another's opportunity is simply a violation of the most basic standards of ethics.

Only a small portion of money goes to the person selling the organ—as little as $800 and not more than $10,000. In fact, there may even be a surplus of kidneys in some places—sellers in India and Iraq actually line up at hospitals willing to part with a kidney for less than $1,000. Most studies and follow-ups report on the recipients, not on

[7] Janet Radcliffe-Richards, et al., "The Case for Allowing Kidney Sales", *The Lancet* 351, no. 9120 (June 27, 1998): 1950–52.

the donors. The last category may not be problem-free, since those who live in abject poverty usually live in conditions of poor diet, low-quality drinking water, and increased risk of infectious diseases. No one seems to say much or report much about these sellers.

Along with the above factors, consider the pertinent directives for Catholic teaching and practice. Directive 30 of the 1994 NCCB *Ethical and Religious Directives* states in part: "Furthermore, the freedom of the prospective donor must be respected, and economic advantages should not accrue to the donor."

The Vatican *Charter for Health Care Workers* also proscribes commercialization:

> The medical intervention in transplants "is inseparable from a *human act of donation.*"... "It is a decision to offer, without reward, a part of one's own body for the health and well-being of another person. In this sense, the medical action of transplantation makes possible the donor's act of self-giving, that sincere gift of self which expresses our constitutive calling to love and communion." [8]

The same *Charter for Health Care Workers*, in footnote 185, makes further reference to a teaching of Pope Pius XII, urging some "intelligent reserve" in this matter. Pope Pius agreed that demanded recompense (for an organ) would be an abuse, but it would also be an exaggeration to say that the acceptance of any recompense is immoral. He argued the case is analogous to that of blood transfusions ("To the Delegates of the Italian Association for Cornea Donors and the Italian Union for the Blind", May 14, 1956).

On the one hand, I know of no moralist who would argue against the donor receiving compensation (cost coverage) for the medical expenses and perhaps loss of wages or other inconvenience for making the organ available, so long as there is no payment for (purchase) the organ itself. On the other hand, organ donation is not truly analogous to blood transfusion. In a healthy person, blood donations do replace themselves, whereas kidneys do not. [9]

---

[8] *Charter for Health Care Workers*, no. 90; the quotations are from John Paul II, "Address to Participants of the First International Congress of the Society for Organ Sharing" (June 20, 1991).

[9] For some early cautions and then increased clarity on this, cf. Albert S. Moraczewski, "A Sour Note in Organ Transplantation: Are Human Organs Saleable?" *Ethics & Medics* (Jan. 1984): 2–3; and J. Haas, "The Sale of Human Organs", *Ethics & Medics* 15 (Feb. 1990): 1–2.

The *Code of Medical Ethics* (2000–2001) of the American Medical Association takes a similar position:

> The voluntary donation of organs in appropriate circumstances is to be encouraged. However, it is not ethical to participate in a procedure to enable a living donor to receive payment, other than for the reimbursement of expenses necessarily incurred in connection with removal, for any of the donor's non-renewable organs. (no. 2.15)

More recently, and more in accord with a sound Christian anthropology, Pope John Paul II addressed this question directly in an address to a Transplant Congress in Rome. In part, the Pope taught:

> It must first be emphasized, as I observed on another occasion, that every organ transplant has its source in a decision of great ethical value: "The decision to offer without reward a part of one's own body for the health and well-being of another person" ("Address to the Participants in a Congress on Organ Transplants", June 20, 1991; no. 3). Here precisely lies the nobility of the gesture, a gesture which is a genuine act of love. It is not just a matter of giving away something that belongs to us, but of giving something of ourselves, for "by virtue of its substantial union with a spiritual soul, the human body cannot be considered as a mere complex of tissues, organs and functions ... rather it is a constitutive part of the person who manifests and expresses himself through it". (CDF, *Donum Vitae*, no. 3)
>
> Accordingly, any procedure which tends to commercialize human organs or to consider them as items of exchange or trade must be considered morally unacceptable, because to use the body as an "object" is to violate the dignity of the human person.[10]

In view of the above, I would judge the sale of organs from living donors immoral and hope that it remains illegal as well.

—August 2001

---

[10] John Paul II, "Address to the 18th International Congress of the Transplantation Society" (Aug. 29, 2000), no. 3.

7

# Justifiable Homicide, Capital Punishment, and War

## *Murder of Abortionist*

Question: Some pro-life friends argue that the murder of Dr. David Gunn in Florida was justifiable homicide. They argue that since the abortionist kills innocent babies, it is justifiable to stop him and save lives. What do you think?

Answer: I think the answer is already in the question. "Murder" is intrinsically evil, and murder for the best of reasons or the worst of reasons is always wrong.

Two preliminary points are not immediately *ad rem*, but they are worthy of consideration. All mainline pro-life groups are against murder, even of those who perform these abortions.

Next, as a tactic, these killings are the ultimate in counter-productivity. The pro-abortion media love such "tragedies" since they use and highlight them to smear and to discredit the whole pro-life movement with the "violence" blanket of a few extremists. We know this tiny extreme is not the center, but all sorts of mainline pro-lifers have to explain and distinguish themselves from activities that they have not and cannot condone. I have no illusions about converting or even reaching the media elite, but a large segment of the general population is misled and manipulated away from the main pro-life message and witness.

The basic argument of those who would try to justify such acts assumes too much and proves too little. The "justifying" comparison that I hear or read most goes like this: this is really an act of justifiable defense against an unjust aggressor.

Thus, as in conventional Christian ethics there can be and are justifying conditions for the use of force (even lethal force) to repel an unjust aggressor, the same, they argue, is true here. That is, the abortionist is really a "serial killer" of innocent babies. Indeed, the abortionist does not act out of passion, nor *pro bono*, but is a hired killer—a medical "hit-man" who kills the innocent for profit and prostitutes the medical profession in the process. Thus, the use of deadly force will prevent him from murdering more innocents.

All of this is true, but it also assumes too much, too quickly.

First, this assumes that one can try to kill a potential killer in order to prevent more killing. The Church repudiates the direct intent to kill. Justifiable self-defense applies only to that killing that is not directly intended, that is a secondary effect.

Moral theology does not permit the faithful Christian individual acting alone (on one's own authority) to intend to kill another person directly. Saint Thomas Aquinas, the usual and classic source of justifiable self-defense, is most insistent about this requirement (cf. *Summa Theologiae* [*ST*], II-II, q. 64, a. 7).

Next, the justifiable defense comparison urges that the guilt of a known intentional killing can be outweighed by preventing another, but as yet unknown, evil. But a good end does not justify an evil means (Rom 3:8).

Shooting the abortionist is not the same as killing in defense of home or family because the latter killing could be incidental, unintended, a secondary effect. Whereas the murder (from what I have read) was intended, premeditated, and not an accident at all.

Further, those who kill on their own authority open a dangerous spiral that all pro-lifers want shut. When the attacker attempts intended lethal force against the abortionist, is not the clinic guard free, and the police officer duty bound to repel the attacker with force, even lethal force? Where does this end? How is it limited?

A useful editorial in *Christianity Today* makes most of these points while providing important Christian reminders.[1] Some things that are understandable are not for that reason justifiable.

Direct abortion is murder. And I am sure we are all as tired of abortion as we are tired of murder. But using evil to fight evil shows our impatience with God. We must fight bad things in God's way: "Do not be overcome by evil, but overcome evil with good" (Rom 12:21).

---

[1] David Neff, "Unjustifiable Homicide", *Christianity Today* 37, no. 14 (Nov. 22, 1993): 13.

While we can hate evil as God surely does, we must as surely do good to our enemies as the same God teaches us. We must fight murder without conforming to it, nor condoning it in any way, but it makes no Christian sense to try to justify murder to limit murder.

It may be that the desperate reach of some extremists to justify killing is not so much an ethical problem as a spiritual one—we need our hearts and minds transformed and renewed by God. "Christians ultimately rest in the knowledge that God's sovereignty over life and death means that even the most tragic events will in eternity be seen to have worked for good and contribute to God's glory." [2]

—May 1994

## Bombing Iraq Not Justified

Question: In your opinion, do the bombing attacks on Iraqi targets fulfill the traditional just war criteria?

Answer: The traditional elements of what is called the "just war" doctrine are listed in the *Catechism* number 2309, along with numbers 2308 to 2314. First, we note the introduction of this teaching in the *Catechism*: "The strict conditions for *legitimate defense by military force* ..." (no. 2309; emphasis in the original, especially "*defense*").

In ways, the *Catechism*'s presentation of the elements or conditions of "just war" theory is overly concise; i.e., the space is small, examples are not given, and some terms are not fully explained. (This is not a criticism of the *Catechism* but simply to note its style—it is not a multi-volume encyclopedia.)

The U.S. bishops in *The Challenge of Peace: God's Promise and Our Response* of May 3, 1983, present a much fuller explanation of the "just war" criteria with several examples and contemporary applications (see nos. 85–110).

For reasons I do not understand, the secular media has been largely silent and offered something of a "free pass" on the morality of the U.S.-British attacks begun in December of 1998.

---

[2] Ibid., p. 13.

Personally, I do not consider Saddam Hussein a nice person; rather, he is a vicious dictator, sometimes aggressive and always shrewd, who does not hesitate to murder his own in-laws. His plots and policies have brought great suffering on his own people, make most of his neighbors understandably nervous, and he has contributed nothing to world peace and stability: no runs, no hits, all errors! Unfortunately, this dangerous character is not unique in this world, and perhaps it is because he is a dangerous character—with a proven track record not just a potential one—that the secular media find no sympathy for him or in him.

While all of this is, I believe, true of this dangerous character, nevertheless, being a dangerous character is not one of the elements of the "just war" criteria.

Shortly after the December 1998 U.S.-British air attacks, Archbishop Theodore E. McCarrick, head of the NCCB Committee on International Policy, properly raised the issue: "These military strikes unduly risk violating just war criteria."

Further, Archbishop Edwin O'Brien, Archdiocese for Military Services, issued a statement on December 30, 1998, sent to all Catholic chaplains noting that military personnel "are not exempt from making conscientious decisions".[3]

The statement asked the American administration to initiate no further military action in the Middle East. In concert with officials of the bishops' conference and the Vatican, Archbishop O'Brien gave voice to serious questions as to the justifiability of this military action: "whether just war requirements for non-combatant immunity, proportionality and probability of success could be met in this situation".

The Archbishop correctly notes that one who judges an action to be in violation of the moral law is bound to avoid that action; whereas, in the face of uncertain evidence the individual is justified in following the presumably better informed decisions of superiors. The last point is in accord with the *Catechism*'s teaching about the importance of "the prudential judgment of those who have responsibility for the common good" (no. 2309).

The air strikes, we are told, were designed to avoid any and every civilian target, which, if so, would surely reduce the probability of noncombatant injury. But, the proportionality and probability of success are serious questions here.

[3] See *Origins* 28, no. 30 (Jan. 14, 1999): 525.

What is "success" here? Some commentators spoke of "degrading Iraq's weapons systems". Sound bites like "degrade weapons" or "send a message" are highly ambiguous and hardly informative. If a policy goal is not stated with some clarity, it is very difficult to offer a judgment on the "probability of success" when there is no clear definition of what success is.

In addition, conventional just-war criteria address the question of being called by "competent authority" (cf. NCCB, *Challenge of Peace*, nos. 87 and 88; cf also, obliquely, *CCC*, no. 2309). It is not clear that these actions are under the mandate or sanction of the United Nations, and clearly, they were not mandated nor sanctioned by the U.S. Congress.

The just-war criteria are, after all, conditions for "*legitimate defense by military force*". I may be wrong in this assessment, but these air strikes (acts of war) can just as reasonably be described as *aggressive* acts rather than strictly *defensive* ones.

Perhaps since the Gulf War of 1991, the media has contributed to the public perception that "air strikes" are some kind of a video game, arranged and scripted for the evening news. When pilots are over ten thousand feet above targets and cruise missile launchers hundreds of miles away, this may not engage people as the conventional combat films and images of WWII, Korea, and Vietnam. However, the bombs and missiles are destructive, and they do land somewhere.

A brutal dictator's unjust invasion of Kuwait and his destructive exit from the same surely can qualify as aggressive acts, but it seems to me, apart from actual or truly imminent aggression, we do not have the moral right to bomb rulers and regimes we do not like, even when there is a good reason not to like them or trust them.

—July 1999

## War on Terrorism Meets Just-War Criteria

Question: Does the current war against terrorism fulfill the just-war criteria?

Answer: As it is now, and thus far, I believe it does. As I understand it, the U.S. bishops' conference supports the same conclusion in their statement *Living with Faith and Hope after Sept. 11* (November 14, 2001).

This is not a conventional kind of war with a nation-state aggressor and a nation-state defender. But, it is not simply a police question either, i.e., the pursuit, arrest, trial, and imprisonment of a murderous gang. Certainly, the mass murder attacks of 9-11 were acts of war against the United States in particular, and perhaps the West in general.

As I understand the just-war tradition and its conditions, it is fundamentally a moral framework rooted in justice and moral realism. When the adversary is not a uniformed army in the conventional sense, that does not really change the reality of the situation or the justice components that can be honored or dishonored.

No sane person likes war, but sanity can also be impaired by addiction to sentimentality. The pursuit of justice is an obligation of the state—indeed a moral obligation not merely a politically correct or incorrect option. A just war of defense is acknowledged by Vatican II (*Gaudium et Spes* [GS], no. 79) and clearly repeated in the *Catechism of the Catholic Church* (nos. 2308–10; also see no. 2240). The *Catechism* teaches "the right and duty to impose on citizens the *obligations necessary for national defense*" (no. 2310, emphasis in original).

The moral criteria (conditions) of the just-war teaching have been presented by scholars as a two-tier framework: first, the justice of the *war decision* (*ius ad bellum*); second, just-war *conduct* (*ius in bello*). While the two are closely connected (even sequential), they are not identical. Selective citation or focus on only one of the latter (conduct) without thoughtfully fulfilling the former (decision) can cause more confusion than clarity.

The war decision (*ius ad bellum*) calls for clear analysis on the "strict conditions for legitimate defense by military force": just cause; upright intention; last resort; hope of success; proportionate or appropriate to the goal (just cause) not producing evils and disorders greater than the evil to be opposed; conducted and called by competent public authority who have responsibility for the common good (cf. *CCC* no. 2309). Thus, the war decision must first find its possible justification in the fulfillment of these justice criteria.

Our difference between these latter (*in bello*) criteria and the first tier (*ad bellum*) criteria is that the *conduct* (*in bello*) criteria inevitably involve contingent and sometimes prudential judgments. To focus first or exclusively on the contingent can blur the political realism or drain the moral justice components of the just-war analysis. This is not the place to reargue the passions of the 1980s Cold-War rhetoric, but in my judgment, some spokesmen of just-war criteria did not state Catholic moral theory well at the time, with the unintended consequence that political correctness replaced political realism and the basic moral wisdom of the just-war analysis was somewhat muddled.[4]

This answer seems to be a convolution of cautions. In ways, it is; in ways, it's not. In the past twenty years, some official and scholarly Catholic commentary on just-war teaching has been, I think, somewhat confusing. Perhaps this was to try to accommodate political correctness, or, unprincipled pacifism, but the results of those misstatements come back to cloud what should be clear in the present case.

For example, the NCCB 1983 pastoral letter, *The Challenge of Peace*, (no. 80) and its update of 1993, *The Harvest of Justice Is Sown in Peace*, (no. 2) says: "The just-war tradition begins with a strong presumption against the use of force ..." This is simply not an accurate statement of the tradition historically or theologically. In fact, Saint Augustine does not begin with that presumption (*City of God*, 19:12) nor does Saint Thomas Aquinas (*ST*, II-II, q. 40, aa. 1–4), nor does Vatican II (*GS*, no. 79), nor does the *Catechism* (nos. 2304, 2308), nor do the pastoral letters of the West German bishops (April 18, 1984) or the French bishops (November 8, 1983).

The traditional analysis, especially the first-tier criteria (*ad bellum*) begins with justice and rights—the just pursuit and protection of justice and human and moral rights. A more accurate initial statement of the question is found in the words Aquinas attributes to Augustine: "Among true worshippers of God those wars are looked on as peacemaking which are waged neither from aggrandizement nor cruelty, but with the object of securing peace, of repressing the evil and supporting the good" (*ST*, II-II, q. 40, a. 1).

In the same past two decades, some official and scholarly Catholic commentary has made a moral equivalence of just-war theory and strict pacifism. For example, the 1983 pastoral letter asserts that just-war and pacifism are complementary (no. 74) that they share a common presumption (no. 120) but differ on *how* to defend the common

---

[4] For an excellent book on just-war theory—attentive both to political realism and to moral principle—cf. James Turner Johnson, *Morality and Contemporary Warfare* (New Haven, Conn. and London: Yale University Press, 1999).

good (no. 74). This is not only un-historical but slightly incoherent. Strict pacifism forbids the use of *any* force, whereas just-war theory holds that force can be justly used when certain moral conditions are fulfilled.

Clearly, just-war theory and pacifism do not share a common presumption against the use of force. One says it can be justified; the other says it is never justified. I cannot read that as complementary. In the tradition, the just use of force can be described as an act of virtue (justice; cf. *ST*, II-II, q. 188, a. 3), whereas strict pacifism holds the opposite conclusion and presumption.

The late Father Richard A. McCormick, writing in the *New Catholic Encyclopedia* (1967) held that strict pacifism was morally indefensible. Quoting John C. Murray paraphrasing Pope Pius XII, a Catholic citizen cannot refuse to give his service to the state and refuse to fulfill the duties affixed by law.[5] The *Catechism* also teaches that it is "morally obligatory ... to defend one's country" (no. 2240). Surely, some humane provision in civil law can be urged for individuals who opt out of politics or for reasons of conscience refuse to bear arms at all *provided*, however, that they accept some other form of service to the human community (*GS*, no. 79; repeated in *CCC*, no. 2311).

What McCormick wrote in 1967 was surely conventional teaching as are the relevant points of the Council and the *Catechism*. There would have to have been a gigantic (stealth) development of doctrine to state in 1983 (and again in 1993) that just-war doctrine and strict pacifism really agree on fundamental principle but differ only on *how* that basic principle (just force vs. no force) is carried out.

Perhaps pastoral teaching documents, produced by committees, have to embrace conflicting compromises to get the support of all committee members. This is the way of labor-management negotiations—give some partial thing to everyone, but don't give everything to anyone. This is the way of resolving disputes over wages, benefits, and work rules, and the same is often true of tortured but necessary legislative compromises. But this is not the way of fundamental moral principles—when you split the difference in principle of a principle, it simply ceases to be a first principle anymore.

---

[5] Fr. Richard A. McCormick, "Morality of War", *New Catholic Encyclopedia*, vol. 14 (New York: McGraw-Hill, 1967), p. 804.

A lack of clarity about political realism or moral principle on the first-tier criteria (*ius ad bellum*) will come back to haunt the advocates and documents that send a muddled message.

Recent examples are not lacking. Archbishop Edwin F. O'Brien of the Archdiocese for Military Service wrote a clear Christmas message (December 13, 2001) to Catholics in the U.S. military accurately reflecting his support and the support of the USCCB.[6]

However, the Archbishop's letter was preceded in the same issue of *Origins* by a statement ("The War ... Must Stop") from a group of U.S. Catholics (i.e., individuals whose organizations and titles are listed for identification purposes only)—in large part, Pax Christi and the Justice and Peace committees and coordinators of several religious orders of men and women. This group does some selective citation from the USCCB statement of November 14, 2001, to question and quibble with episcopal support for the war against terrorism. They argue that the 9-11 attacks on U.S. cities and citizens should be dealt with by police investigations and trial before such a tribunal as the World Court at the Hague. Significantly, however, they add: "[W]e invite our bishops and all Catholics to rethink the 'just-war' tradition and seek a new paradigm for judging questions of war and peace today" (p. 506).

Surely, there is no harm in rethinking settled doctrine or any work in progress. But it seems to me pretty clear that prior but relatively recent statements that just-war doctrine and pacifism are really two complementary branches of the same Catholic trunk can also be rethought. They do not share the same first principle while differing only on *how* that principle is carried out. They differ not only in application but differ in principle at root.

In a sense, these so-called "peace groups" are consistent—they *don't* include themselves in the just-war paradigm, as they call it; they ask and seek a different paradigm, i.e., a doctrine different from Augustine, Aquinas, the Council, or the *Catechism*.

Yes, I do believe the present war against terrorism, as it is and thus far, is justified on the just-war analysis. However, I do not believe that all mentions of just-war theory accurately reflect the tradition they claim to represent.

—April 2002

---

[6] *Origins* 31, no. 30 (Jan. 10, 2002): 508.

## Questioning the Invasion of Iraq

Question: Do you a think a U.S. war with Iraq would fulfill the conditions of the just-war criteria?

Answer: On this, I am somewhat conflicted because I am not entirely sure that the traditional just-war criteria perfectly fits this case (and even less so for the contemporary fight against terrorism).

I do accept the received teaching on the conditions for *legitimate defense by military force* that is concisely summarized in the *Catechism* (nos. 2308–14, esp. 2309). The statement of the 1992 *Catechism* is not novel; indeed, it accurately reflects the formal teaching of Vatican II (*GS*, nos, 79, 80).

In the time from the Council (1965) to the *Catechism* (1992), it has been my impression that not every Catholic spokesman for or of the so-called just war tradition has done justice to the tradition they claim to expound. Yet, on the positive side, I found two book-length works to be particularly helpful in presenting the Catholic tradition and trying, conscientiously, to apply it to contemporary and newer challenges: George Weigel, *Tranquillitas Ordinis*, and James Turner Johnson, *Morality and Contemporary Warfare*.[7]

In the present context of international terrorism, i.e., warlike acts that directly target innocents, we are forced to confront aggression. The *Catechism* teaches that "terrorism" is "gravely against justice and charity" (no. 2297).

It is not aggression in the conventional sense, as when armies cross borders and invade the territory of another country; it is rather a seemingly organized effort of we know not whom, we know not where, nor do we really know what they are up to. The harm, damage, and unjust loss of life of these aggressive acts are all too real, but their agents rarely give notice, warning, or explanation for the unjust damage they do.

At first, military action against the Taliban in Afghanistan was seen by most, I think, as a just and measured response. Clearly, that regime was a safe haven and welcome harbor for protecting, training, and

---

[7] George Weigel, *Tranquillitas Ordinis: The Present Failure and Future Promise of American Catholic Thought on War and Peace* (Oxford: Oxford University Press, 1987); see footnote 4 on p. 94 above for Turner publication details.

exporting terrorists in all directions, not to mention what they unjustly imposed on the diverse Afghan people.

Iraq seems to be a different case. What I have read, especially by Catholic authors and Catholic authorities, is a near-unanimous condemnation of military action against Iraq. The condemnation by European Catholics is most emphatic with near unanimity that any U.S.-British–led military action against Iraq is a clear violation of the just-war doctrine and is clearly immoral. To this point, I do not share their intensity or their emphatic certitude.

Some call this a "preemptive" war, thus a war of aggression, and by this claim contrary to the Council and the *Catechism*. I am not convinced that that is the only way to frame this question. Is this the first act of a *new* war, or, the last act of an *old* war? Could it not be described as "treaty enforcement", i.e., after repeated international warnings and resolutions since 1991, Iraq has not done what they agreed and pledged to do at the completion of the 1991 Gulf War?

Conventional just-war conditions: "just cause", "last resort", "hope of success", "competent authority", not producing evils and disorders graver than the evil to be eliminated—all these raise questions, the answers to which are not immediately obvious to me.

It is surely an anomalous situation that in the name of enforcing U.N. resolutions, the formal authority (even willingness) of the U.N. (in the Security Council) is not present. But, the substantive justice of this "cause" must count for something and not simply the legal or procedural aspects of what percentage of what majority renders an action moral or immoral.

Some argue that "containment" and full "inspection" can accomplish whatever military action is meant to do. Thus, this would not be a "last resort" in the conventional analysis since less drastic measures could accomplish "containment".

It is true that "containment" was a standard feature of post-WWII and Cold-War policy. However, when "containment" meant deterring Soviet tanks from rushing west to the North Sea in fifty-five hours or some fleet from crossing observable naval boundaries, this provided some security—strained and tense for sure, but some kind of security.

On the other hand, biological and chemical weapons of great destruction are readily delivered, even by single agents, and are not secure simply because they are "contained" within the geographical limits of

Iraq. Genuine inspections simply cannot work unless there is genuine and positive cooperation on the part of the host country. Iraq is a land of 16,700 square miles; no amount of inspectors can check all of it without cooperation. Thus far, Iraq has pledged this cooperation and verification, but the track record of genuine compliance has never been full and sometimes nonexistent.

The Social Justice Secretariat of the Society of Jesus has stated that the reasons for attacking Iraq are "not convincing", and the effects of a possible war will turn out to be so devastating that "it becomes very difficult, if not impossible to justify a military intervention".[8] Without question, the doctrine of "unanticipated consequences" poses serious and grave factors in "not producing evils and disorders graver than the evil to be eliminated". What will such an attack unleash within the already troubled area of the Middle East? What will a post–Saddam Hussein Iraq become with its deeply divided factions and rivalries? What will heighten tensions between Muslims and the West?

Yet, along with the "unanticipated consequences" that no one can now predict with certitude, there are the anticipated consequences of continuing a criminal regime that unjustly, even violently, oppresses large segments of its own population.

There is and should be respect for legitimate and sovereign states. But, state sovereignty should not become a shield to deflect criticism from homeland injustice while using international forums to lecture other sovereign states how to behave.

Certainly, the United Nations is the international organization for peace and peaceful cooperation among sovereign states. However, the number of functioning democracies in the U.N. is actually a modest number. The dedication of some U.N. members to its democratic procedures and procedural legalities that can summon a majority vote sometimes produces stunning contradictions. Some vigorously vote for democratic procedures for others to observe while such procedures are neither tolerated nor permitted in their own countries.

Recently, the Sudan had a vote on a U.N. human rights commission. Sudan! One of the few places on earth that tolerates slavery and even the commercial buy-back of slaves. That regime does not deserve an international human rights vote. Just as truly, Iraq is not

---

[8] Fernando Franco, S.J., Secretary, Letter to the Provincial Co-ordinators of Social Apostolate, "War Is a Defeat for Humanity" (Feb. 7, 2003).

the only country to be in violation of clear and long-standing U.N. resolutions.

In sum, I am conflicted and somewhat ambivalent about the justice of the anticipated war with Iraq. I do not share the emphatic certitude of the many European critics who judge this question so clearly as immoral. While I respect the traditional just-war criteria as part of our received teaching, given the nature and reality of the new war of and on international terrorism, the application of the traditional criteria is difficult but not unreasonable.

To me, the justice of the cause looms very large in the conventional just-war analysis. This concerns, as well, the rule of law. State-sponsored terrorism, or sovereign states that protect, allow, or permit terrorists safe haven by that fact, gravely contradict the rule of law and formally cooperate in evil.

—April 2003

## Confusion about the Invasion and Occupation of Iraq

Question: In the war and occupation of Iraq, some Catholics say this fits the "just-war" criteria, and some others say no. Can you add some clarity to this?

Answer: Maybe; maybe not! Usually, I do try to be clear. At present, several aspects of the just-war doctrine are in dialogue as is, to some extent, the doctrine itself. Two recent articles review some of the aspects of this question at some length: Brian Johnstone's "Pope John Paul II and the War in Iraq" and Kenneth Himes' "Intervention, Just War, and U.S. National Security".[9]

Johnstone notes what is well known—that Pope John Paul has challenged the doctrine of preventive war that some proposed as a justification for the war in Iraq. In his Christmas message (2002), the Pope repeated his warnings to the United States and Great Britain and pronounced himself against any "preventative war". All commentators (that

---

[9] Brian V. Johnstone, "Pope John Paul II and the War in Iraq", *Studia Moralia* 41, no. 2 (2003):.309–30; and Kenneth R. Himes, "Intervention, Just War, and U.S. National Security", *Theological Studies* 65, no. 1 (2004): 141–57.

I am aware of) have accepted the responses of the Pope and the Vatican as a rejection of the war in Iraq.

Nevertheless, the same Pope has reiterated the right to self-defense in his encyclical *Evangelium Vitae* (no. 55). For Johnstone, John Paul II's categoric rejection of war ("Violence never again! War never again! Terrorism never again!")[10] is not just utopian rhetoric but rooted in his profound convictions about human solidarity (common humanity). The Pope also has a positive evaluation of available means to contain conflict and foster peace, namely, international law and the practices of dialogue and diplomacy. As Johnstone notes, it was "without major war, many of the divisions of Europe were overcome, Poland was liberated, Germany was reunited, and South Africa achieved major political change and reconciliation".[11]

Papal statements generally have a "prophetic" quality and are cast in general terms: denouncing violence and calling for peace. Usually they do not attempt public judgments as to which side has the "just cause" or even which concrete acts violate specific just-war conditions.

Johnstone notes something of a paradox in the Catholic tradition—that the teaching gives a clear priority to the imperatives of peace, and yet, does not repudiate the "just war" doctrine. While John Paul II has not defended the just-war doctrine, neither has he repudiated it and adopted pacifism.[12]

At times, at least to me, the Pope's talks and pronouncements sound like "functional pacifism"; nevertheless, official Catholic teaching affirms the right and the duty on the part of governments to defend their citizens (*GS*, no. 79; *CCC*, no. 2308). This is not a moral option; it is a moral duty.

As Johnstone correctly points out, at least two issues remain: (1) the foundation of the right of defense and (2) the justification of force, in some form, as the means of exercising this right. Johnstone suggests a semantic distinction between the word "*war*" and "disarming the aggressor". He uses this to interpret the Vatican position that war put forward as a positive means for peace probably won't work, whereas defense in a form of disarming violence might preserve the conditions necessary for peace.

---

[10] See "Day of Prayer for Peace in the World" (Jan. 24, 2002), pt. 4, no. 2.
[11] Johnstone, "John Paul II and the War in Iraq", p. 312.
[12] Ibid., p. 322.

The *Catechism of the Catholic Church* as it now reads and teaches does present "strict conditions" for the "legitimate defense by military force", (no. 2309). The presumption is and has been for a long time (e.g., Pope Pius XII) that the only so-called "just war" is a just war of defense.

The present intervention in Iraq (and before that, Afghanistan) has raised many serious questions about the grounds for a "just cause" in the just-war thinking. The classic case of one sovereign state aggressively invading the accepted borders of another sovereign state is not the direct focus here.

The Himes article in *Theological Studies* raises many nuanced questions that deserve serious study. In the 1990s, there were calls to send armed forces into countries where a humanitarian crisis occurred; for some, genocide justifies intervention, and many justify intervention to stop ethnic cleansing or to restore civil order within failed states. Another argument for intervention arose from terrorist attacks in the United States and elsewhere.[13] The latter could be seen as "self-defense" against state-sponsored terrorism and/or so-called "rogue states". This could be seen as a war of aggression by proxy.

Of late, much attention has focused on the proliferation of weapons of mass destruction. This raises questions about evaluating attacks that are either preemptive or preventative. Preemptive actions can find some support within the just-war tradition where it is not necessarily seen as aggression (anticipatory defense).

Preventive war was viewed differently since it was seen as an attack on a future but uncertain threat—the focus being more on capability than intent. It is here, I believe, that the United States' attack on Iraq is heavily criticized because, many argue, it was not a preemptive response to an imminent danger but a war of prevention that many judge unnecessary. For some, a multilateral (i.e., international, U.N. Security Council) authorization could justify such intervention, for others, not so.

Other conditions that seemed to loom large in the discussions and pastoral letters of the 1980s seem less acute in Iraq. Direct and even indirect civilian casualties have been greatly reduced. So-called "smart weapons" seem to have performed as advertised, reducing greatly the number of direct civilian casualties. Yet, an unanticipated consequence of this may be an increase of potential targets. It may well be

[13] Himes, "Intervention, Just War, and U.S. National Security", p. 143.

that highly sophisticated air power requires fewer foot soldiers, but securing the peace and some kind of restoration may require more personnel.

"If the war with Iraq was fought with the purpose of regime change and the liberation of the Iraqi people, it is imperative that the postwar situation be factored into any ethical assessment of the American-led war", Himes observed.[14] If the purpose was to alter the internal situation of that nation to increase stability and the chances for peace in the region, it is not yet clear what kind of Iraq will emerge from that effort.

Large-scale troop movements and battles have long ceased, but challenges of occupation and transition remain—much of which seem closer to police work (against criminal activity) than classic military efforts: intelligence gathering; interdiction of materials and funding; detection leading to arrest; and the prosecution of individuals.

This may well be the present challenge of terrorism in general and al Qaeda in particular. There is no sovereign state to confront or that confronts. Rather, some ideological fanatics issue their own fatwas to sanction the killing of any Americans (civilian or military) to further an agenda known fully and only to themselves.

Right reason requires that dialogue and diplomacy be the first steps in resolving controversy, but neither dialogue nor diplomacy can even engage terrorism. Everything I read tells me that this is not a "clash of civilizations", yet those who energize, sanction, and practice terrorism simply do not qualify as civilized. Murderous terrorism has to be resisted and repelled. If the conventional just-war conditions do not structure and/or allow such a defense, then a reasoned and revised moral framework must be developed to confront terrorism and the expanded calls for intervention.

I do not pretend to know the clear or complete answer to this challenge, but it seems to me that both the Johnstone and the Himes studies are a needed beginning for serious and sober reflection.

—October 2004

---

[14] Ibid., p. 156.

# II

# Sex and Marriage

# 8

# The Meaning and Purpose
# of Conjugal Love

## The Ends of Marriage

Question: Has the Church changed her teaching about the primary and secondary "ends of marriage"?

Answer: There is hardly a more nuanced and intricate question in sacramental theology than the central question of the "ends of marriage".

In response to the question of "changed" definition, I would answer in terms of a positive "development of doctrine" rooted in the teaching of Popes Pius XI and Pius XII. "Change" for some people connotes a contradiction. The authentic teaching of the present *Code of Canon Law* (1983) and the present *Catechism of the Catholic Church* (1992) offer no contradiction to traditional Catholic teaching but rather a positive development of that Catholic teaching.

The question of the "ends of marriage" has been the object of study and controversy, at least since the publication of *Casti Connubii* (1930) up to and through Vatican Council II (1962–1965). A reliable summary of that development and contributors is provided by R.J. Levis in the *New Catholic Encyclopedia*.[1]

However, it is the postconciliar teaching—especially after *Gaudium et Spes* (1965) numbers 47–52, *Humanae Vitae* (1968), and after and throughout the voluminous teaching of Pope John Paul II (well reflected in the revised 1983 *Code*, can. 1055, §1, and the *Catechism*, no. 1601)— that has generated some truly amazing charges, for instance, that

---

[1] R. J. Levis, "Ends of Marriage", in *New Catholic Encyclopedia*, vol. 9 (New York: McGraw-Hill, 1967), pp. 267–70.

from the omission of some 1917 canonical language of primary and secondary ends has been the occasion, if not the cause, of the rise in marriage annulments.

To answer this misguided charge and to explain competently a correct version of the Church's teaching on the "ends of marriage", I heartily recommend as required reading a recent article, "Marriage, Annulment, and the Quest for Lasting Commitment" by Cormac Burke. Monsignor Burke is a renowned canonist (a judge of the Roman Rota) and a very fine theologian as well. (I apologize to readers for singling out a periodical publication six months late, but this column of mine is written almost that many months prior to publication.)

Monsignor Burke correctly points out that both the *Code* and the *Catechism* state clearly the two ends of marriage, which "is by its very nature ordered to the good of the spouses and the procreation and education of offspring" (can. 1055, §1, and *CCC*, no. 1601, quoting the same canon verbatim).

Some see this as the abandonment of the terminology of the "hierarchy of ends" with their numerical specification of the "primary" and "secondary" ends. Rather than departure, Burke is correct in his description of the development in the Church's teaching on the ends of marriage; i.e., the Church defines marriage with two equal (co-essential, if you will) but interrelated primary ends: the good of the spouses and the transmission of life. Rather than a hierarchy between them, "it is their mutual interdependence and inseparability which are now emphasized." [2] This is an "ordered relationship" insisted upon by Pope Pius XII and the interdependence and inseparability so much insisted upon by Paul VI in *Humanae Vitae* (*HV*), number 12, and John Paul II in *Familiaris Consortio* (*FC*), number 32.

The "good of the spouses" (*bonum coniugum*) cited in both the *Code* and the *Catechism* should not be confused with the classic Augustinian "goods of marriage". The *bona matrimonii* of Augustine are positive and essential features of matrimony that give it dignity. As Burke notes here, "Augustine is speaking of the values or essential properties of marriage, not of its ends or finalities." The "good of the spouses" involves something that is good for them; it denotes not a property of marriage but something marriage should cause or

---

[2] Cormac Burke, "Marriage, Annulment, and the Quest for Lasting Commitment", in *Catholic World Report* 6, no. 1 (Jan. 1996): 55.

lead to—again, not in the line of a property, but in the line of finality or end.[3]

For a correct canonical and pastoral application, Burke spells out the rich Christian anthropology of *Gaudium et Spes* and the extensive Magisterium of John Paul II expounding that anthropology. The real enemy of lasting marital commitment (or any Christian commitment) is not a few words present or missing in or from canon 1055, section 1; the real enemy is selfishness ("inordinate self-love ... the opposite of charity", *HV*, no. 21), the same radical, autonomous selfish individualism so thoroughly repudiated by *Veritatis Splendor* (*VS*), in numbers 36 to 41.

Burke is correct: the essence of true "personalism", the genuine papal and conciliar anthropology is the now signature citation so often invoked by John Paul II: "[M]an ... cannot fully find himself except through a sincere gift of himself" (*GS*, no. 24; cf. Lk 17:33).

Again, Burke is correct. This is the key to marriage preparation, marriage ceremonies, and all the support mechanisms in place or to be developed that support and sustain stable marriage and family life. For priest readers especially, I strongly recommend reading the Burke article line by line and to incorporate its insights into any marriage or marriage preparation work.

—June 1996

## Previous Explanation of Marriage Questioned

Question: In a prior Q/A about the ends of marriage, you seemed to downplay, even avoid, the classic terminology of the *primary* and *secondary* ends of marriage. Was this a deliberate omission?

Answer: The previous Q/A (June 1996) was an attempt to defend and agree with the published article of Monsignor Cormac Burke of the Roman Rota.[4] A printed and telling letter called me on the same point.[5]

First, the thrust of Monsignor Burke's article was to respond to those critics who assert that it was the omission of the canonical language—

---

[3] Ibid., p. 56.
[4] See footnote 2, on p. 108 above.
[5] P. J. McDonald, *Homiletic and Pastoral Review* (*HPR*), December 1996.

"primary and secondary ends of marriage"—in the new (1983) *Code* (can. 1055, §1) and the new *Catechism* (no. 1601) that was the occasion, even the cause, of the great rise in annulments. Burke denies this cause-and-effect relationship and looks elsewhere for the rise in annulments. I believe he was correct and agree with him.

What then of the "primary-secondary" language? No one can question that this was the language of the *canonical* definition of marriage in the 1917 *Code of Canon Law*. Canon 1013, section 1, of the 1917 *Code* was as clear as it was concise: the primary purpose of marriage (*finis primarius*) is the procreation and education of children (*procreatio atque educatio prolis*); the secondary (*secondarius*) purpose is to furnish mutual aid (*mutuum adiutorium*) and a remedy for concupiscence (*remedium concupiscentiae*).

Note well! "Conjugal love" is not mentioned at all in that 1917 *canonical* definition. While no orthodox Catholic theologian questions the canonical wording of the 1917 *Code*, many Catholic theologians and writers did probe and question the *theological* adequacy of this very concise *canonical* definition. Some in the 1930s and 1940s went too far in personalist, even existentialist, revisions (e.g., H. Doms; B. Kremple), but others—Ford-Kelly, and significantly, Karol Wojtyla in his *Love and Responsibility* (1960)—insisted on the correct *theological* point that "conjugal love" is not a secondary end of marriage.

Vatican Council II did not employ the canonical terminology of "primary-secondary" in its teaching on marriage.[6] Some Vatican II commentators did overwork this "omission", implying that the Council had redefined marriage canonically.[7] But, as the official *Acta* of that Council explain, in a *pastoral* text which intends to begin a dialogue with the whole world, precise juridic elements are not required. Even so, the goods and ends of marriage are cited over ten times throughout the texts of the Council.[8]

The Council, of course, did not nor did it claim to "redefine" marriage *canonically*; rather, it was the new (1983) *Code* that *did* "redefine" marriage canonically in canon 1055, section 1, accurately and adequately reflecting the theological teaching of the Ecumenical Council (Vatican II), as did the *Catechism* (no. 1601).

[6] Cf. *Documents of Vatican II*, ed. Walter M. Abbott, S.J. (London: Geoffery Chapman, 1966), p. 250, n. 155.

[7] Cf., e.g., Donald R. Campion, Introduction to *Gaudium et Spes*, in ibid., pp. 189–90.

[8] *Acta Synodalia*, vol. IV, pars vii, p. 477.

Further, we must ask: Just how "traditional" was the so-called classic terminology "primary-secondary"? In a splendid article, the late John R. Connery, S.J., noted:

> It was not until the nineteenth century that theologians began to use the terms *primary* and *secondary* in regard to the specific goals of marriage. They gave the primary to procreation and considered mutual assistance and the relief of concupiscence as secondary ends. This new terminology made its way into the *Code of Canon Law* published in 1917. What should be emphasized here is that setting up this priority in no way affected the traditional role love has played as the dynamic force underlying marriage. Unfortunately, in some pre–Vatican II treatises on marriage, love is identified as mutual assistance and given only a secondary role in marriage. This seemed to be dictated by a concern for the problem of contraception, but in light of the tradition this identification is misleading.[9]

To verify Father Connery's assertion about the relatively recent vintage of the "primary-secondary" language, we might consult the very "traditional" (even classic) *Roman Catechism* of 1566 on the reasons or purposes of marriage:

> The first reason is the instinctive mutual attraction of the sexes to form a stable companionship of the two persons, as a basis for mutual happiness and help amid the trials of life extending even to sickness and old age.... The second reason is another instinctive desire: to have offspring. This desire should not be so much to have heirs for one's property, as rather to provide new recipients for the gift of faith and new heirs for heaven.[10]

Indeed, the numerical listing there ("first reason, second reason") is the reverse of the 1917 *Code*, and clearly there was no concession to or for contraception; on that the *Roman Catechism* was emphatic: "Whoever, therefore, in marriage artificially prevents conception, or procures an abortion, commits a most serious sin: the sin of premeditated murder".[11]

Again, Father Connery is not inventing nor deconstructing history here. No less an authority than Pope Pius XI, in number 24 of his classic encyclical, *Casti Connubii* (December 31, 1930), cites the

---

[9] John R. Connery, S.J., "The Role of Love in Christian Marriage", *Communio* 11, no. 3 (1984): 251.
[10] *Roman Catechism* (1566), pt. II, 7—Matrimony, n. 13.
[11] Ibid.

same paragraph from the *Roman Catechism* as to the "chief reason and purpose of matrimony" (*primaria matrimonii causa et ratio* in *AAS* 22 [1930], p. 548) provided some necessary distinctions are made (DS 3707).

Indeed, the most traditional of Western classic Fathers, Saint Augustine, in his peerless treatise on the goods of marriage, *De Bono Coniugali* (A.D. 401), makes no mention of "primary-secondary" but begins this classic work with the great and natural good of friendship (1) and the great good of natural companionship between the two sexes, even more so sacramentally, between husband and wife (3). Augustine, of course, makes no concession to contraception; indeed, it was his classic "Aliquando" text from *De Nuptiis et Concupiscentia* (A.D. 420) that was the traditional citation for theology from the fifth century to today and still is.

Thus, I believe there were valid *canonical* and social reasons for the "primary-secondary" terminology in the 1917 *Code*, but that it is *theologically* misleading to define marriage only in that stated priority. Whereas, attentive to Catholic theological tradition, recent and ancient, I would argue that the definitions of the new *Code* and the new *Catechism*, correctly reflecting the theological teaching of Vatican II, emphasizing the inseparability of the goods and purposes of marriage concede nothing to permissive contraception nor to permissive annulments.

—February 1999


## Non-contraceptive Masturbation

Question: The question is an intimate one, but it is posed frequently enough that a straight answer may be a useful reference. The question refers to those married and beyond childbearing years. When long past menopause, since conception is not possible (and thus contraception is not relevant), is singular or mutual masturbation still considered wrongful activity?

Answer: Yes. Masturbation is a disordered use of human sexuality for the single, the married, or the widowed precisely because it is an intrinsically disordered act. Some seem to think that the Church's only teaching is against contraception; thus, where contraception is not a question, there are no other questions vis-à-vis human sexuality.

The core doctrine of *Humanae Vitae*, number 12, *and Familiaris Consortio*, number 32, is, I believe, the basic principle for all sexual ethics. That is—"the inseparable connection, established by God, ... between the *unitive* significance and the *procreative* significance which are both inherent to the marriage act" (*HV*, no. 12, emphasis added). This can be called the *Love-Life Link*: Love, the *unitive*, personal, two-in-one-flesh dimension of human sexuality; and Life, the *procreative*, also personal, generous dimension of not being self-contained nor self-enclosed.

The fundamental principle here is *not* that both have to be fully realized in *every* instance, but that we should never act against either good in *any* instance.

For much of the twentieth century, a great amount of attention was focused on how to foster the love dimension while preventing the life dimension (contraception, i.e., how to have sex without babies). But the close of this century has also focused of late on the opposite, the life dimension while separating the love dimension (*in vitro* fertilization and other reproductive technologies, i.e., how to have babies without sex).

As sexual activity, masturbation fosters neither of these goods of human sexuality: it is not two-in-one-flesh love, nor is it procreative as such. Thus, it fails on both counts and is properly described as intrinsically disordered.

The core teaching of *Humanae Vitae* and *Familiaris Consortio* above is organic and consistent, which is why those who dissent from *HV* inevitably dissent from the extended, repeated, and connected teaching in CDF documents *Persona Humana* (1975) and *Donum Vitae* (1987) and dissent as well from the Church's authentic teaching on homosexual acts (CDF, "*On the Pastoral Care of Homosexual Persons*", 1986) since homosexual activity is, reductively, masturbatory activity.

Objectively, the teaching of the Church on the immorality of masturbation is clear and often repeated in our time (cf. CDF, *Persona Humana*, no. 9; *CCC*, no. 2352; *VS*, no. 47). The same authentic teaching directs our attention to subjective factors that can mitigate or lessen personal responsibility, but such do not change the nature ("moral object") of this disordered use of human sexuality.

Further, there are excellent and reliable theological explanations that present this authentic teaching in normal and understandable American

English. See, for instance, *Catholic Sexual Ethics*; *The Courage to Be Chaste*, and a truly magisterial and comprehensive treatment by John F. Harvey, "The Pastoral Problem of Masturbation".[12]

It is now common in some social science and muddled theological circles to dismiss masturbation as a nonevent. This is completely contrary to constant Christian teaching and the moral sense of the Christian faithful.

The trendies usually compare masturbation with something else, saying, "Well, it's not as bad as abortion and probably worse than skipping grace before meals." Such comparisons are meaningless and irrelevant precisely because they are the wrong comparisons. The morally relevant comparison is the freedom of contradiction: to abort or not to abort; to pray or not to pray. To compare one moral disorder with a different species of moral disorder proves or disproves nothing, because it's the wrong comparison.

Pastorally and really, masturbation is not a "nonevent". Masturbatory sex (what Germain Grisez once called "Pseudo-Sex") is far more prevalent than we care to admit.

Many critics of received Church teaching describe that authentic teaching as the enemy of "spontaneity" in their sex lives, even their married lives. However, a careful look at alleged "spontaneity" reveals not so much spontaneity as a thoroughly mechanical view of sex; i.e., every attraction must cause stimulation; every stimulation must cause arousal; every arousal must be gratified; and every gratification must end in complete orgasm—if one takes away or even questions this causal, necessary sequence, the relationship will fold, love will wither, and marriage break down.

But, if one grants the truly mechanical nature of this nearly physiological compulsion, contraception, for one, is inevitable—surely any thinking person needs some "protection" from the consequences and outcomes of this physiological necessity.

In truth, this confuses sex with eros—an eros that seeks only a transient electrical discharge in the brain's pleasure center, prompted by

---

[12] Rev. Ronald Lawler, O.F.M. Cap, Joseph Boyle, Jr., and William E. May, *Catholic Sexual Ethics* (Huntingdon, Ind.: Our Sunday Visitor Publishing, 1985), pp. 172, 187–95. Benedict J. Groeschel, *The Courage to Be Chaste* (Mahwah, N.J.: Paulist Press, 1985), pp. 64–69, with pastoral suggestions, pp. 100–108. John F. Harvey, O.S.F.S., "The Pastoral Problem of Masturbation", *Linacre Quarterly* 60, no. 2 (May 1993): 25–49.

appropriate venereal stimulation. This is the "freedom" brought by the Pill, the freedom to separate acts from their consequences.

But, in fact, there is nothing spontaneous about such a mechanical view of sex; it is a euphemism for obedience to a masturbatory impulse. Since it presumes no "self-mastery", it precludes any meaning to "self-donation". No one gives what he does not have, nor what he has no possession of. This is the literal antithesis to what Paul VI praises and recommends in *Humanae Vitae*: "the application of human intelligence to an activity in which a rational creature such as man is so closely associated with his Creator" (no. 16).

Upon investigation, much of modern contraception is reductively masturbatory activity, as is all unnatural sex. No, masturbation is not a nonevent in any state of life. The Church's received teaching is the correct teaching for every state in life, for it is the only teaching that puts together and keeps together "the inseparable connection, willed by God ... between the two meanings of the conjugal act: the unitive meaning and the procreative meaning" (*FC*, no. 32, quoting *HV*, no. 12).

—June 1994

## Pornography: An Enemy of True Love

Question: I rarely hear or read condemnations of pornography. Is it so insignificant that it deserves no mention?

Answer: In my judgment, it's not insignificant but more like a large elephant in the living room that no one wants to mention.

In 1998, Americans spent $4 billion on pornographic video sales and rentals, yet that literally is not the half of it: the full porn business is estimated between $10 billion and $14 billion annually when you include porn television networks, pay-per-view movies on cable and satellite, Internet websites, in-room hotel movies, phone sex, toys, and magazines, according to an article by Frank Rich in the *New York Times Magazine*.[13]

[13] Frank Rich, "Naked Capitalists", *New York Times Magazine*, May 20, 2011, pp. 51ff.

The low-end $10 billion figure is more income than that made by professional football, basketball, and baseball together. Commercially, porn is a huge industry, not a sideshow. Porn also has silent business partners in high places—two of the more prominent, quiet purveyors being Marriott (in-room X-rated movies) and General Motors (owns satellite giant DirectTV).

The quiet engine that revolutionized and expanded the porn explosion was the arrival of the home video (VCR). In the early 1980s, the VCR (later the Internet) conquered America by offering easier and more anonymous access to porn. Prior to home video, pornography had a far smaller audience, often limited to "adult theaters" in the seedy part of town. The VCR took porn into the living rooms and the bedrooms of America. Hardcore porn is now available at chains like Tower (though not at Blockbuster). And while Hollywood released four hundred movies in 2000, eleven thousand "adult titles" were released in the same calendar year.

Too many Fortune 500 corporations with clout (e.g., AT&T and AOL Time Warner) make too much money on porn for restrictive legislation to move, and Rich is probably right that the Supreme Court's 1973 "community standards" for obscenity may now be a legal *non sequitur*.

What is to be said morally? The *Catechism* provides a fine summary: "Pornography consists in removing real or simulated sexual acts from the intimacy of the partners, in order to display them deliberately to third parties. It offends against chastity because it perverts the conjugal act, the intimate giving of spouses to each other." The *Catechism* also points out that the dignity of all those involved—from actors to producers to consumers—is injured, because each of them is being used by others, either as "an object of base pleasure" or "illicit profit". Further, all of them are engrossed in a "fantasy world". Finally, the *Catechism* makes clear that pornography is a "grave offense" and that governing bodies should prohibit its "production and distribution" (no. 2354).

The likelihood of our civil authorities preventing the production or distribution of such material is next to zero. Thus, since little can be done to prevent the pollution of our external (even in-home) atmosphere, all the more reason to construct and sustain our own internal moral atmosphere and convictions.

Authentic Church teaching on human sexuality got seriously mugged some time ago by the major media. Thus, we must instruct and convince our own people that pseudo-sex is not harmless—indeed, it has consequences. It is simply a moral mistake and bad pastoral advice to pretend that masturbatory sex is just an adolescent problem— surely it is not just a small tribe of young teens who come up with $10 billion annually. Auto-erotic activity is not so easily bored; auto-erotic activity is regressive and habitual, which is why it feeds and fuels so much commerce.

It is not an accident that pornography thrives on anonymity; it is rather essential to it, which is why the privacy of the VCR revolutionized its expansion. Auto-erotic activity is the first refuge of the insecure (immature) and the last refuge of the isolated (lonely of any age)—there is no authentic gift of self in it but only selfishness, the real enemy of true love.

Anyone—single, married, widowed—who has not integrated his sexuality (*CCC*, no. 2337) into his real life and personal vocation so that he can love well will be attracted to sexual fantasy, and he can get locked in there regardless of age or state in life.

My hunch is that civil authorities will not solve or lessen this problem. The only defense that I see is the correct formation of a Catholic conscience in true virtue—chastity and all other Christian virtues.

I suspect that a number (perhaps a large number) of Christian parents financially support this big business. How convincing can such parents be when they look for ways to block the transmission of materials to their children that they themselves watch? I suspect that only sound teaching and genuine lived example can help form correct consciences against this moral poison that will surely expand rather than shrink in our lifetime.

—January 2002

## Indissolubility of Marriage

Question: In presenting or explaining indissoluble marriage, I find it not so much denied as disarmed when someone describes it only as an "ideal". Is there a way to approach this?

Answer: A step-down or side-step "ideal" is applied of late to a good deal more than marriage, but, as you say, it seems to emerge most often in discussions about indissolubility.

The word "*ideal*" has evolved loosely in standard English. The dictionary meaning once was a strong one: high perfection; excellence; normative model for imitation. Yet, for some today, "*ideal*" means a goal worth aiming at, but not-to-worry if you don't make it, or don't even come close. After all, it's *only* an "ideal".

In this usage shift, "ideal" seems to connote more "unreal" than "real" as in the put-down: "but in the real world". This misleading use of "ideal" was noted long ago by C. S. Lewis in his *Mere Christianity*.[14]

Moral perfection for Lewis is not a matter of private taste, as in one's ideal house, ideal ship, ideal movie, but rather necessary norms and rules. To be sure, he argues, perfect arithmetic is "an ideal", and yet we all make mistakes in arithmetic. Still, there is nothing particularly high-minded about aiming for arithmetical perfection when doing your checkbook. It would be idiotic not to try for that perfection, for every mistake will cause you trouble later on. In the same way, every moral failure causes trouble.

On the indissolubility of monogamous marriage, the first time I noticed Church doctrine described as "ideal", in a serious work of theology, was Walter Kasper's, *Theology of Christian Marriage*.[15] As C. S. Lewis predicted, this would cause trouble later on, and it did.[16]

In the morally comprehensive encyclical *Veritatis Splendor* of Pope John Paul II, this tactic of characterizing authentic Church teaching as only "an ideal" is thoroughly critiqued and repudiated (no. 103).

In the third chapter of *VS*, about the truth of the moral good for the life of the Church and of the world (nos. 84–120), the Pope focuses closely on the reality of God's grace and God's law (nos. 102–5) precisely because the *reality of redemption* is at stake—"lest the cross of Christ be emptied of its power" (1 Cor 1:17).

The Pope's emphasis is important as is its seriousness for all true moral teaching.

---

[14] See pt. 3, "Christian Behavior", no. 1—The Three Parts of Morality, in Lewis' *Mere Christianity* (1943; reprinted often).

[15] Walter Kasper, *Theology of Christian Marriage* (German, 1977; New York: Seabury Press, 1980).

[16] Cf. Bishops Karl Lehmann, Oscar Saier, and Walter Kasper, "Pastoral Ministry: The Divorced and Remarried" (issued Aug. 10, 1993), published in *Origins* 23, no. 38 (Mar. 10, 1994): 670–76; and the CDF rejection of same: "Concerning the Reception of Holy Communion by the Divorced and Remarried Members of the Faithful" (Sept. 14, 1994).

Man always has before him the spiritual horizon of hope, thanks to the *help of divine grace* and with *the cooperation of human freedom.* . . .

. . . .

*Only in the mystery of Christ's Redemption do we discover the "concrete" possibilities of man.* It would be a very serious error to conclude . . . that the Church's teaching is essentially only an "ideal" which must then be adapted, proportioned, graduated to the so-called concrete possibilities of man, according to a "balancing of the goods in question." But what are the "concrete possibilities of man"? And of *which* man are we speaking? Of man *dominated* by lust or of man *redeemed by Christ*? This is what is at stake: the *reality* of Christ's redemption. *Christ has redeemed us!* This means that he has given us the possibility of realizing *the entire* truth of our being: he has set our freedom free from the *domination* of concupiscence. And if redeemed man still sins, this is not due to an imperfection of Christ's redemptive act, but to man's will not to avail himself of the grace which flows from that act.[17]

— May 1995

---

[17] *VS*, no. 103, emphasis in original; quoting "Address to Those Taking Part in a Course on 'Responsible Parenthood'" (Mar. 1, 1984), no. 4, cf. *Insegnamenti* VII, 1 (1984), p. 583.

# 9

# Invalid Marriages

## *Cohabitation*

Question: News reports state that two U.S. dioceses no longer consider cohabitation a moral obstacle to marriage. Is this so?

Answer: From what I have read, that is not exactly what they said, but what is reported is misleading.

I know of two statements: (1) the Diocese of San Angelo, Texas, published "Couples Living Together before Marriage", and (2) the Archdiocese of Miami issued "marriage preparation guidelines" that the *Miami Herald* so highlighted (distorted?) that that paper offered the Archbishop of Miami op-ed space to respond to their page-one presentation four days earlier.[1]

Both dioceses do emphasize that "cohabitation is not a canonical impediment to marriage". That, of course, is true in a sense. but it's not all that's true. It is also true that astigmatism is not a canonical impediment to marriage, but without corrective lenses you just can't see clearly.

While cohabitation (trial marriage; living together) is not a canonical impediment, it is a sin. It is surely objective grave matter (cf. *CCC*, no. 2353) and a reliable source of grave scandal.

No authority below the Holy See has the competence to establish an impediment to marriage (cf. can. 1075, §2, and *FC*, no. 66). But clearly, this is not simply a canonical question—a canonical impediment or no canonical impediment. Since marriage is a sacrament of

---

[1] Bishop Michael Pfeifer, "Couples Living Together before Marriage", *Origins* 27, no. 4 (June 12, 1997): 49, 51–53.

the living, the celebration of marriage must be *per se* valid, worthy, and fruitful (*FC*, no. 67).

If a couple is living together, and has no intention of separating—even for a time—or indeed explicitly and arrogantly refuses to do so, the pastor is confronted with a serious pastoral and moral problem. It may well be that this couple does not want what the Church really has to offer. In that case, it is not the Church that invents an "obstacle" in the way of their celebration, but the couple themselves (*FC*, no. 68). Just what is it they have come to Church to celebrate? If someone refuses to live chastely before marriage, then how, apart from magic, will he live a chaste marriage?

If diocesan directives (guidelines) announce that cohabitation "is not grounds for the priest to delay or refuse marriage preparation" (or, as one news report has it, the priest "may not refuse"), such directives almost invite misunderstanding. To announce what is not an impediment in Church law while ignoring God's law (one of the Ten Commandments) is neither good preparation nor sound pastoral practice.

These policies are presented under the rubric that we want to be "pastoral" rather than "legalistic" about cohabitation. Let's start by being honest. The word "*pastoral*" is sometimes abused. When "pastoral" means being understanding, open, polite. and all other Christian virtues, all is well. When "pastoral" is a code word to finesse a commandment of God, that is neither pastoral nor true. Obviously, as "living together" becomes more frequent and more open, dumbing-down Christian standards does not solve the problem but only camouflages it.

Every sober pastor knows and meets serious challenges in this regard—some friendly, some not; some out of ignorance and some from smart alecks pushing their own self-indulgent envelopes. I am not sure that there is a single simple answer for every possible case without patient and candid discussion and explanation of Church teaching and an honest discussion of actual circumstances. Some celebrations will have to be simple, to avoid obvious scandal. Some will have to be delayed in the face of adamant refusal to accept the Church's moral teaching. My own feeling is that general guidelines here do not fit all sizes, and guidelines should not remove competent pastors from exercising sound judgments reflecting all of the Church's teaching, not just parts of it.

With the escalation of divorce and annulments at the other end of marriage, all voices seem to be crying out for improvements in marriage preparation. It seems to be a counter-value, even a disservice, to convey or imply (even unwittingly) that standards before or prior to marriage are lessened or negotiable and then pretend shock and surprise that marriages in America don't stand up too well. Distortions of the term "*pastoral*" only increase the counter-values.

Pope John Paul II has taught clearly in *Familiaris Consortio* on "Trial Marriages" (no. 80) and so-called "Free Unions" (no. 81) along with "Marriage Preparation" (nos. 66–68). The Pontifical Council for the Family published "Preparation for the Sacrament of Marriage" (May 13, 1996, nos. 1–73). Germain Grisez also presents marriage preparation and engagement with the seriousness it deserves.[2]

"The 'pastoral' nature of theology does not mean it should be less doctrinal" (John Paul II, *Pastores Dabo Vobis*, no. 55). Thus, especially in view of the pontifical teaching above, one should not convey even the impression that this is only or merely a canonical problem; it is indeed a moral and sacramental problem of difficulty and complexity that pastors have to confront consistently—to speak the truth in love (Eph 4:15). Lovingly? Yes! But truthfully too! Or, it's just not the truth about love, which is, of course, what true marriage is—*the truth about love!*

—October 1997

## Pre-nuptial Agreements

Question: I read of Hollywood and media types who have signed pre-matrimonial agreements. Does this amount to an intention against permanence?

Answer: After doing some homework, I am informed by some Catholic lawyers that pre-matrimonial agreements are not limited to just Hollywood and big media types. Apparently, some young professionals (who tend to marry later) agree that what they earned and saved as singles is their individual possession and not to be nor to

---

[2] Cf. his *Living a Christian Life*, vol. 2 of *The Way of the Lord Jesus* (Quincy, Ill.: Franciscan Press, 1993), pp. 737–52, esp. 749–52.

become common property. Others have highly detailed agreements specifying who gets to keep what, even *before* they have said "yes" for keeps.

Is this an intention against permanence? I have not found very much written on this by expert canonists. However, from what I read, it is not seen to be an invalidating intention against marriage, but surely it is a "red flag" that deserves serious pastoral discussion and instruction *before* marriage.

On the one hand, no authority below the Holy See can establish a genuine impediment to marriage (can. 1075). Also, this does not seem directly to involve a "future condition" or the other important distinctions of canon 1102. Yet, post factum, it might later serve as some kind of corroborative evidence of an intention against marriage.

There are, of course, some forms of pre-marriage agreement that are not so recent. European royal houses sometimes had arrangements to make sure their castles and crown jewels did not pass out of their families. Some super-wealthy Americans also constructed legal trusts designed to ensure that large stocks and big properties did not pass from their grasp and control.

However, the legal life of royal types or Wall Street royals was not usually a parochial concern. My lawyer friends tell me this is much more widespread now amid the general population. The media may have hyped the Trumps and the Kennedys, but the hype has sparked the interest and signatures of a wider audience.

The first casualty here seems to be the most traditional promise: "for better, for worse; for richer, for poorer; in sickness and in health". For some, this now reads: "for better, for richer, that's healthy". This, of course, is far removed from one of the beautiful characteristics of "conjugal love" in the unread section of *Humanae Vitae*, where Paul VI taught that "married love ... is a love which is total—that very special form of personal friendship in which husband and wife generously share everything, allowing no unreasonable exceptions and not thinking solely of their own convenience" (no. 9).

The genuine "gift of self" to the other has been a key principle of the conciliar (*GS*, nos. 24, 48) and pontifical teaching on marriage (*HV*; *FC*; *Letter to Families* [February 2, 1994], no. 11). While the language of total self-giving enjoys prominence in the literature and the ceremonies, I wonder whether the written words of these agreements do not undermine the spoken words of the intended. It's one thing to be businesslike in your outlook and mentality, but the sacrament of marriage is not a business.

As above, I don't think such agreements constitute a canonical impediment, but they can and do present a pastoral problem. In health terms, it's not exactly an obstacle to commitment, but more like an aneurysm—a soft spot, a thinness that could break, bubble, or bleed that commitment and thus deserves serious pastoral discussion before and not just after it happens.

—March 1997

## Intention Not to Have Children

Question: My niece plans to marry soon. She and her fiancé emphatically inform me that they will never have children; they want only a "child-free" marriage. Is this a valid marriage?

Answer: Sometimes, couples will state doubts, hesitations, or temporary conditions—"not right away", "not till we're settled", "not till we are ready or can afford it". All of these can and do raise questions, but none is as emphatic as the case you send.

In the case you propose, both parties are emphatic about their intention to have "a child-free marriage". That, of course, is a positive act of the will on their part, and if it is as certain and as specific as you describe, there is no marriage—it is null and void. In effect, this couple wants something which the Church does not offer, and, by a positive act of the will, rejects what the Church does offer.

The *Code of Canon Law* speaks, in part, of a positive act of the will to exclude marriage itself or any essential element of marriage (can. 1101, §2). This is precisely the problem here. Marriage, by definition, is a covenant which of its nature is ordered to the well-being of the spouses and to the procreation and raising of children (can. 1055, §1).

Sexual acts, the most intimate expression of conjugal love, are, according to *Humanae Vitae*, number 9, not exhausted only in a communion of the spouses but destined to perpetuate themselves by cooperating in the work of creation.

As Vatican Council II taught—God is the Author of matrimony: "The intimate partnership of married life and love has been established by the Creator and qualified by His laws. . . . By their very nature, the institution of matrimony itself and conjugal love are ordained for the procreation and education of children and find in them their ultimate crown" (*GS*, no. 48). This is the received and certain Christian teaching reflected in universal law (can. 1055, §1) and in universal teaching (*CCC*, nos. 1601, 1652).

This couple may intend "togetherness", "companionship", or "living together", but they do not intend marriage of God's design—established by the Creator and qualified by *his laws*. Rather, they intend their own institution, of their own design, qualified by their own limits. Quite literally, they are on their own—this is no sacrament and there is no sacramental grace.

If they are as frank and emphatic with some priest (as witness) as they have been with you, they put that priest in an impossible situation. They ask him to witness what he cannot witness, for this is not a "marriage"; it is a sacramental nullity and void by ecclesiastical and natural law.

—October 1997

## Attending an Invalid Marriage

**Question:** I read the following in an advice column in a Catholic newspaper: "My older daughter married a divorced non-Catholic in a Christian church. I refused to give her away because I felt she was entering an invalid and adulterous relationship." The father wanted to know if his decision had been right, and the advice columnist wrote that there are "no black-and-white answers" in such cases.

**Answer:** I have never been convinced that moral answers had to be colorful, even neutral, but surely this one is not entirely gray. In the case presented (with normal facts presumed), a baptized Catholic is marrying "outside the Church" (i.e., without any dispensation), but here also attempting to marry someone whom she could not validly marry in any church, anywhere.

Clearly, her intended spouse is already married (i.e., "divorced non-Catholic"). Thus, in this case, there is no possibility to witness to the truth, all one could do is witness a nullity.

I doubt that there is any more painful family problem than this, which has only grown worse over the past twenty-five years. The most searing pain involves those Catholic parents who have truly lived and loved the faith as the very center of their lives—and one or more of their grown children for whom the faith means little, or nothing; and in the most extreme cases deliberate defiance of the "laws of the Church" is used as a tool to test or taunt the natural family love parents have for their own children.

Prior to the Council (1962–1965), "approved authors" treated this subject of participation in or attendance at the invalid marriage of baptized Catholics under two perspectives: (1) an impermissible form of cooperation contrary to the virtue of faith and (2) a question of theological scandal.[3]

Now, while it is true that Vatican Council II greatly revised ecumenical rules about participation and cooperation in sacred and mixed things,[4] the case of baptized Catholics marrying outside the Church (without dispensation) is not really an ecumenical matter at all. It is truly a matter of consistent versus inconsistent Catholic practice, and the question of scandal very much remains.

Theologically, "*scandal*" is not mere shock or upset, nor eyebrow raising; rather, it is "an attitude or behavior which leads another to do evil. The person who gives scandal becomes his neighbor's tempter. He damages virtue and integrity; he may even draw his brother into spiritual death. Scandal is a grave offense if by deed or omission another is deliberately led into a grave offense" (no. 2284). In the section on scandal (nos. 2284–87), the *Catechism of the Catholic Church* calls for a "respect for the souls of others". "Temptations to sin are sure to come, but woe to him by whom they come" (Lk 17:1).

Also, the "cooperation" question does not entirely disappear. Surely, the Catholic parents by their stated disagreement and their expressed disappointment are not "formal cooperators" in evil (they expressly

---

[3] Cf., Henry Davis, S.J., *Moral and Pastoral Theology*, vol. 1 (London, New York: Sheed and Ward, 1949), p. 286; H. Noldin, A. Schmitt, and G. Heinzel, *Summa Theologiae Moralis* vol. 2 (Rauch, 1961), p. 3.

[4] Cf. e.g., *Decree on Ecumenism* (Nov. 21, 1964); and especially the postconciliar *Ecumenical Directory* (May 14, 1967), nos. 25–63.

do *not* agree with what is going on); but participation or attendance does raise the question of "material cooperation". In this, together with the theological scandal involved, I would adhere to the conventional guide that "presence means consent", and that in the case given, the pained parent was correct in neither attending nor participating.

Clearly, the primary "wrongdoer" is and remains the marrying adult who marries invalidly. This is doubly unfair since it will pain and hurt observant Catholics much more than nominal ones, who can hardly frame the question in religious terms at all.

It seems to me that the same maxim—"presence means consent"—also holds for less blatant cases.

Keeping, or trying to keep, family bonds of love and friendship intact remains an important value too. Explaining (not advertising) your absence, if asked, together with gift-giving, even attending a reception or party afterward would not, in my opinion, cause scandal in most cases. On this matter, moralists are divided; some hold that one should not give gifts or attend a reception.[5] But most wedding receptions these days could not possibly be described as or confused with a "religious event".

Some might think it inconsistent to attend a reception celebrating an event which you just chose not to attend. (I would respect those who could not do this.) Yet, the ambiguous no-show and show-up could convey two needed messages: the absence would testify to the unacceptance of the religious nullity; the presence could affirm family bonds of love and friendship, admitting candidly, this is not an entirely happy solution, overall, because it cannot be a happy event for practicing Catholics.

—June 1993

## Marrying Outside the Church

Question: Our daughter, age thirty, left the Church at age fifteen. She has been an active member of an Evangelical church for the past fifteen years, and she insists she is Christian and not Catholic! She is

[5] See Regis Scanlon, O.F.M. Cap., *HPR*, Feb. 1988, pp. 20–27.

now engaged to be married to an Evangelical in their church. As Catholic parents are we free to attend this?

**Answer:** Under normal circumstances, it is my opinion that attendance at an invalid marriage causes scandal on the basis that "presence means consent". (I am aware that many moralists no longer hold to that standard.)

Now, the usual question involves the canonical *form* of marriage. That is, canon 1108, section 1, states clearly: only those marriages are valid which are contracted in the presence of a priest (bishop, deacon) and two witnesses. In the new *Code of Canon Law*, it is possible for Catholics to get a dispensation from "canonical form" (cf. can. 1127, § 2) from their local Ordinary (bishop), but that is clearly not the case you ask about.

Your letter notes, after receiving different opinions, whether your daughter (a validly baptized Catholic) is even subject to canonical form.

This is a practical question because of what one canonical commentary describes as an "important innovation". This refers to canon 1117 of the 1983 *Code*. This canon states that the "prescribed form" is to be observed if at least one party was baptized in the Catholic Church or received into it and "has not by a formal act defected from it". This particular canon is an innovation; there was nothing near it or like it in the 1917 *Code*.

Now, twenty years after the promulgation of the 1983 *Code*, canon 1117 is still difficult to interpret and just as difficult to apply. My own custom (and limitation) is to consult three available canonical commentaries: (1) *Code of Canon Law Annotated* (a Spanish-Canadian effort); (2) *The Canon Law* (of the Canon Law Society of Great Britain and Ireland); and (3) *The New Commentary on the Code of Canon Law* of the Canon Law Society of America.

These three commentaries all treat canon 1117 in some detail, with many careful distinctions and much nuance.[6] One makes the point that the term "a formal act" in canon 1117 "has not by a formal act defected from it (the Church)" requires a "careful exegesis". This is neither Spanish nor Canadian understatement, it is quite true.

---

[6] *Code of Canon Law Annotated*, ed. Ernest Caparros, et al. (Montreal: Wilson and Lafleur, 1993), pp. 707–8; *The Canon Law: Letter & Spirit* (Collegeville, Minn.: Liturgical Press, 1995), pp. 603, and 629; and *New Commentary on the Code of Canon Law* (New York/Mahwah: Paulist Press, 2000), p. 1335.

It seems that neither an irregular life or irregular upbringing, nor even adult rejection of Catholic principles suffices to free oneself from the obligation to observe the canonical form. What is required is a public fact—a fact that both involves a formal withdrawal from the Catholic Church and adhesion to or registration in a non-Catholic denomination; a written declaration made to the pastor or to the proper Ordinary, that is "an external juridical act from which one infers without any doubt formal withdrawal from the Catholic Church".[7]

In view of the above collective comments and the specific details of your letter, it seems to me that your daughter has defected from the Catholic Church by "a formal act"—i.e., for over fifteen years she has separated herself from the Church, repeatedly and emphatically rejected the description "Catholic", and is an active and registered member of a non-Catholic denomination. Because of that, I don't think she is bound to the Catholic form since she has defected from the Church by a formal act.

Since she has never been married, nor has her intended spouse, and since there is no other obvious impediment from what you tell me, I come to presume that this intended wedding will be a valid Christian ceremony. Thus, the conventional expression—"marrying outside the Church"—as the source of scandal does not to my mind apply here. If there are other possible reasons for not attending this ceremony, I simply do not know, but the lack of canonical form in this case is not one.

Apart from your case but about this canon 1117, although I am not a canon lawyer, this particular canon does not strike me as good law. I don't question the good intent or purpose of this law, but here we are twenty years after its promulgation and its application on a case-by-case basis is very difficult—it is difficult to say with certitude that the application is a correct one.

Good human law is for the generality of cases; highly specific applications that almost defy certain classification actually raise more questions than they answer. Unless the Pontifical Council for the Interpretation of Legislative Texts makes future or further clarifications to render canon 1117 more readily applicable, I, for one, would not lose any sleep if this canon were quietly revised or retired.

—January 2003

---

[7] *Code of Canon Law Annotated*, p. 708.

# 10

# Divorce and Remarriage

## Catholic Divorce Lawyer

Question: May a Catholic lawyer assist a Catholic in getting a civil divorce?

Answer: Prudence, sound experience, and the possibility of scandal have always made this a difficult and delicate question. The answer offered here will differ from what was the standard answer of the textbooks years ago.

Prior to 1965, when civil divorce was a much rarer event both culturally and statistically, most Catholic lawyers were trained to and did generally avoid taking part in divorce cases.

A popular and concise booklet, *Legal Moral Principles* by Reverend R. P. Murray was probably typical of pre-conciliar authors. In section 9, "Marriage—The Law—The Lawyer", Murray argued: Catholic lawyers may plead the case of one resisting divorce from a valid marriage; may plead the case of one whose marriage has been declared null by the Church; and may plead the case of one who does not intend to remarry but only get their legal rights secured. "Accordingly, apart from these rare cases, the Catholic lawyer must practically refuse to prosecute a petition for divorce even though the parties involved are non-Catholics, presumably believing in good faith that their marriage can be dissolved." [1] This short booklet did then reflect what more prominent authors had published at great length: e.g., Francis J. Connell, Bernard Haring, and several summaries by renowned Jesuit moralists Gerald Kelly and John J. Lynch, writing in the "Moral Notes" of *Theological Studies*. [2]

[1] Rev. R. P. Murray, *Legal Moral Principles* (Buffalo: Rauch-Stoeckl, 1949), pp. 14–15.
[2] Francis J. Connell, *Morals in Politics and Professions* (Westminster, Md.: Newman Press, 1951), pp. 110–11; Bernard Haring, C.Ss.R., *The Law of Christ*, vol. 2 (Westminster, Md.:

Prior to 1965, that is prior to the explosion of the so-called "no-fault" divorce legislation, many civil jurisdictions had relatively serious, even strict, criteria for civil divorce. For example, pre-1965 New York state law permitted divorce for adultery only. This led some to leave the state (for a Mexican divorce or a Reno divorce), or those who stayed within the jurisdiction often engaged in all sorts of known perjury to secure their civil divorce.

This known perjury on all sides was still another reason why all sorts of honest Catholic lawyers simply avoided involvement in divorce proceedings—a situation perhaps not well known to the general public, but well known within legal circles and another obvious source of scandal.

In ways, of course, so-called "no-fault" divorce knew no limits and helped produce a divorce mentality and an expanded industry to service this sorrow. There were 393,000 divorces in the USA in 1960; 700,000 in 1970; and by 1975, there were and are 1,000,000-plus divorces every year.

At almost the same time, Vatican Council II lamented the "plague of divorce" as one of the "disfigurements" that obscures the excellence of marriage (*GS*, no. 47). It is not simply the good of the individual but also the good of the human and Christian society that are intimately linked with stable marriage and family life, according to the same Council.

Yet, the Church's own canon law can and does permit lawful separation (cann. 1151–55) without, of course, any alleged "right" to remarry. The same canon law, motivated by Christian charity and solicitous for the good of the family, urges the offended spouse to pardon grave faults and not sunder conjugal life (can. 1152, §1). Yet, where there is grave danger of soul or body to the other or to the children, or where "common life" is unduly difficult, separation by decree or one's own authority is possible (can. 1153, §1).

Further, it is now common tribunal practice in this country to presume or require the possession of a civil divorce prior to seeking an annulment. Church law and practice is dedicated to upholding marriage. Thus, the first step, even in a dissolution procedure, is to mention the possibility of attempting reconciliation. The possibility

Newman Press, 1964), pp. 511–12; Gerald Kelly, S.J., "Notes on Moral Theology, 1949", *Theological Studies* (*TS*) 11 (1950): 69–79; Kelly, "*Notes on Moral Theology, 1950*", *TS* 12 (1951): 88–89; John J. Lynch, "Notes on Moral Theology", *TS* 22 (1961): 249.

of a civil divorce effectively says "no" to that last hope of reconciliation, and, having the civil divorce prior to the canonical annulment (if granted) would prevent the Catholic party from suffering
adverse civil penalties or consequences simply for acting in accord
with Church law.

Thus, the same canons and their stated goals—Christian charity and
family good—should motivate a Catholic lawyer to make at least a
first mention and effort at reconciliation, which, even if it fails, attests
to the importance of indissoluble marriage and is virtue attempted
rather than avoided. A *what's-the-use?* attitude no more ennobles the
legal profession than it does any other learned profession.

With that background, we read the following in the *Catechism of the
Catholic Church*: "If civil divorce remains the only possible way of ensur-
ing certain legal rights, the care of the children, or the protection of
inheritance, it can be tolerated and does not constitute a moral offense"
(no. 2383).

If it is not a moral offense, then it seems clear to me that a Catholic
lawyer can assist a Catholic to secure a civil divorce when this is the
only way to secure or ensure the protection of certain legal rights.

—July 1995


## Communion for Divorced and Remarried Catholics

Question: Although the Church has responded to this pastoral problem, I continue to hear and read about the acceptability, even the
advocacy, of "internal forum" solutions for divorced and remarried
Catholics [who have not been granted annulments] to receive Communion. Am I mistaken that this is wrong?

Answer: No, you are not mistaken. Yes, you are correct that the
highest authorities in the Church have clearly and repeatedly taught
the unacceptability of this so-called solution and forbidden pastors to
teach or practice this contradiction. Further, you are also correct that
some authors continue to print and promote the opposite.

First, all do agree that this is a serious pastoral problem; i.e., married
Catholics who are civilly divorced, who then remarry (invalidly) and
now desire to receive Holy Communion. At one time or another, every

pastor has encountered this situation—the first valid union is indeed the impediment that disqualifies the second invalid union; this objective circumstance precludes the worthy reception of Holy Communion.

Thus, when this couple is unable to separate, apart from the possibility of not living as husband and wife and avoiding scandal, the Catholic is simply unable to make the necessary "purpose of amendment"— i.e., amending the invalid union, or, amend by abstaining from marital acts and avoiding scandal.

I doubt, in the history of the Church, that this difficult case has ever been answered with more pastoral explicitness than by Pope John Paul II in *Familiaris Consortio*, number 84. The Pope explicitly mentions the most difficult case—those who are "subjectively certain" in conscience that their previous marriage was not valid.

Next, he encourages those in this situation not to quit the Church but to participate as fully as they *can* in Church life: hear the Word of God; attend Mass; persevere in prayer; participate in works of charity and justice; raise children as Christians; and cultivate the spirit and practice of penance day by day.

> However, the Church reaffirms her practice, based on Sacred Scripture, of not admitting to Eucharistic Communion divorced persons who have remarried. They are unable to be admitted thereto from the fact that their state and condition of life objectively contradict that union of love between Christ and the Church which is signified and effected by the Eucharist. (no. 84)

This is not a singular mention of the Holy Father but a consistent teaching, consistently repeated in the most formal manner (cf. his *Reconciliatio et Paenitentia* [December 2, 1984], no. 34; *CCC*, no. 1650).

In view of the clear and formal teaching, it is also, sadly, true that some "authors" continue to teach, even advocate, the opposite practice under the rubric of "internal forum" solution, or, the so-called "good conscience" solution. Some do not even hesitate to distort this teaching in order to justify unsound practices that contradict it.

At least two recent examples promote this distortion. *The Tablet* (of London) ran a series of articles in 1991, wherein Theodore Davey (in the issue of July 27, 1991) clearly misrepresented authentic Church teaching and tried to twist a prior position of Cardinal Ratzinger to make it further distort the official response of Cardinal Seper, Cardinal Ratzinger's predecessor as Prefect of the Congregation for the Doctrine of the Faith.

Cardinal Ratzinger, in turn, took the unusual step of writing a lengthy letter of correction to *The Tablet* to refute its distorted teaching on divorced and remarried Catholics and the Eucharist.[3]

Sadly, the London *Tablet* has for some time taken on a very anti-Roman spirit. In this instance, *The Tablet* did not even bother to mention correct Catholic teaching (*FC*, no. 84) while trying to make the CDF Prefect look like a dissenter against that teaching. It's a sad day when one of the highest officials in the Catholic Church can't get even a fair hearing in an allegedly "Catholic" publication and has to write a personal letter to refute distortions of Catholic teaching.

A similar, but less eminent, distortion has appeared in a national Catholic monthly in New Zealand—a five-part series in *Marist Messenger* by the Reverend John Hosie. In particular, part 4 concerns "Remarried Catholics and Holy Communion". Here, Father Hosie concedes that Pope John Paul spoke in "a general way" that such Catholics (divorced and remarried) "may not participate in the Eucharist". But, he continues, most Catholics are not aware of what he calls a "second level" of teaching at the "level of conscience".[4]

In such situations, he writes, the Catholic may make a decision in what is called "internal forum" or in "good conscience" and "may then continue to receive Holy Communion". This, he says, is a perfectly "correct moral principle" and "totally orthodox" (pp. 9–10) and appeals to a April 11, 1973 letter to the CDF (the late Cardinal Seper) the concluding words of which state: "the approved practice of the Church in the internal forum".[5]

Father Hosie then forwards the strange conclusion that priests "should apply the *approved practice* of the good conscience solution", and, even more, "Pope John Paul was certainly implying this outcome in his reference, quoted above".[6]

In the space of two pages, Father Hosie would have us believe that the same Pope said such Catholics "may not participate in the Eucharist" (p. 9) but was certainly "implying" the opposite (p. 10).

---

[3] Joseph Cardinal Ratzinger, "Church, Pope and Gospel", *Tablet* 245, no. 7891 (Oct. 28, 1991): 1310, 1311.

[4] John Hosie, S.M., "Remarried Catholics and Holy Communion", *Marist Messenger* 63, no. 11 (Dec. 1992): 9.

[5] Cf. *Canon Law Digest*, vol. 8 (Chicago Province S.J., 1978), p. 504.

[6] Hosie, "Remarried Catholics", p. 10.

What the Pope explicitly taught in *FC*, number 84, in 1981, was repeated verbatim in 1984 and 1992; the opposite practice was nowhere "implied"; indeed it was condemned.

Further, Cardinal Seper's mention of the "approved practice" of the Church in "the internal forum" must be read honestly.

First, it has never been the "approved" practice for the divorced and remarried to receive Holy Communion—so it can't mean that. The only "approved" practice of "internal forum" can be the sincere confessional solution of agreeing to live as brother and sister and avoiding scandal.

Also, there was and is the remote and rare possibility of some long-standing canonical case that lacks some small but technical proof—a case that looks invalid, with moral certitude, but some canonical point is lacking—which could then be sent to the Sacred Penitentiary in Rome, which has jurisdiction in the "internal forum" and can issue a declaration of freedom that has external effects.[7]

This is the only "approved" practice envisioned or sanctioned by Cardinal Seper in 1973 or Cardinal Ratzinger in 1991. To say or suggest that the Pope "implies" a practice contradictory to his own formal teaching is not only insulting to the Pope but badly misleading to Catholics in this difficult situation. This is not a "good conscience" solution, but rather, advice on how to form a "bad conscience", and those who follow such bad advice are likely to be hurt not once but twice.

—November 1993

---

[7] Cf. J. McGrath, "Good Conscience Procedures", in *New Catholic Encyclopedia*, vol. 17 (New York: McGraw-Hill, 1979), p. 243.

# Birth Control

## Contraception and Marriage Preparation

Question: Have you read the treatment of "Responsible Parent-hood" in *Together for Life*? Would you give this to couples preparing for marriage?

Answer: Have I read it? Yes! Would I give it to couples? No! Monsignor Joseph M. Champlin's booklet was first published in 1970.[1] It is now in its 39th printing (March 1993) with some five million copies in print.

*Together for Life* (hereafter, *TL*) is, perhaps, the most widely distributed pre-Cana publication in this country. It surely has some advantages that help account for its great distribution.

First, it is an easy read; the copy I am looking at has ninety-six pages. It is attractively laid out, with many "nice" pictures, but with only a light overlay of text and comment of a doctrinal nature.

Perhaps, the biggest plus is that the booklet contains all the optional prayers and readings that can be chosen for the marriage ceremony. This alone makes it truly convenient for pastors, who can hand a couple this booklet, and they, in turn, can peruse the possibilities without plodding through the giant Lectionary or Sacramentary. In fact, the last page is a convenient tear-out sheet which is a neat tally sheet of the readings, prayers, and blessings chosen by the couple.

On the level of liturgical choreography and dialogue, *TL* is the handiest of handouts. On the level of Catholic doctrine and morals on marriage, this is Catholic "Lite"—a kind of ultra-slim-fast in theology. While the booklet does have an "imprimatur", this imprimatur says

[1] Msgr. Joseph M. Champlin, *Together for Life* (Notre Dame, Ind.: Ave Maria Press, 1970).

more about who granted it than it does about what an imprimatur should guarantee. *TL* is of the Dutch Catechism genre, i.e., it does not say all that much that's wrong, rather it does not say enough of what's right!

You ask specifically about the treatment of "Responsible Parenthood". On the precise question of harmonizing married love and the responsible transmission of life, Monsignor Champlin refers to Vatican II, *Gaudium et Spes*, but not in an accurate nor consistent way. The author cites what I take to be number 50 of that document, that married couples ultimately make this judgment before God, "but in their manner of acting spouses should be aware that they cannot proceed arbitrarily" (*TL*, p. 67).

The Council is, of course, quite specific that this judgment does not rest on good intentions or the evaluation of motives alone, but is determined by "objective standards": "objective standards . . . based on the nature of the human person and his acts, preserve the full sense of mutual self-giving and human procreation in the context of true love" (*GS*, no. 51; also cited fully in the *CCC*, no. 2368. Indeed, the few summary paragraphs 2366 through 2372 of the *Catechism* would be a far superior treatment than the one-page [p. 67] gloss of *TL*).

After correctly citing the Council in part, *TL* then proceeds to do what the Council said not to do—*TL* asks only about motives and intentions through three questions: Are we being selfish? Or too trusting? Or not trusting enough? Nowhere is contraception, the term, or its wrongfulness ever mentioned in this single-page summary of *TL*, nor for that matter is the word chastity or married chastity ever mentioned!

Rather and instead, *Together for Life* then positions those who "feel caught in a dilemma"—with God "seeming to say one thing in their hearts and another [thing] through his Church" (p. 67).

Here, of course, Vatican II is not appealed to since the same Council clearly taught that "a true contradiction cannot exist" between divine laws governing the transmission of life and the fostering of authentic married love (*GS*, no. 51). Just what this voice "in the heart" is remains unexplained. Personally, I know of no example of public or private revelation where God tells someone in private to do what the Church forbids in public and private. Again, as above, on this very matter, the Council is explicit that couples are not to proceed arbitrarily, and more specifically, this is not a question of good intentions or motives alone;

yet, *TL* asks only and alone: selfish? trusting? too much? too little?—only about motives or intentions.

The *conscience* card!

If this is not already ambiguous enough, *TL* now sets up a conflicted conscience ("There is no easy resolution ...", "torn between conflicting commands"); readers are now given very misleading advice: "At those times we purify our hearts, search for God's light in this special circumstance, then *decide what is the best course to follow*. And follow it without any fear or anxiety" (*TL*, p. 67, emphasis added).

One would think that, in a Catholic publication, the teaching of God's Church might be the "God's light" one searches for, but that is not stated clearly. Rather, readers are told "then decide the best course to follow". Presumably, if they decide for the contraception, that is the "best" course for them. If they decide against contraception, that is the "best" course for them. It's all winners and no losers in this set-up.

Notice there is no mention of a *correct* conscience nor an *erroneous* conscience—whatever course you decide is best if, of course, the best course for you. In effect, the formal teaching of the Church on this subject has just been rendered inoperative. Just in case someone might miss the *situational* spin of this solution, readers are told that should they ever be "unable to cope with the conflict" to seek out not just a priest but an "understanding priest" who will not and should not make your decision but help to ensure "continued peace" with whatever decision you come to—right or wrong. In other words, shop around till you find an affirmative cleric who will support the peaceful possession of your decision—regardless of the decision. Some people call this a "pastoral solution".

This final paragraph of conscience mis-formation pretty much undoes whatever vestiges of Catholic teaching that may have survived to this point.

Clearly, this misconstructed half-truth (decide what is best for yourself) is very much at odds with the treatment of conscience in *Veritatis Splendor*, numbers 54 to 64, and equally at odds with the excellent treatment of conscience in the *Catechism of the Catholic Church* (nos. 1776–802). Again, as above, the *Catechism* presents a masterful summary—in almost the same space as *TL*—of conjugal love, fidelity, and the fecundity of marriage (nos. 2360–72).

A practical problem remains: *Together for Life* is still the handiest of handouts, largely because of its copyright grip on the ICEL translation of the Rite of Marriage and the Jerusalem Bible's translation of the various readings from the Lectionary. Few pastors like to drop something unless and until they can put something else in its place.

John F. Kippley has published *Marriage Is for Keeps*. This booklet lists the readings but does not include them.[2] The Kippley booklet, however, is so far superior, so much richer in the doctrine and morals of marriage, that there is no serious comparison with *TL*, which is not so much a poor second, but just poor in doctrine and anemic in morals.

—November 1994


## Reasons for Natural Family Planning

Question: How "serious" are the "serious reasons" for practicing natural family planning (NFP)? Some call NFP Catholic contraception; others say the opposite. What official teaching answers this directly?

Answer: First, NFP is not any kind of contraception, which we understand to be any action that deliberately renders sexual intercourse incapable of causing conception. Some style themselves "providentialists" in their claim that God will provide for whatever number of children you have. Of course, married couples (and all Christians) should trust in divine providence. "But", as Germain Grisez points out, "providence has given the Christian couple reason enlightened by faith and the power to act in accord with it."[3] Piety should not be confused with presumption.

As for the "serious" or "just" reasons, more, I think, can be said about their generic kind than about their specific weight in a given case or life.

---

[2] Almost simultaneous with the publication of my November 1994 column, I received a new copy of *Marriage Is for Keeps* (1994) "Wedding Edition", which does contain the Rite itself and all the possible Readings for the ceremony, together with the last-page selection forms. Thus, this booklet is now complete and as practical as any available. Source: The Couple to Couple League, P.O. Box 111184, Cincinnati, OH 45211; Phone 1-513-661-7612.

—March 1995

[3] Germain Grisez, *Living a Christian Life* (Quincy, Ill.: Franciscan Press, 1993), p. 682.

The classic encyclical *Casti Connubii* of Pope Pius XI does not mention this precise point but speaks only of "virtuous continence which Christian law permits in matrimony when both parties consent" (DS 3716).

It was, rather, Pope Pius XII in his famous and extensive "Address to the Midwives" who first spoke of a positive obligation for transmitting life. But as a positive obligation it can admit of excusing causes, i.e., "grave motives" independent of the good will of those obliged. These "serious motives" he categorized as four kinds: "medical, eugenic, economic and social".[4] These can exempt from this positive duty for a long time, even for the entire duration of the marriage.

Thus, according to Pius XII, the choice to avoid or postpone birth can be licit under just and reasonable conditions. But, without serious or just reasons of this kind, the deliberate will to avoid the fertility of this union must derive from a false appreciation of life or motives foreign to right ethical norms.[5]

Next, the *ex professo* treatment of marriage by the Second Vatican Council (in *GS*, nos. 47–52) is both helpful and pertinent to this question. The Council teaches: "Marriage and conjugal love are by their nature ordained toward the begetting and educating of children. Children are really the supreme gift of marriage and contribute very substantially to the welfare of their parents" (no. 50).

Within that context which will shape and form the new *Code* (can. 1055, §1) and the new *Catechism* (no. 1601), the Council mentions factors couples should consider: their own welfare and their children (already born or foreseen); material and spiritual conditions of the times and state in life; and even the interests of the family group, temporal society, and the Church herself. The Council then teaches: "The parents themselves ... should ultimately make this judgment in the sight of God" (*GS*, no. 50).This cannot be an arbitrary decision but a conscience judgment conformed to divine law and Church teaching which authentically interprets that law in light of the gospel.

---

[4] Pope Pius XII, "Address to Italian Association of Catholic Midwives" (Oct. 29, 1951), see *AAS* 43 (1951): 846.

[5] For a close commentary on this teaching, see John C. Ford, S.J., and Gerald Kelly, S.J., *Contemporary Moral Theology*, vol. 2: *Marriage Questions* (Westminster, Md.: Newman Press, 1963), pp. 396–430.

Lastly, in harmonizing conjugal love with respect for human life, the Council taught that the moral aspect of choices here "does not depend solely on sincere intentions" (motives only), but also on *objective standards* "based on the nature of the human person and his acts [that] preserve the full sense of mutual self-giving and human procreation in the context of true love" (*GS*, no. 51).

Next, Pope Paul VI in *Humanae Vitae*, numbers 10 and 16, continues the same teaching of Pius XII and the Council. The Pope teaches: "With regard to physical, economic, psychological and social conditions, responsible parenthood is exercised by those who prudently and generously decide to have more children, and by those who, for serious reasons and with due respect for moral precepts, decide not to have additional children for either a certain or an indefinite period of time" (no. 10).

Two small points here. The "eugenic" reference of Pope Pius XII has been replaced by the "psychological" reference of Paul VI. And *Humanae Vitae* speaks of an "indefinite period of time" instead of "for the entire duration of the marriage".

Curiously, in the magisterial exhortation of John Paul II, *Familiaris Consortio*—a document many times longer and larger than *Humanae Vitae*—there is no mention of the "reasons" for practicing NFP where you would surely expect it.

However, the same Pope, John Paul II, in a book-length series of talks, *Reflections on Humanae Vitae* (1984), does address this question specifically.[6] He notes that NFP can be an abuse if used for "unworthy reasons". And that a morally correct standard takes into account not only the good of the family, but the health and means of the couple, along with the good of society and the Church (repeating the factors mentioned in *GS*, no. 50).

Lastly, in his encyclical *Evangelium Vitae*, in the part devoted to building up a new "culture of life", John Paul speaks of the work of education, training couples in responsible procreation: "This happens when the family is generously open to new lives, and when couples maintain an attitude of openness and service to life, even if, for serious reasons and in respect for the moral law, they choose to avoid a new birth for the time being or indefinitely"(no. 97; both in Latin and in translation, this is verbatim *HV*, no. 10).

---

[6] General Audience, "Responsible Parenthood Linked to Moral Maturity" (Sept. 5, 1984).

Where does this leave the question? I think John Kippley is correct when he writes: "You cannot decide for anybody else what generosity means in their case." [7]

The providentialists say, do nothing to interfere with procreation (including NFP). The seculars say, have 1.78 children. The Catholic position is neither of these but calls for generosity, while recognizing there can be serious reasons for spacing children or limiting family size. The point is to get the couples to ask themselves are they really answering God's call to generosity in the service of life. Kippley is correct—a good place to start is to read reflectively *Gaudium et Spes*, numbers 50 and 51.

—February 2005

## Contraception as a Lesser Evil

Question: This is not a single question but a summary of questions invoking the justification of or counseling the "lesser evil". Isn't contraception better than abortion? Contraception preferable to family break-up? Better for a Catholic hospital to provide contraception and sterilizations than cease to exist? Does not a truly proportionate reason modify lesser evils?

Answer: This manner of posing moral dilemmas has a modern and frequent usage that bears little resemblance to the careful distinctions of classic moralists.

First, the expression "lesser evil" can have several meanings. Joseph Boyle, at a Dallas workshop for bishops (1984), noted that "lesser evil" can refer to the difference between light and grave matter, an unjust and more unjust state of affairs, or a morally right but difficult choice compared to undesirable consequences but not morally required. Boyle's basic critique is that of the prevalent misuse of the so-called "lesser evil" by proportionalists. [8]

[7] John F. Kippley, *Sex & the Marriage Covenant* (Cincinnati: Couple-to-Couple League, 1991), p. 205.

[8] Joseph Boyle, "The Principle of Double Effect: Good Actions Entangled in Evil", in *Moral Theology Today: Certitudes and Doubts*, ed. Rev. Donald G. McCarthy (St. Louis: Pope John Center, 1984), p. 257.

Germain Grisez notes: "Classical moralists were not of one mind on the permissibility of counseling the lesser of two moral evils." Grisez is correct that the classical moralists who did approve of "counseling the lesser evil" assumed as a condition "that the other was already determined to carry out the greater evil".[9]

Grisez himself correctly argues that it is always "direct scandal" to encourage anyone to do any moral evil in order to avoid any non-moral evil, however great. To intend a lesser sin is, obviously, to intend sin and thus give scandal. Therefore, to counsel a "lesser evil" can only be permissible when, rather than lead a wrongdoer to choose an evil, the counselor only tries to persuade the other to bring about less harm.[10]

Classic and reliable moralists, such as Hieronymus Noldin, S.J., Albert Schmitt, S.J., and Marcelino Zalba, S.J., teach the same.[11] Henry Davis, S.J., in his *Moral and Pastoral Theology*, goes to great lengths to make proper distinctions while defending Jesuit authors against charges that they endorse violations of the end justifies the means.[12]

Father Ludovico Bender, O.P., presents the most stringent analysis: to choose an action as the lesser of two evils is illicit (if both are moral evils). One evil does not become good simply because a greater evil could have been chosen. Bender argues this is a nonexistent dilemma wherein one is required to choose between two sinful acts. One can always refrain, he argues, from positive action altogether when, if to do neither, would itself be no sin. If serious damage results from this omission, the individual would not be responsible for such consequences because no one can be morally required to sin.[13]

Is it permissible to *advise* a person bent on committing sin to commit another but less grave sin? Bender argues not! For to advise or suggest is to "induce", and there is always scandal in that. However, to *dissuade* another from part of a total evil already planned and insofar as the wrongdoer cannot be deterred from the complete wrong is, for

[9] Germain Grisez, *Living a Christian Life* (Quincy, Ill.: Franciscan Press, 1993), p. 237.
[10] Ibid.
[11] See H. Noldin, A. Schmitt, and G. Heinzel, *Summa Theologiae Moralis* (Rauch, 1961), p. 105, n. 113; and Marcellino Zalba, *Theologiae Moralis Compendium*, vol. 2 (Madrid, 1958), pp. 112–13.
[12] Henry Davis, S.J., *Moral and Pastoral Theology*, vol. 1, 6th ed. (London, New York: Sheed and Ward, 1949), pp. 247; 339.
[13] Fr. Ludovico Bender, O.P., *Dictionary of Moral Theology* (Westminster, Md.: Newman Press, 1962), pp. 705–6.

Bender, a good deed. The classic example: to suggest to a thief, who wants to kill the owner and take his property, to take only the money, is not advising theft but advising against murder. The theft, already decided upon, is not caused by the advice: this particular advice is to deter the thief from murder also decided upon.

Thus, he argues that there is a difference between *counseling* the lesser of two evils and *advising* against part of a proposed evil. The first employs an evil act for a good end; the second, a good act for a good end.[14]

The subtleties and distinctions of classical moralists are a far cry from the quantitative and careless comparisons of most proportionalists. In my opinion, old and new authors can use the same terms ("lesser evil") but use it in ways that have no resemblance to each other. Grisez's brief treatment is a good example of good examples that clarify modern dilemmas instead of confusing them.[15]

Thus, for example, the *Catechism* teaches: "The gravity of sins is more or less great: murder is graver than theft. One must also take into account who is wronged: violence against parents is in itself graver than violence against a stranger" (no. 1858; cf. also nos. 1854–64; *VS*, nos. 69, 70; *Reconciliatio et Paenitentia*, no. 17).

It is surely true that murder is graver than theft. But, theft (grave or light) is never a "good", and is only a "lesser evil" by comparison to something worse. This kind of "comparison morality" has the quantitative attraction of damage control—but morally it is the wrong comparison.

The morally relevant comparison presented to moral choice is the basic freedom of contradiction (freedom of exercise): to do or not do the same thing under the same circumstances. Thus, to steal or not steal $1,000 from a specific person. To compare this with other acts (other and different moral choices)—this owner or this company grosses one million dollars per annum, or at least I am not killing him when I steal—these other facts (choices) do not change the moral species of grave theft. Morally, it is the wrong comparison and easily misleads to an uncountable calculus of subjective reasons in place of an objective moral principle.

Thus, the question is posed: Is not contraception "justified" as a "lesser evil" to avoid an abortion or a family break-up?

---

[14] Ibid., p. 706.
[15] Cf. Grisez, *Living a Christian Life*, pp. 237–38.

John Paul II's encyclical *Evangelium Vitae* addresses this question. Some might try to justify contraception as an abortion preventative, but this is an empirical illusion. Widespread contraception does not reduce abortion; indeed, it is in societies where contraception is most available that permissive abortions flourish.

Although contraception and abortion differ in nature and moral gravity—abortion destroys a life (Fifth Commandment) while contraception opposes the virtue of chastity in marriage (Sixth Commandment)—despite these differences they are closely connected "as fruits of the same tree" (*EV*, no. 13). They share an anti-life mentality, a distorted refusal to accept responsibility in matters of sexuality; and a self-centered concept of freedom that sees human life as an obstacle to personal fulfillment (EV, no. 13). Thus, abortion comes to be seen as back-up for failed contraception.

Acts that are intrinsically evil—as both contraception and abortion are (*VS*, nos. 47, 80)—never become "good", nor permissible when done with the intention of bringing about some "good" or lesser evil. Intrinsically evil acts are, in the end, objects of human choice that by their very nature are "incapable of being ordered to God because they radically contradict the good of the person made in his image" (*VS*, nos. 79, 80).

Lastly, there can be a complete confusion of categories when some argue on the basis of the "lesser evil" that a Catholic hospital can "materially cooperate" in nontherapeutic sterilizations (and perhaps other proscribed "services") considering that, if the Catholic hospital does not merge or co-sponsor or joint venture prohibited services, that geographic area will be under-served by a diminished or disappearing or closed Catholic facility. The argument for cooperating in what the Catholic facility is prohibited from providing often confuses loss of money (a real loss but not a moral evil) with nontherapeutic contraception and/or abortion referrals (moral evils).

Morally, this is not a "lesser evil" case at all. In fact, when a Catholic facility begins to provide so-called "services" that it is ethically and institutionally opposed to, one could ask whether the loss, reduction, or closure of such a facility is only a qualified loss since it already institutionally contradicts its own ethics—itself a scandal. In terms of Catholic witness, it is not clear what "good" is lost or "lesser" when a religious institution self-contradicts its religious identity and its religious purpose.

—December 1997

## Contraceptive Fornication

Question: Some Catholic parents have asked me (as pastor) about their unmarried adult children using contraception. Granted nonmarital intercourse is wrong, but isn't their use of contraception here a "lesser evil"?

Answer: The so-called "lesser evil" theory is, unfortunately, more often invoked than explained. This particular case and its rationale is, again unfortunately, all too common.

There are two distinct but related moral questions here: (1) fornication and (2) contraception. Both are moral evils. To declare one a "lesser" evil inevitably involves the agent in unacceptable proportionalism, and the practice of either evil here cannot be a genuine preparation for true Christian marriage or even single Christian living.

Germain Grisez gives the same answer in his *Living a Christian Life*. He argues: first, the argument is an example of proportionalism, which is not a workable method of moral judgment (with the subsequent publication of *Veritatis Splendor* one can call proportionalism a condemned method of moral judgment). Second, couples who cannot responsibly engage in sexual intercourse open to new life always have an alternative to contraception—they can and should abstain. If such a couple chooses contraception, they irresponsibly risk pregnancy, because contraceptives sometimes fail.

Then precisely to the question raised, Grisez writes:

> A man and a woman who are not married to each other should not engage in sexual intercourse in any case; if they not only do so but practice contraception, they only facilitate one immorality by another. Moreover, using contraception aggravates rather than mitigates the sinfulness of fornication, since to the specific malice of fornication it adds that of a contralife will and the associated injustice to the unwanted child if contraception fails.[16]

Thus, contraceptive fornication is not a so-called "lesser evil", it is rather a different evil, or different evils. They are distinct acts of choice, separate and separable, both of which are intrinsically evil (*VS*, no. 47).

[16] Grisez, *Living a Christian Life*, p. 515.

Intrinsic evils are not "lessened" or "improved" morally by adding on another intrinsic evil as if it were some kind of reverse compound interest.

The language of "lesser evil" is both confusing and misleading here. It is not a lesser evil; it is a different and another evil. "Lesser" connotes and commits to some kind of subtraction from "gross" evil, suggesting a "net" evil not quite as bad as the total. That kind of moral arithmetic misleads because it pretends that moral "goods" and "evils" are measurable things of a given size, shape, or weight. This is not so.

In any case, contraceptive fornication is just about the worst possible preparation for a chaste Christian marriage. When contraception is perceived or lived as "not so bad" or "lesser" before marriage, it will inevitably return as "not so bad" in the face of any later problem or inconvenience faced in true marriage.

There are authors who try to make a case for nonmarital contraception as a "lesser evil" to an unwanted child (?) or to head off a possible or future abortion.[17] I believe that effort is flawed both in theory and in actual practice.

Pope John Paul II taught in *Evangelium Vitae* that while contraception and abortion are related they are specifically *different* evils—as they contradict different virtues and commandments. Furthermore, the negative values inherent in the "contraceptive mentality" foster and strengthen the temptation to abort when "unwanted" life is conceived. The pro-abortion culture is strongest where the teaching against contraception is most rejected (no. 13).

Thus, rather than being a "lesser" evil, contraception is simply another and different evil which fosters and engraves the other evil by pretending to mitigate what it actually deepens.

—May 2000

## Emergency Contraception

Question: Various bills and regulations propose to mandate "emergency contraception". Not all Catholic responses to this movement seem to say the same thing. How does this stand?

[17] Cf. Jean-Marie Hennaux, "Risques de viol et inhibiteurs de fecondation", *Nouvelle Revue theologique* 120, no. 2 (1998): 196–215.

Answer: I agree with your uncertainty: not all Catholic responses are the same response to this challenge. What I take to be the clearest and best response is that of Dr. Eugene F. Diamond: "The Ovulation or Pregnancy Approach in Cases of Rape?"[18] Indeed, Dr. Diamond writes in response to and presents a critique of Drs. Ronald Hamel and Michael Panicola's "Emergency Contraception and Sexual Assault".[19]

A first problem is terminology, i.e., the very expression "emergency contraception" seems to beg the question that needs to be answered. Is this simply a question of contraception or does it risk abortion and is called "emergency contraception" to distract attention away from the abortion problem? Once this is called "contraception", the public relations effort is probably lost.

Some of the general public will give some space for Catholic institutions and Catholic individuals to distance themselves from any participation in abortion procedures and abortifacients. However, the same general public is not so willing to allow or acknowledge Catholic reluctance about contraception. Thus, by calling this "emergency contraception", the impression is given and taken that the only point at issue is "contraception" when, of course, the crucial point at issue is the risk of abortion and abortion consequences.

In the conventional terms of the 1950s, when the term *contraception* meant diaphragms, the case for self-defense against rape was and remained a defensible opinion. This was the reported advice of the German bishops to German women in post-war Berlin, then occupied by the Red Army, an army not known for good manners.

However, during the "Nuns in the Congo" case in the early '60s and the rapes in Bosnia in the early '90s, the contraceptive in question was no longer a simple barrier method to prevent conception, but rather the birth control pill—at first called an anti-ovulant or anovulant.

This is and remains the problem. The pill is not simply or only a chemical method of preventing ovulation. All commercially available

---

[18] Dr. Eugene F. Diamond, "The Ovulation or Pregnancy Approach in Cases of Rape?" *National Catholic Bioethics Quarterly* 3, no. 4 (Winter 2003): 689–94.

[19] Ronald P. Hamel, Ph.D., and Michael R. Panicola, Ph.D., "Emergency Contraception and Sexual Assault", *Health Progress* 83, no. 5 (Sept./Oct. 2002): 12–15, 51. I presume this article from *Health Progress* to be the formal position of the Catholic Health Association, and, if it is, I judge that to be both unfortunate and imprecise.

birth control pills marketed in the United States have some abortifacient properties. This element raises some moral questions that simply
did not exist in the post-war Berlin context.

To approach this dilemma today, some Catholic authors speak of a
"Pregnancy Approach" while others speak of an "Ovulation Approach"
in the aftercare of rape victims. An example of the former is the Hamel
and Panicola article in *Health Progress* cited above; an example of the
latter is Peter Cataldo in *Catholic Health Care Ethics*.[20]

In the pregnancy approach, only a pregnancy test is given. If a woman
has been raped while pregnant, the need for post-rape hormone therapy is moot, indeed counterproductive. If she is not pregnant, this
approach presumes the emergency contraceptives will only prevent ovulation, sperm migration, or sperm conception—these are seen as self-
defensive contraceptives in this context. However, multiple-dose oral
contraceptives can also have the effect of disturbing the receptivity of
the endometrium, which does not prevent conception but prevents
implantation and is thus in effect abortifacient.

This is why the "ovulation approach" tests not only for the presence of pregnancy but also for the time or timing of ovulation to free
one from that abortifacient possibility. It does require more effort, but
that effort seems necessary in order to avoid an abortifacient practice.

There is no technology or chemistry presently available to prevent
sperm capacitation in the fallopian tube, or to prevent the advance of
spermatic pronucleus to the ovum's pronucleus to full syngamy (zygote)
hours later. The only possible effect available at this point is to prevent
implantation, and that is an abortifacient effect.

In a given case, we may not factually know, and that's the problem.
When (post-zygotic) human life is at stake, it is not enough not to
know, rather we must know that we do no harm to human life and
thus must here take the safer course.

Thus, I believe the ovulation approach is the more correct because
the real question is whether or not potentially abortifacient medications should or should not be given to every woman who presents
herself to an emergency room with a history of sexual assault. It seems
to me that the December 15, 2003, "Fact Sheet on Emergency Contraception" of the U.S. Bishops' Committee for Pro-Life Activities

[20] *Catholic Health Care Ethics: A Manual for Ethics Committees*, ed. Peter J. Cataldo and
Albert Moraczewski (Boston: National Catholic Bioethics Center, 2002), pp. 8–14.

makes the same point: "Tests are available to determine whether ovulation has occurred." [21] Thus, it is not simply a pregnancy test but also concern about ovulation as well.

Of course, no one questions the obvious need for pregnancy testing in these cases. On the other hand, the routine or automatic administration of oral contraceptives without reference to or knowledge of the timing or status of her menstrual cycle is not without moral risk.

Directive 36 of the 2001 *Ethical and Religious Directives* of the USCCB is largely correct as it reads, but, it is also a bit ambiguous since it mentions "after appropriate testing" without specifying or indicating which tests or methods are "appropriate".

The Ovulation Approach (e.g., the Peoria protocol and the like) requires a pregnancy test and tests to specify the range and time of ovulation. The Pregnancy Approach is just that—after a negative pregnancy test then any oral contraceptive is administered.

Personally, I wish some of the science were clearer than it is. However, I am not an expert in science, and my basic reservation is elsewhere.

My reservation concerns "moral certitude". Advocates of almost all positions claim to have "moral certitude" for their position, so that no wrong (evil) or risk of evil is placed. They support that claim by appealing to Probabilities as a "traditional" principle.

Some make this claim but muddle their point in making it. Classic *Probabilism* has to do with doubts of law (at base, the principle is *lax dubia non obligat*). There is no doubt of law here. The law is certain: Thou shalt not kill! No Catholic questions that when it means "[D]o not directly kill the innocent or risk the same".

What is sometimes in doubt here is instead a doubt of fact—in fact, has conception taken place or not? No amount of probable opinions or approved authors will make a woman pregnant if she is not, nor can the same authorities make her un-pregnant if she is.

As I understand Catholic moral teaching, this is one of the three areas to which Probabilism cannot be applied: i.e., the rights of a third party, specifically, the right of an innocent third party not to be injured.

Since the Hamel-Panicola article in *Health Progress* represents, I presume, the position of the Catholic Health Association, and claims the

---

[21] U.S. Bishops' Committee for Pro-Life Activities, "Fact Sheet on 'Emergency Contraception' and Treatment of Victims of Sexual Assault", *Origins* 33, no. 30 (Jan. 8, 2004): 507–8.

status of "moral certitude", my reservation and objection is that the article makes a claim that is neither available nor permissible. Since Probabilism cannot apply here, then the safer course with its extra efforts must be followed. Dr. Diamond's critique is correct, I believe, and will reward a careful reading.

—March 2004


## Repairing Vasectomy

Question: If someone has a change of mind and heart after having had a vasectomy, is there a moral obligation to have this repaired?

Answer: I presume the question concerns a nonmedical, i.e., directly contraceptive sterilization (elective vasectomy). There is no question that this is a sin, and since it involves a bodily mutilation that is usually irreversible, it is more seriously wrong than other forms of temporary contraception.

I do not know of any Church documentation that deals explicitly with this question. However, reliable moralists usually argue that there is no further obligation than sincere contrition, absolution, and penance.

Traditionally, we hold that all people are bound to *ordinary* means to take care of their health, life, and bodily integrity. Also, usually no one is held to *extraordinary* means, but they are free to do so if they choose.

Reversing a vasectomy is itself medically problematic; the success rate is not too high, and the procedures involved are quite expensive. In view of the doubtful outcome and the undoubted costs, such an effort is usually deemed "extraordinary". Thus, it is not obligatory.

Germain Grisez presents the same conclusion in his moral textbook:

> But sometimes people do sincerely repent being sterilized.... Must they now either abstain entirely from marital intercourse or try to have the sterilization reversed? While Church teaching does not deal explicitly with this question, general principles point to a negative answer, at least for most cases. On the one hand, having repented sterilization, married couples have the same right to intercourse and reasons for it which other couples have after the wife's menopause. On the other

hand, there usually are good reasons not to try to have the operation reversed: doing so involves costs and other burdens, the attempt often fails to restore fertility.[22]

Grisez cites Thomas J. O'Donnell for the same conclusion.[23] Both of these are reliable Catholic moralists who present a solid opinion with which I agree and support.

—May 1996

## Sex Selection Intercourse

Question: According to Dr. L. Shettles, a combination of the timing of intercourse (before ovulation vs. at or after ovulation) together with different douches (acid vs. baking soda) can achieve an 85 to 90 percent success rate in conceiving a child of a particular sex. Is this moral?

Answer: The world of science does not share Dr. Landrum Shettles' great enthusiasm for this "method". A sober review and assessment of this "method" can be found in John and Sheila Kippley's *The Art of Natural Family Planning*.[24]

First, the Couple-to-Couple League responds correctly to the question with some hesitation because too much concern about sex selection can detract from seeing the child as a gift and lead instead to seeing the child as a product or construction. This concern is a valid one (cf. *DV*; and *EV*, nos. 22, 39, 63 et passim).

The Shettles theory starts with facts but postulates answers that are either non-factual or simply unknown. The premise is that sperm with "Y" chromosomes are smaller and swim faster, but don't live as long as those with "X" chromosomes, which are larger and slower but last longer. "The longer the theory is around, the more controversial it becomes, and some researchers, however, question this claim."

[22] Grisez, *Living a Christian Life*, p. 545.

[23] Thomas J. O'Donnell, S.J., "Repentance Following Directly Willed Contraceptive Sterilization," *Medical-Moral Newsletter* 26 (Jan. 1989): 4.

[24] John and Sheila Kippley, *The Art of Natural Family Planning*, 4th ed. (Cincinnati: Couple-to-Couple League, 1996), pp. 302–3, with documentation on p. 304.

Concerning different kinds of douches—one supposedly killing male-bearing sperm, the other killing female-bearing sperm—this practice is to be discouraged. The objection is not primarily that it is partly or potentially contraceptive (since plenty of sperm are presumably unaffected), but douche-damaged sperm can cause birth defects, a problem associated with spermicides in general.

The process itself is morally ambiguous at best, since it raises questions about the limits of technological intervention and manipulation of the life processes. For these reasons, it is to be discouraged and avoided and simply does not belong in any presentation of natural family planning.

I find that *The Art of Natural Family Planning* together with all the publications of the Couple-to-Couple League present clear explanations of the most technical questions and always with complete fidelity to formal Catholic moral teaching. The CCL is a good and reliable source.

—May 1997

## 12

# Infertility Treatments

## Fertility Clinics

Question: Newspapers report that fertility clinics are being sued for unethical practices. Most of the same reports claim that we need further and fuller legislation since there are hardly any laws in this area. Is legislation needed?

Answer: I doubt it. When writers claim there are no laws they presume, of course, that the laws of God and the natural law do not pertain. It is willful ignorance of the laws of God and the natural law that has helped bring about this mess.

Some offer cautions that with better record keeping, better auditing, and more "quality control" in reproductive technology, we can slow the slide down the "slippery slope". My hunch is that "slippery slope" is too polite a term; indeed, we have gone off the cliff entirely.

You are correct, newspapers now report oddities worthy of Aldous Huxley's imagination. Eggs were stolen from nine anesthetized women and implanted in other women resulting in three births at the University of California's Irvine Center for Reproductive Health.[1] Two Rhode Island couples sued that state's only fertility clinic for losing nine embryos.[2] "Almost Anything Goes in Birth Science in Italy" read a headline from a report on "granny moms" and baby Elisabetta, who was supposedly conceived from an egg taken from a woman who died two years before and carried to term by her father's sister.[3] The

---

[1] "Fertility Clinic Is Blamed in Theft of Eggs from Sedated Women", *New York Times* (*NYT*), Nov. 12, 1995, p. 28.

[2] "Fertility Clinic Is Sued over Loss of Embryos", *NYT*, Oct. 1, 1995, p. 26.

[3] Celestine Bohlen, "Almost Anything Goes in Birth Science in Italy", *NYT*, Apr. 4, 1995. p. A-14.

prestigious University Hospital at Utrecht (Netherlands) announces the birth of two healthy twin boys: one white, one black.[4] The Genetics and IVF Institute of Fairfax, Virginia regularly advertises donor egg services "available now with no waiting list", with "over 100 fully screened donors immediately accessible". Perhaps your list is longer than mine, but I don't think legislated "quality control" is the answer.

Our society and its vaunted technology has taken a wrong turn, a very wrong turn not merely down some slippery slope but really off the cliff.

With the birth of baby Louise Brown in 1978, the first *in vitro* fertilization birth was a technical success. With all other people of good will, I wish Louise well, but she was, however, misconceived. That technical event was not an ethical giant step forward. Rather, and unfortunately, it opened a door to a new level of human manipulation that seems now only to get deeper and wider.

In the USA, given our legal obsession with absolute individual autonomy, some pretend it is all a matter of "choice". There is no right or wrong in "reproduction" (as they call it), only "choices". If all is *choice*, then get prepared for some strange choices *and* the inevitable consequence of the "choices" of others that you did not choose at all.

There is a cryptic passage in the *Catechism of the Catholic Church* (no. 2275) which refers three times to the "introduction" of the Instruction on Bioethics, *Donum Vitae* of the Congregation for the Doctrine of the Faith. That "introduction" has five points which can serve as a concise Christian anthropology far more necessary for correctly evaluating this field than any catch-up civil legislation.

Procedures make it possible to intervene "not only in order to assist but also to dominate the processes of procreation" (*DV*, pt. 1, no. 1). The Church does not intervene here to teach science as science, but the Church does offer criteria for moral judgment regarding the application of research and technology to human life and its beginnings.

It is an illusion to claim that research and technology are morally "neutral". They are not. The fundamental moral insight is that research and technology must be "at the service of the human person", of his inalienable rights, and his true and integral good according to the design and will of God (*DV*, pt. 1, no. 2).

---

[4] Marlise Simons, "Uproar over Twins and a Couple's Anguish", *NYT*, June 28, 1995, p. A-3.

An intervention on the human body affects not only tissues, organs, and their functions, but involves the person himself. Thus, applied biology and medicine can work together for the integral good of human life when they come to the aid of a person stricken by illness or infirmity and when they respect that person's dignity as a creature of God (*DV*, pt. 1, no. 3).

No biologist or doctor, no mother or father, no technician or advertiser can reasonably claim, by virtue of scientific competence, "to be able to decide about people's origin and destiny". Human life is a gift, not an achievement. Humans are begotten, not made nor manufactured.

*Donum Vitae* then focuses on two central points: the life of the human being and the special nature of the transmission of human life in marriage (pt. 1, no. 4). The larger parts (1 and 2) of that document take up these two points in detail, and part 3 addresses both moral and civil law.

However, it is the "introduction", the Christian anthropology if you will, that must be read with care and thoroughness—read it with a copy of the New Testament and the *Documents of Vatican II* at hand. The laws of God and the natural moral law offer true perspective and corrective here; additional human legislation—apart from or contrary to divine law—will probably only make worse, by arbitrary inclusion or exclusion, what is already a very wrong turn against life and against marriage.

— April 1996


## GIFT Infertility Treatment

Question: What is the morality of GIFT? Is it a procedure that a Catholic facility should promote?

Answer: First, some definitions. *GIFT* means "Gamete Intra-Fallopian Transfer". Many procedures are required: (1) ova are collected from the wife through laparoscopy; (2) semen is collected from the husband either illicitly by masturbation, or licitly by using a perforated condom or Silastic® sheath after intercourse; (3) sperm are "washed" ("scrubbed down") to remove prostaglandins and antibodies and by centrifuging to capacitate better sperm with more potential for fertilization; (4) the ovum and processed sperm are placed in a catheter separated by an air bubble and deposited in the fallopian tube. If successful, conception takes place *in vivo* rather than *in vitro*, which is how it differs from *in vitro* fertilization.

The CDF instruction on bioethics, *Donum Vitae*, did not explicitly consider GIFT. Indeed, at the press conference presenting the instruction in 1987, one Vatican presenter said the document left GIFT open to further research and theological discussion.

And discussion there has been. The Dallas workshop for Bishops (February 1988) was published as a book, *Reproductive Technologies, Marriage and the Church* (1988) with two opinions: Donald T. DeMarco (against GIFT) and Donald G. McCarthy (pro GIFT).[5]

Both authors (DeMarco and McCarthy) accept Church teaching, where they disagree is whether or not GIFT "assists" or "replaces" a marital act in this procedure. If it assists, one can argue it is a licit procedure; if it separates so as to substitute and/or replace a marital act, it is not a licit procedure.

This debate has continued especially in *Ethics & Medics* and the *Linacre Quarterly*. For example, John M. Haas argues no to GIFT, while McCarthy argues yes to GIFT.[6] Thomas J. O'Donnell in his *Medicine & Christian Morality* argued against GIFT but saw it open to discussion.[7] Germain Grisez argues that "since the ovum and semen ... do not pertain to any act of marital intercourse, this procedure, when successful, produces a baby by technology rather than contributes to a marital act's fruitfulness." [8]

Similarly, Benedict Ashley and Kevin O'Rourke argue: "The technology involved seems to replace the conjugal act as the sufficient cause of the uniting of the sperm and ovum rather than simply to assist it." [9] Similar arguments against the moral permissibility of GIFT

---

[5] Donald T. DeMarco, "Catholic Moral Teaching and TOT/GIFT", and Donald G. McCarthy, "Catholic Medical Teaching and TOT/GIFT: A Response to Donald DeMarco", in *Reproductive Technologies, Marriage and the Church* (Braintree, Mass.: Pope John Center, 1988), pp. 122–39 and 140–45, respectively.

[6] John M. Haas, "GIFT? No!", *Ethics & Medics* 18, no. 9 (1993): 1–3; McCarthy, "GIFT? Yes!", *Ethics & Medics* 18, no. 9 (1993): 3–4.

[7] Thomas J. O'Donnell, S.J., *Medicine & Christian Morality* (Staten Island, N.Y.: Alba House, 1991), p. 263; cf. also his 3rd ed. (Staten Island, N.Y.: Alba House, 1996), p. 263.

[8] Germain Grisez, *Difficult Moral Questions*, vol. 3 of *The Way of the Lord Jesus* (Quincy, Ill.: Franciscan Press, 1997), p. 245.

[9] Benedict M. Ashley, O.P., and Kevin D. O'Rourke, O.P., *Health Care Ethics*, 3rd ed. (St. Louis, Mo.: Catholic Health Association of the United States, 1989), p. 285.

can be found in William E. May, Nicholas Tonti-Filippini, and John Doerfler.[10]

On the other hand, Peter J. Cataldo, of the Pope John Center, considers most of these criticisms and argues for GIFT in two articles.[11] Cataldo summarizes these criticisms as two: ontological and numerical. Ontological in the sense of causality: Does GIFT assist or replace the marital act? When sperm is collected another way (e.g., masturbation—a method not advocated by Cataldo) in that order of causality, a marital act is not essential at all to GIFT.

Further, most of the above critics see GIFT and its mechanics as the principal cause of conception and the marital act as only a subordinate cause—more and more remote depending on the number of interventions and clinical preparations prior to injection into the fallopian tube.

Apparently in response to O'Donnell, Cataldo rejects the argument that the sheer number of interventions is relevant or decisive in severing the required link between the marital act and fertilization.[12]

I would not argue that the sheer *number* of interventions is decisive in itself, but the *kind* of interventions is surely relevant. What is politely called "washing" or "scrubbing" sperm is no mere aid to facilitate a marital act. These are separate and separable human acts that seem to me to be no different from artificial insemination—which all of the above authors agree is not morally permissible.

If, indeed, the technical mechanics of processed sperm and its subsequent injection are not artificial insemination—what is? If catheter-delivered processed sperm were injected without air bubble and ovum, it would surely be described morally as artificial insemination. If that is true of the simpler, is it not also true of the more complicated delivery?

---

[10] Cf. William E. May, "Catholic Teaching on the Laboratory Generation of Human Life", in *The Gift of Life: The Proceedings of a National Conference on the Vatican Instruction on Reproductive Ethics and Technology*, ed. Thomas Hilgers, M.D., and Marilyn Wallace, R.S.M. (Omaha, Neb.: Pope Paul VI Institute Press, 1990), p. 80; May's *Marriage: The Rock on Which the Family Is Built* (San Francisco: Ignatius Press, 1995), pp. 89–90; Nicholas Tonti-Filippini, "'Donum vitae' and Gamete Intra-Fallopian Tube Transfer", *Linacre Quarterly* 57, no. 2 (1990): 74–75; and John F. Doerfler, "Is GIFT Compatible with the Teaching of Donum Vitae?" *Linacre Quarterly* 64, no. 1 (1997): 16–29.

[11] Briefly in Peter J. Cataldo, "Reproductive Technologies", *Ethics & Medics* 21, no. 1 (1996): 1–3, and more fully in chapter 6 of *The Gospel of Life* (Pope John Center, 1996), pp. 61–94.

[12] Cataldo, *Gospel of Life*, p. 90.

I would agree with Grisez and Ashley-O'Rourke that this procedure "replaces" rather than "assists" a marital act and that GIFT in its clinical execution is really a form of high-tech insemination. For these reasons, I do not believe a Catholic facility should promote or provide this procedure.

—January 1998

## Adoption of Frozen Embryos

Question: A couple volunteers to "rescue" a frozen embryo not of their own making. They do not approve of *in vitro* fertilization, but they want only to rescue and adopt this unborn and raise the child. Is this a licit option?

Answer: I suspect that this answer is not an absolute one, but it is, I believe, a reliable one.

First, all can agree that this attempt is not an "ordinary" means and thus is *not* ethically obligatory on any one. Might it be considered an "extraordinary" means, that is, not obligatory but ethically optional for her (or those) who so choose?

The most extensive and concise collection of relevant moral wisdom with which to address this question is found in the "instruction" of the Congregation of the Doctrine of the Faith, *Donum Vitae.*

The questioners believe that *in vitro* fertilization (IVF) is wrong; they offer no approval of it and seek no gain from it; their only interest and question is—Is it licit for a woman to volunteer her womb in an attempted rescue of a frozen embryo?

One can argue that *Donum Vitae* does not directly answer this precise question. However, it does state principles relevant to the resolution of this question.

First, the document addresses the use for research purposes of embryos obtained by IVF. One can suggest that this effort is not for "research purposes" but for "rescue purposes". Yet, the full answer of *Donum Vitae* notes: "It is therefore not in conformity with the moral law deliberately to expose to death human embryos obtained 'in vitro'" (pt. 1, no. 5).

The questioners and I myself can accept that moral truth, but given the fact that the frozen embryo came to be in an illicit fashion, what of the possibility of trying to help or "rescue" this frozen embryo from no man's land?

The instruction continues: "In consequence of the fact that they have been produced *in vitro*, those embryos which are not transferred into the body of the mother and are called 'spare' are exposed to an absurd fate [*sorti absurdae obnoxii permanent*], with no possibility of their being offered safe means of survival which *can be licitly pursued*" (pt. 1, no. 5, emphasis added).

No safe means that *can be licitly pursued*. Perhaps, the CDF did not intend to address this precise case, but I read here a first principled insight indicating that this volunteer "rescue" is *not* a licit option.

Is it relevant to ask whether the woman who volunteers her womb and herself for this project is married or single?

*Donum Vitae* also addresses and rejects "surrogate motherhood" (pt. 2, no. 3). It is true that the "surrogacy" there condemned—in its definitional footnotes A and B—is the surrogate who plans to carry the pregnancy but plans to surrender the baby once born, whereas the questioner plans to accept and adopt (if necessary) the child.

But it seems to me that the foundational reasons for rejecting "surrogacy" as licit also apply to this project—a failure to meet the obligations of maternal love, conjugal fidelity, and responsible motherhood; and the facts offend the dignity and right of the child to be conceived, carried in the womb, brought into the world, and brought up by his own parents, setting up to the detriment of families, a division between the physical, psychological, and moral elements which constitute families (*DV*, pt. 2, no. 3).

Further, *Donum Vitae* proposes a principled conclusion that pertains, I think, to this question: "The moral relevance of the link between the meanings of the conjugal act and between the goods of marriage, as well as the unity of the human being and the dignity of his origin, demand that the procreation of a human person be brought about as the fruit of the conjugal act specific to the love between spouses" (pt. 2, no. 4) which this project is not.

Surely, the intention is a good one, even generous, but the means are not, I think, licit means to achieve that good and generous purpose. This is not dissimilar to the Church's repudiation of other means of artificial reproduction, even homologous or artificial insemination by the husband.

No one questions the goodness of intention here, nor is the ethical objection entirely the artificiality of the means alone, but rather, the complete separation of the unitive and procreative dimensions of the conjugal act and the goods of marriage, which are not mere physical acts, isolated kinds of activity open to endless recycling.

Human "procreation" is a far better expression than human "reproduction". "*Reproduction*" is basically a manufacturing term. In a technological society like ours, the reproductive process is already viewed by too many as mere divisible parts (phases), somewhat like a wash-dry cycle, or a tape recording that can be stopped, started, restarted, or jump-started anywhere along the line like a machine, which is quite different from the integrated aspects of "procreation", reflecting God's wise design for love and life.

In sum, this cannot be ethically obligatory, nor do I consider it an ethical option, but I would not be surprised if all do not agree and would welcome reasons why the above is incorrect.

—October 1995

## Surrogate Motherhood

Question: I read in the paper that a Buffalo grandmother was the "surrogate" mother for her own grandson and that this took place in a Catholic hospital. Doesn't the Church oppose surrogacy?

Answer: It is reliably reported both in the *Buffalo News* and the *New York Times* that a 53-year-old Orchard Park grandmother served as the surrogate for her own son and daughter-in-law who could not have children themselves because the daughter-in-law underwent a hysterectomy eleven years ago, after her divorce.[13] It is further reported that this child (Matthew, 6 lbs., 8 oz.) was delivered December 28, 1992, at Sisters Hospital in Buffalo, New York Sisters Hospital is operated by the Daughters of Charity of St. Vincent de Paul.

---

[13] Henry L. Davis, "Hospital Ethics Clash with Methods That Let Woman Bear Grandson", *Buffalo News*, Jan. 3, 1993, pp. B l, 16; Lindsey Gruson, "When 'Mom' and 'Grandma' Are One and the Same", *New York Times*, Feb. 16, 1993, pp. B, l, 6.

Grandma is one of the first women in the USA to be the gestational mother for her own grandson, and she is probably the oldest (53).

First, let's consider the Catholic hospital; then some unhelpful commentaries. The *in vitro* fertilization did not take place at Sisters Hospital, only the delivery, seven and a half months later, did. To their credit, the hospital did see discontinuity between a prior violation of Catholic ethics, and they tried to put some discreet distance between the hospital and the media event.

It was pointed out, quite properly, that a Catholic facility often treats and takes care of results while not approving what caused those results: emergency rooms treat gun-shot victims whether the victim was holding-up or upholding the bank. Similarly, children are delivered of unwed mothers, without any moral comment or approval of the circumstances of conception.

So the birth of a child is good; I hope little Matthew lives to be 100; but no Catholic institution could approve or facilitate the wrong means of this child's conception.

Given the impending notoriety of this case (and there was some), you would think that simple prudence might suggest that the child be delivered elsewhere. To their credit, Sisters Hospital did try to distance themselves from the media hype—perhaps they offered alternatives, I do not know—in any case, they did nothing morally wrong. Maybe not the brightest event in a Catholic facility last December, but not a wrongful event.

However, the other players and commentators are not so clean. The ever-predictable, Catholic-bashing, *New York Times* presented it as a "parable for the growing chasm dividing Roman Catholics from their Church", portraying Dr. William Cooper, head of the Christian Fertility Institute in Easton, Pennsylvania (the actual site of the *in vitro* fertilization and embryo transfer) as a born-again Christian saying: "This is the work, I believe, God called me to do." [14]

Now, because of this grandma's age, he first had to reverse chemically her menopause. The first two attempts with another surrogate failed, then Dr. born-again suggested a family member might be the best surrogate. What the *NYT* did not report about Dr. Cooper is that he "faces several hundred charges of medical misconduct and billing improprieties filed by the Pennsylvania Licensing Board"; at least

---

[14] Gruson, "'Mom' and 'Grandma' Are One", B6.

fourteen women claim he "performed minor surgery on them without consent and without anesthesia". Dr. Cooper claims this is all a misunderstanding and that "God will protect me from any obstacle." [15] Would that he was as solicitous for God's good creation as he apparently is for hawking his wares.

Even more problematic is the "moral" comment of the rector of the local Catholic seminary (Reverend Frederick Leising): "There is not as much rigidity as people think. It's an area of ongoing reflection brought about by the fact that we are caught in a historical moment of great changes in medical moral issues." [16]

It's hard to take Father Leising's comment as serious—authentic Catholic teaching should not be disparaged as "rigidity".

In the most formal and comprehensive instruction ever on the subject, the Congregation for the Doctrine of the Faith taught clearly in *Donum Vitae* that surrogate motherhood is not morally licit (pt. 2, no. 3) and that homologous *in vitro* fertilization is not morally licit even when everything is done to avoid the death of the human embryo (pt. 2, no. 5).

No teacher nor media type can be denied "ongoing" personal reflection, but to say or suggest that Church teaching is somehow "caught" in some moment of change is simply untrue and unscholarly.

"Ongoing reflection" for some theologians really means that no matter what the Church formally teaches, their "reflection" will "go on" until the Church adopts or sanctions the erroneous view of the dissenting reflector.

It's good we have Catholic hospitals, not theological hospitals, or even Ongoing Reflection hospitals, for the latter two would have practices as varied as are their speculations.

How true the sober warning of Pope Paul VI in *Humanae Vitae*, number 17, about the grave and dire consequences of rejecting the Church's authentic teaching on human sexuality—those consequences clearly now are as many and as unnatural as human ingenuity can distort.

—June 1993

[15] Davis, "Hospital Ethics Clash with Methods", B16.
[16] Ibid.

# 13

# Homosexuality

## Sexual Orientation

Question: I read articles on celibacy and even on fitness for ordination that argue that sexual orientation is not relevant. All that matters is not acting out one's sexuality. Is this correct?

Answer: I think not. Indeed, a distinct and rather formal part of
authentic Catholic teaching gets left out of such presentations which,
I believe, have real consequences—bad and misleading consequences.
Also, I would question how much practical and pastoral realism there
is in such overworked blackboard distinctions.

To locate an important part in Church teaching, two explicit instruc-
tions of the Congregation for the Doctrine of the Faith must be read
together, not apart. The first is the 1975 *Declaration on Certain Questions concerning Sexual Ethics* (*Persona Humana*), number 8, and the second, the 1986 letter *On the Pastoral Care of Homosexual Persons* (*PCHP*),
number 3.

The 1975 declaration did mention a seemingly reasonable distinction between a homosexual tendency that seems to be transitory and
one that seems to be definitive. Some argued that the latter seems so
"natural" as to justify homosexual relations in those instances. While
approaching pastoral cases with understanding and prudence as to cul-
pability, the CDF taught clearly that "homosexual acts are intrinsically
disordered and can in no case be approved of" (*Persona Humana*, no. 8).

One should note in that declaration that while a distinction in orientation is mentioned, absolutely nothing is said or speculated about
the moral status of that orientation (tendency or inclination).

For purposes of continuity and honesty, one might also acknowledge that the treatment of homosexuality in the 1975 declaration is

just four short paragraphs, in a very concise document covering several subjects. Whereas the 1986 *Pastoral Care of Homosexual Persons* is a much more extensive and nuanced eighteen-point document only and entirely on homosexuality.

It is precisely number 3 of the *Pastoral Care of Homosexual Persons* that clarifies explicitly the point at hand. Number 3 says that the Congregation (in 1975) "took note of the distinction commonly drawn between 'the homosexual condition or tendency and individual homosexual actions'." Actually, the 1975 declaration took note of a distinction between a tendency that seems to be transitory and one that seems to be definitive. *Persona Humana* does not explicitly distinguish orientations and actions; nevertheless, almost all subsequent comments and commentaries did and do.

Now, it is precisely here that the 1986 letter brings more focused clarity that "an overly benign interpretation was given to the homosexual condition itself", with "some going so far as to call [that condition] 'neutral' or even 'good'". The Congregation then specifies that although this particular inclination (or any other) is not (as such) a sin, "it is a more or less strong tendency ordered toward an intrinsic moral evil; and thus the *inclination itself* must be seen as an *objective disorder* [*ipsa propensio . . . obiective inordinata est iudicanda*]" (emphasis added). Clearly, the CDF teaches that this tendency (inclination or orientation) is *not* neutral, nor good, but an inclination to an objective disorder. The reason for this clarification is then stated "lest they be led to believe that the living out of this orientation in homosexual activity is a morally acceptable option. It is not" (*PCHP*, no. 3).

Thus, those who write or teach or set policies that effectively present the homosexual orientation as "neutral" or merely "indifferent" do not accurately represent authentic Catholic teaching. Most often this sleight of hand misleads by what it leaves out rather than what it includes. It is now common in some policy statements to state that homosexual acts are intrinsically disordered (objectively immoral) and then say nothing at all about the orientation.

A curious middle (and I take it deliberately muddled) position appears in the sex-ed guidelines approved by the U.S. bishops in the document *Human Sexuality* (November 21, 1990). In chapter 4 of that document, a special category for "Persons with a Homosexual Orientation" is given three pages (54–56) but the clear and pertinent teaching above ("the inclination itself must be seen as an objective disorder" from

CDF, *PCHP*, no. 3) is removed from the text of the document and buried in a footnote to which two somewhat gratuitous further qual-ifications are added that do not increase theological clarity but tend to camouflage it.[1] While what qualifies for footnote status may be an honest editorial judgment, it does seem to me that this footnoting has the net effect of trying to water down or apologize for the shining theological clarity of the *Pastoral Care of Homosexual Persons*.

In any case, the failure to mention that this orientation is an objec-tive disorder gives ground and provides fuel for more "overly benign interpretation[s]", which is precisely the result that the 1986 letter aimed at refuting.

The above is wholly objective and can be documented in authentic texts of the Magisterium. What follows is largely personal in terms of pastoral and practical realism when authentic teaching is not presented completely.

Policy statements (regarding religious employment, candidacy for orders, or membership in religious communities) should be careful not to flatten out the distinction between homosexuality and hetero-sexuality by saying (only) that celibates follow Christ by not acting out their sexuality.

Celibacy or consecrated virginity is properly a virtue, indeed a per-fection, of the heterosexual who has a desire for wife and family. The homosexual orientation has no such desire; his desire, by definition, is for others of the same sex. By not acting out this disorder, it is not clear to me he is living celibacy or virginity in the same way as the heterosexual.

To consider orientations as neutral or *ex aequo* seems to neglect the theological basis of celibacy and put in its place merely a psycholog-ical one. The ultimate reason for celibacy is the free choice to follow Jesus Christ as closely as possible and to choose to live as he did— celibate. This involves giving up a *good*, not giving up or putting off an *evil*. The latter is commanded, mandated for all Christians in every state in life; embracing evil is never the moral choice. Nor is it par-ticularly heroic virtue.

Jesus sacrificed (made "sacred") his life and natural desire for wife and family by positively giving them up for the sake of the kingdom and doing the will of him who sent him. In imitating this life choice of Jesus, God is honored still today by any creature who trusts him to

---

[1] USCC, *Human Sexuality* (Washington, D.C.: USCC, 1991), p. 55, n. 49.

fulfill perfectly in the next life any loss or lack voluntarily offered in this life. God is honored by any creature who gives up a high natural gift and witnesses thereby an afterlife in which God will fulfill those who have served him faithfully. In the next life, there will be no marriage nor giving in marriage (Mt 22:30; Lk 20:25), whereas misused or disordered sexuality has no moral place at all in this life or the next life.

Another bad consequence of studied silence on this disordered inclination is the pastoral confusion that muddled policies cause. Some candidates for priesthood and religious life are now labeled "homophobic", rigid, patriarchal, and intolerant if they are not positively enthusiastic about and open to "alternate" orientations and personal expressions of a deep and caring kind. The wrong candidates are required to undergo required counseling, sometimes with predictably negative effects—the right people leave the seminary for the wrong reason.

If the homosexual orientation were even neutral, then one so inclined should be encouraged to "rejoice" in this gift; heterosexuals should be mandated to respect this orientation in the same way they respect their own; and someone should be charged with preaching against those who consider the homosexual orientation disordered or unnatural. Clearly, these politically correct mandates truly contradict the authentic teaching cited above (CDF, *PCHP*, no. 3).

We are all obliged to "[speak] the truth in love" (Eph 4:15). We will all be better served in this regard by speaking the whole truth, lovingly to be sure, but the whole truth, not selective parts of it.

—December 1994

## Correction to the Catechism

Question: I read that the Latin *Catechism* (1997) somewhat corrected the *Catechism's* teaching on homosexuality. I have no access to the Latin; is this so?

Answer: Yes. The 1994 English translation of the *Catechism* now in print says: "The number of men and women who have deep-seated homosexual tendencies is not negligible. *They do not choose their homosexual condition*; for most of them it is a trial" (no. 2358; emphasis added).

Our English version is an accurate translation of the original French (1992): "Ils ne choisissent pas leur condition homosexuelle." The Spanish and Italian translations do the same.

However, in the now official (September 8, 1997) Latin *Catechism*, there is a correction of this ambiguity. The second sentence of number 2358 now reads: "Haec propensio, obiective inordinata, pro maiore eorum parte constituit probationem" (*Catechismus Catholicae Ecclesia* [1997], p. 598; "This inclination, which is objectively disordered, constitutes for most of them a trial)." [2]

While the first publication in French was authentic, only the Latin version is official and, where corrected, definitive. Thus, the "they do not choose their homosexual condition" has been eliminated and replaced with "[t]his inclination, which is objectively disordered".

In fact, this small correction was both needed and logical. The prior version of number 2358 was really at odds with the preceding paragraph in number 2357: "Its psychological genesis remains largely unexplained." If, in number 2357, you make the correct social-science statement that its psychological genesis is largely unexplained, it makes no sense to say in the next paragraph that "they do not choose" this condition, for in saying that one takes for granted an "explanation" of what it just said is "unexplained".

Also, in the atmosphere of political correctness and "advocacy theology", this small ambiguity in the original version of the *Catechism* did not go unnoticed. For whatever reason, *America* magazine seems dedicated to providing friendly space to gay Catholics and their special pleading.

*America* published a lengthy interview with Andrew Sullivan, whose basic point was that he is openly "Catholic" and openly "gay". Sullivan cites the *Catechism* as incoherent:

> Q. "Have you seen it?"
> A. "I've read it in French, yes."
> Q. "What does it concede?"
> A. "That homosexuality is, so far as one can tell, an involuntary condition." [3]

---

[2] Cf. *Origins* 27, no. 15 (Sept. 25, 1997): 261.

[3] Thomas H, Stahel, "I'm Here: An Interview with Andrew Sullivan", *America* 168, no. 16 (May 8, 1993): 7.

From this, Sullivan argues that the Church position is philosophically and fundamentally incoherent.

Another, and more recent, article in *America* by Stephen Rossetti and Gerald Coleman overworks the same ambiguity.[4] Perhaps, with the official *Catechism* now corrected, *America* will publish some correctives too. That "perhaps" is a faint hope.

Unfortunately, an NCCB Committee on Marriage and Family issued *Always Our Children: A Pastoral Message to the Parents of Homosexual, Children* (October 1, 1997), which is not that pastoral nor theologically accurate.

*Always Our Children* (*AOC*) teaches that generally, homosexual orientation is experienced "as a given"[5] and therefore cannot be considered sinful (p. 289), and more emphatically, speaks of "a homosexual orientation" as "not immoral in itself" (p. 290).

Roman documents from the Congregation for the Doctrine of the Faith to the *Catechism* (1992, 1997) use the more theologically accurate terms *"condition"* or *"tendency"*, whereas the NCCB *AOC* seems locked into *"orientation"* terminology. In any case, a "tendency", "condition", "inclination", or "orientation" prior to choice (i.e., what does not proceed from the will with a knowledge of the end) is not properly placed in the categories of moral choice.

However, as the CDF letter *On the "Pastoral Care of Homosexual Persons"*, number 3, took careful note of the common distinction between the homosexual *condition* or *tendency* and homosexual *actions*, the CDF noted as well that the post-1975 discussion of this distinction gave an "overly benign interpretation" to the "homosexual condition" itself. Some went as far as to call that condition neutral or even good. To avoid continuing confusion, the CDF taught with precision that although a particular inclination is not a sin, "it is a more or less strong tendency ordered toward an intrinsic moral evil; and thus the inclination itself must be seen as an objective disorder" (*PCHP*, no. 3; cf. also *CCC* [1997], no. 2358).

Thus, in categories prior to moral choice, this "condition" or "tendency" is to be seen as an objective disorder. When NCCB *AOC* teaches that the homosexual inclination is "not immoral", it must mean

---

[4] Stephen J. Rossetti and Gerald. D. Coleman, "Psychology and the Church's Teaching on Homosexuality", *America* 177, no. 13 (Nov. 1, 1997): 6–23, see p. 6.

[5] Cf. "Always Our Children", *Origins* 27, no. 17 (Oct. 9, 1997): 289.

that it is moral or neutral, which is precisely in contradiction to what the CDF taught so clearly in *Pastoral Care of Homosexual Persons*.

Further, the NCCB *AOC* as a "pastoral message" does not strike me as very pastoral. *AOC* teaches: "If ... an adolescent ... may be experimenting with some homosexual behaviors.... Sometimes the best approach may be a wait-and-see attitude".[6] I know of no authentic moral or pastoral teaching that suggests a "wait-and-see" attitude toward an occasion of sin, much less sinful acts by adolescents. I can't imagine any pastor or parent in the Church suggesting "wait-and-see" to adolescents who may be experimenting in grave theft, perjury, or incest. That is not pastoral and will not foster a correct conscience; it can easily foster an erroneous conscience, which is not the goal of loving and caring parents or pastors.

Thus, the correction in the *Catechism*, number 2358, is a welcome correction. It is not new teaching but the same teaching of the CDF letter, which some did not accept then and apparently some still do not accept.

—February 1998

## The Sin of Sodom

**Question:** According to Daniel A. Helminiak's *What the Bible Really Says about Homosexuality*, "The sin of Sodom was inhospitality, not homosexuality.... And from the bible's positive teaching about heterosexuality, there follows no valid conclusion whatsoever about homosexuality."[7] Is there a response to this?

**Answer:** There is, indeed, a correct response because that statement is both false and misleading. To correct and refute this distortion, this

---

[6] The paragraph in *AOC* to which Mgsr. Smith refers has since been replaced, and the former quotation now reads: "What is called for on the part of parents is an approach which does not presume that your child has developed a homosexual orientation and which will help you maintain a loving relationship while you provide support, information, encouragement and moral guidance. Parents must always be vigilant about their children's behavior and exercise responsible interventions when necessary."—*Ed.*

[7] Daniel A. Helminiak's *What the Bible Really Says about Homosexuality* (San Francisco: Alamo Square Press, 1994), pp. 107–9.

Q/A limits itself to the Sodom passage in Genesis 19:1–29. No attempt is made here to review the other negative biblical condemnations of homosexual acts in Leviticus 18:22, 20:13; Romans 1:26, 27; 1 Corinthians 6:9; 1 Timothy 1:10; Jude 7.

First, it's important to read Genesis 19 even in translation. I cite here the revised New American Bible (1987). The townsmen of Sodom come out to the house of Lot and demand: "Bring them out to us that we may have *intimacies* with them" (Gen 19:5), and Lot responds: "I have two daughters that have never had *intercourse* with men" (19:8).

The opinion that this refers to inhospitality instead of homosexuality is not a recent opinion. This "revision" was once suggested by the Anglican author D. Sherwin Bailey in his book: *Homosexuality and Western Christian Tradition*.[8] The thrust of Bailey's argument is to question *any* reference to homosexual sin in Genesis 19:5. He argues that the Hebrew word. *YADA* ("to know") although sometimes means to "have intercourse with" (e.g., Gen 4:1 and Gen 19:8) may only mean "get acquainted with" in Genesis 19:5. Thus, the demand to "know" the visitors Lot entertained would imply a serious breach of the rules of hospitality rather than any sexual connotation at all. The popular reach of this "revision" has gone far beyond any biblical evidence to support it.

Bailey's interpretation is open to profound criticism and refutation.[9]

1. It is difficult, if not impossible, to understand the weight of biblical tradition regarding the "sin of Sodom" in terms of the rules of hospitality; consider, Genesis 13:13, 14:11, 18:20; Deuteronomy 29:23, 32:32; Isaiah 1:9, 13:19; Jeremiah 49:18, 50:40; Lamentations 4:6; Ezekiel 16:46–58; Amos 4:11; Zephaniah 2:9—these are not references to inhospitality!

The New Testament refers to Sodom as a pointer to divine judgment: Matthew 10:15; Luke 10:12, 13:19, 17:29; 2 Peter 2:6; and Jude 7, which reads: "Sodom and Gomorrah . . . , which . . . acted immorally and indulged in unnatural lust, serve as an example by undergoing a punishment of eternal fire." These passages, and many others, do not refer to inhospitality; the "sin of Sodom" is seen in the Bible as the proud defiance of God-given norms, with a clear *sexual* component.

---

[8] Derrick Sherwin Bailey, *Homosexuality and Western Christian Tradition* (London, 1955; reprint: North Haven, Conn.: Shoestring Press, 1975), p. 155.

[9] Cf. Donald J. Wold, *Out of Order: Homosexuality in the Bible and the Ancient Near East* (Grand Rapids, Mich.: Baker Books, 1998), pp. 77–89.

2. It is not acceptable to decide the meaning of *YADA* ("to know") by statistics, lest the less common meaning would never be the probable meaning of the word. The word *YADA* does have a range of meanings in the Bible: to know; to have experience; to be wise; to have relations with; sexual intercourse; etc. This word appears 943 times in the Old Testament: seventeen refer to sexual intercourse; twenty-eight times it means "get acquainted with". Thus, only the context can determine its meaning in a given passage. Since everyone, even Bailey, admits that *YADA* can only refer to sexual intercourse in Genesis 19:8, it is difficult to deny the same meaning to the same word three verses earlier (19:5) in the very same passage. The *Hebrew-English Lexicon* and *Theological Dictionary of the Old Testament* both make this exegetical point.[10]

3. Whatever questions might be raised or suggested concerning the historicity of the event (Sodom), it is part of the canon of Scripture, and the moral judgment conveyed is no less valid regardless of the form used to convey that judgment. It is true that there are various literary forms of expression in the Bible (e.g., poems, song, saga, prose, tale, story, etc.), but the point here and in every other mention of homosexual acts in the Old or New Testament is the moral judgment conveyed in a negative judgment of prohibition.

4. The punishment (raining down "on Sodom and Gomorrah brimstone and fire", Gen 19:24) makes no sense if the offense is merely one of inhospitality. Where else in the Bible do you read of effectively "nuking" a city for a breach of hospitality? This makes no biblical nor logical sense. Inhospitality is not a "crime that cries out to heaven" (cf. *Catechism*, no. 1867, esp. note 140), rather it cries out to Barnes and Noble for a copy of Emily Post.

Thus, the opinion of Bailey (along with Helminiak) is not simply open to criticism, it is indeed erroneous. Consider instead the scholarly conclusion of Donald Wold:

> We have studied in detail the meaning of the Hebrew verb *YADA* in Genesis 19 and the related story of the Gibeahites in Judges 19. On the basis of ancient Near Eastern parallels and the Septuagint translation, we can say with confidence that the verb *YADA* means sexual intercourse

---

[10] Francis Brown, S. R. Driver, Charles Briggs, *A Hebrew and English Lexicon* (Oxford: Oxford University Press, 1962), p. 394; G. Johannes Botterweck, *Theological Dictionary of the Old Testament*, vol. 5 (Grand Rapids, Mich.: William B. Eerdmans Publishing, 1986), p. 464.

in these texts, a view that is supported by logical and psychological data. The inhospitality interpretation of the Sodom story should be rejected. The men of Sodom appeal to Lot to release the strangers for the purpose of homosexual relations—if not rape.... The view that homosexuality should be replaced by inhospitality in the Sodom story cannot be supported from biblical sources.[11]

In a remarkable and authoritative letter to the bishops of the Catholic Church, the Congregation for the Doctrine of the Faith issued *On the Pastoral Care of Homosexual Persons* on October 1, 1986. This "letter" addresses both the generic question of the misuse of Scripture and this particular text itself (Gen 19).

For authentic "pastoral care", the CDF correctly notes we should first identify sources of confusion that undermine Church teaching.

> One [source of confusion] is a new exegesis of Sacred Scripture which claims variously that Scripture has nothing to say on the subject of homosexuality, or that it somehow tacitly approves of it, or that all of its moral injunctions are so culture-bound that they are no longer applicable to contemporary life. These views are gravely erroneous and call for particular attention here. (*PCHP*, no. 4)

The CDF also rightly points out "that the Biblical literature owes to the different epochs in which it was written a good deal of its varied patterns of thought and expression" (no. 5). Truly, the Church today addresses the gospel to a world different from the ancient world. Indeed, the world in which the New Testament was written was already diverse from the situation in which the Hebrew Scriptures were written and compiled.

But what is crucial here is that "in the presence of such remarkable diversity, there is nevertheless a clear consistency with the Scriptures themselves on the moral issue of homosexual behavior" (no. 5). This is quite true. The narrative form of Genesis 19 differs from the Holiness Code of Leviticus 18:22 and 20:13, both of which differ again from the Epistles of Saint Paul (Rom 1:18–32; 1 Cor 6:9; 1 Tim 1:10). All these Scriptures were written from and for diverse situations, but the remarkable truth is that all of them convey the exact same negative moral judgment on homosexual behavior. There is then a "constant biblical testimony. The community of faith today, in unbroken continuity with

---

[11] Wold, *Out of Order*, p. 89.

the Jewish and Christian communities within which the ancient Scriptures were written continues to be nourished by the same Scriptures and by the Spirit of Truth whose Word they are" (*PCHP*, no. 5).

Above, Helminiak asserts: "And from the Bible's positive teaching about heterosexuality, there follows no valid conclusion whatsoever about homosexuality." That assertion is gravely erroneous. Authentic positive teachings clearly address and refute their negative contradiction. For instance, the CDF "letter" teaches:

> Providing a basic plan for understanding this entire discussion of homosexuality is the theology of creation we find in Genesis. God, in his infinite wisdom and love, brings into existence all of reality as a reflection of his goodness. He fashions mankind, male and female, in his own image and likeness. Human beings, therefore, are nothing less than the work of God himself; and in the complementarity of the sexes, they are called to reflect the inner unity of the Creator. They do this in a striking way in their cooperation with him in the transmission of life by a mutual donation of self to the other.
>
> In Genesis 3, we find that this truth about persons being an image of God has been obscured by original sin. There inevitably follows a loss of awareness of the covenantal character of the union these persons had with God and with each other. "The human body retains its 'spousal significance' but this is now clouded by sin." Thus "in Genesis 19:1–11, the deterioration due to sin continues in the story of the men of Sodom. There can be no doubt of the moral judgement made there against homosexual relations." (*PCHP*, no. 6)

Thus, both unbiased research and the highest teaching office in the Church (CDF) reject the substitution of inhospitality for homosexuality in Genesis 19 as gravely erroneous.

—March 2001

## Clerical Sex Abuse

Question: Media coverage of clerical sex scandals seems to be of two minds. Headlines announce "pedophilia" but many of the stories under those headlines report cases of homosexual activity with young teenagers and others. Is there any accurate science here?

**Answer:** It seems to me, the first point of reference should be the moral one: i.e., moral truth. Immoral sexual activity is not simply less adequate, inappropriate, or, as some say, dysfunctional. It is first of all evil. Here, grave evil that is both scandalous and sacrilegious evil. In addition, grave unjust harm has been wrongfully inflicted on innocent parties—the younger the innocent, the more unjust the grave harm inflicted.

I too have noticed what your question raises—if not a media bias at least some varied tones of selective outrage. It seems that everybody (?) condemns pedophilia, but political correctness ·seems to require nuance or near silence about homosexual activity. Indeed, some groups (secular and religious) seem more concerned that so-called gay activists and the gay lobby not be or become the scapegoat of the current scandal and crisis.[12] It appears that apologists for the gay lobby are more concerned about what might tarnish their agenda than they are about morality as such.

In any case, is there real science here? My guess is that there is not much. Some of what passes for "science" is simply surveys and samples of radically humanistic psychology (or sociology), "humanistic" in the sense that no theological or moral norms exist. Since the secular media is wedded to the same thoroughly relativistic outlook, they often report and repeat what is not science at all.

Also, I presume that genuine pedophilia is such a tiny percentage of the whole population that there may just not be that many serious clinical studies to evidence or support reliable conclusions.

Nonetheless, there is moral science: moral both general and specific. As above, I know of no *specific* works or studies that connect or equate pedophilia with homosexuality. However, the *generic* question seems, at least to me, to have an obvious answer and a clear connection.

Generically, what kind of activity are we talking about? In conventional moral theology, this is what the textbooks call the "moral object" (*finis operis*). That is, what *kind* or *type* of activity is this in its moral estimation? Surely none of this activity has anything to do with authentic love, i.e., the marital, heterosexual generous gift of self that is open to both life and love (*HV*, no. 12; *FC*, no. 32; *CCC*, no. 2338).

---

[12] E.g., a signed report in *Newsweek* magazine; a signed article in the *London Tablet* (May 11, 2002); and then a full-page ad in the *New York Times*, May 24, 2002, p. A-17, stating bluntly, "Catholic Church Hierarchy: Don't Blame Gay People".

Indeed, it is the contrary on both counts: against love and against life; it is always and in all cases masturbatory sex. This is precisely what all Christians are called to avoid and reject: "Those who belong to Christ Jesus have crucified the flesh with its passions and desires" (Gal 5:24). This call is addressed to all Christians: single, married, or widowed. There are no exceptions; this is the Christian norm and standard; any other norm is simply not Christian.

Masturbatory sex with minors of any age is a moral nullity—it cannot be an authentic gift-of-self open to love and life. All complete homosexual acts are of the same moral nature and species—masturbatory sex, not open to love and life. Even some forms of modern contraception are, reductively, masturbatory sex.

This truth of moral science is either unknown or deliberately forgotten by many. We live in a society that widely rejects this Christian standard. For all too many, the exercise of human sexuality is a highly personal and completely subjective "choice"—it has no intrinsic meaning or purpose. For many moderns, its only purpose is whatever the acting subject decides for: auto eroticism; self-pleasuring (Planned Parenthood's term of choice); relief of tension; it is and means whatever one chooses: sometimes for procreation, sometimes for recreation. Since in this mind-set it has no intrinsic meaning, it all depends on what the deciding subject wants and likes and above all "chooses".

Not too long ago, moral textbooks referred to "masturbation" as "self-abuse". [13] For Bernard Haring (during his orthodox phase), "self-abuse" or what he calls the "solitary sin" is egoistic self-inclusion that so fixes and finalizes the mind and heart as to shut out the *thou*, the other person—all other persons, in fact. [14]

The focus of auto-eroticism is indeed *auto*, that is, *self*. Thus, it is not entirely illogical to discern a link between abuse of self *and* abuse of others. The more one is fixed, even fixated, on self and self-pleasuring, the less one regards or even sees the good and worth of the other or others. Even the Golden Rule can be tarnished in this distortion: "Do unto others as you would have them do unto you." If you don't really mind downgrading your own dignity, then perhaps others won't really mind so much either since you downgrade yourself first.

[13] Cf. Bernard Haring, *Law of Christ*, vol. 3: *Moral Theology for Priests and Laity* (Paramus, N.J.: Newman Press, 1966), p. 301. The same reference can be found in Webster's *Dictionary*, 2nd ed. (New York: Simon and Schuster, 1979), p. 1645.

[14] Haring, *Law of Christ*, p. 302.

Every Christian virtue suffers in that calculus because the self (myself) is *not* the center of the universe. Indeed, as Pope John Paul II never tires of saying, quoting the Council, we will only find and fulfill ourselves "through a sincere gift of [self]" (quoting *GS*, no. 24).

While the Church clearly teaches the evil of masturbation (*CCC*, no. 2352), our society and many of its teachers (secular and religious) clearly do not. For many, it is not a moral question but merely a psychological one explained (or explained away) in terms of adequate maturity. Many simply do not believe that masturbation has any moral or life consequences.

Moreover, the wisdom of authentic Church teaching is further compromised by a kind of comparison morality: masturbation is not so bad compared to abortion; one abortion is not so bad compared to genocide. The moral outcome of that litany is predictable. Nothing is really bad *in se*, as long as one can cite greater and graver evils above it. Of course, the morally relevant comparison ("freedom of contradiction") is to do or not to do the same thing under the same circumstances, not to engage in a can-you-top-this comparison.

I prefer to accept the collective moral wisdom of the Church that masturbatory sex ("self-abuse") is a disordered use of human sexuality; indeed, a misuse that has consequences—moral consequences and life consequences—not just for the self, but for others too.

From the point of view of moral science, it seems to me that there is a connection between homosexual activity and the present sex scandals and that connection is masturbatory sex.

—July 2002

## Same-Sex Union

Question: I read of some priests' councils that, while they do not approve of same-sex marriage, say it is intolerant discrimination to work against its legalization. Is there a Catholic position on this?

Answer: I believe there is a Catholic position—a position rooted in revelation, in unanimous Catholic tradition, in the teaching of Vatican II and the papal Magisterium of John Paul II.

First, I offer a word about "words". I realize, as all readers do, that the print and video media always refer to "same-sex *marriage*". To use a vintage Buckleyism, same-sex *marriage*, is, I think, an oxymoron. Same-sex marriage is a nullity, *not* a marriage. It is as meaningful and available as dry water. That is, it ain't and cannot be. Nonetheless, pervasive media designation of this relationship as a "marriage" tries to invest it with a status and dignity that it does not and cannot have.

What is marriage? Canonically, the 1983 *Code* defines marriage as "a covenant, by which a man and a woman (*quo vir et mulier*) establish between themselves a partnership of their whole life, which of its nature is ordered to the well-being of the spouses and to the procreation and education of children" (can. 1055, §1; cf. as well *CCC*, no. 1601; and *GS*, no. 48).

Fortunately, the 1983 *Code* is specific (*vir et mulier*). In the pre–politically correct days of the 1917 *Code*, the definition of matrimonial consent was generic two "persons capable by law" (*inter personas iure habiles*, can. 1081, §1).

The 1983 *Code*, the *Catechism*, and the Council are all at one—marriage was instituted by God the Creator and qualified by his laws. God himself is the Author of matrimony; God has endowed marriage with various benefits and purposes (cf. *GS*, no. 48; *CCC*, nos. 1602–5).

It is simple but simply essential to repeat over and over—God is the Author of matrimony. No court, no congress, no convention, no cabal can erase Divine Authorship; marriage is of God's design, and no human source or authority can alter that. Human authorities can respect and honor this fact, or they can disfigure and distort it, but they cannot change it; it is beyond human competence.

As the *Catechism* (no. 1602) teaches, Sacred Scripture hymns a consistent song—beginning with the creation of man and woman in the image and likeness of God (Gen 1:26–27) and concluding with the vision of "the marriage supper of the Lamb" (Rev 19:7, 9).

Divine revelation is consistent and specific about the nature of true marriage: "Therefore a man leaves his father and mother and clings to his wife, and they become one flesh" (Gen 2:24, emphasis added). This marital purpose and passage is solemnly invoked and proclaimed by Jesus Christ (Mk 10:7) and emphatically insisted on by Saint Paul (Eph 5:31). To repudiate this essential teaching of marriage is nothing less than sheer moral heresy against the ordinary and universal magisterial teaching of the Church to be held by all believing Catholics.

The words, teaching, and solemn condemnation of the Council of Trent are easily extended to the present case: "Since impious men of this age, madly raging against this teaching [sacramentality of marriage] have not only formed false judgments concerning this venerable sacrament [marriage], but according to their custom, introducing, under the pretext of the gospel, a carnal liberty [*libertatem carnis*] have in word and writing asserted many things foreign to the mind of the Catholic Church" (DS 1800).

Presciently, the Council of Trent repudiates a gospel distortion, i.e., "a carnal liberty", which is, precisely, what the advocates of so-called "same-sex marriage" advocate today. Holy Scripture repudiates the same error. Those who belong to Christ Jesus are called to crucify their flesh with its passions and lusts (Gal 5:24). Thus, believing Christians are called to crucify self-indulgent lusts, not to celebrate them, much less legalize them.

This is not a question of tolerance—if by tolerance we mean the patient virtue to bear with opinions or practices different from our own without bigotry. There is no such thing as a "moral right" to self-indulgent lust. Thus, to work or speak against the canonization or legalization of a nonexistent "right" to which no one has any conceivable "moral right" is to discriminate against no one.

Heterosexual marriage is the only sexual activity and state that properly enjoys the sanction of our civil and moral law. Bigamy enjoys no such sanction; nor does polygamy; nor does any other self-indulgent failing. If so-called "same-sex marriage" were to be granted a privileged place (sanction) in civil law, then we as a society disfigure, distort, and demean the privileged place of heterosexual marriage in society.

Rather than retreat into vacuous slogans, Vatican Council II called upon all Christians and public authorities to promote authentic marriage and family life. Indeed, "Public authority should regard it as a sacred duty to recognize, protect, and promote their [marriage and family's] authentic nature, to shield public morality, and to favor the prosperity of home life" (*GS*, no. 52).

The toleration, escalation, celebration, or legalization of so-called "same-sex marriage" accords in no way with the teaching of the Council; instead it repudiates the specific call and challenge of the Council.

With clarity and true Christian compassion, Pope John Paul II addressed this very point when the European Parliament took a giant step in the wrong direction in 1994. Of the mistaken sanction of the European Parliament, the Pope taught in his Angelus address of February 20, 1994:

> It does not merely defend people with homosexual *tendencies* by rejecting unjust discrimination in their regard. The Church agrees with that—indeed, she supports and approves it. She does so because every human person is worthy of respect.
>
> What is not morally acceptable is the legal approval of homosexual activity. Being understanding towards the sinner who is unable to free himself from this tendency is not the same as lessening the requirement of the moral norm [*VS*, no. 95].... The Parliament's resolution seeks to *legitimize a moral disorder*. The Parliament has unduly institutionalized deviant kinds of behavior not in conformity with God's plan; they are weaknesses, as we know, but Parliament has *supported those weaknesses*. It is not recognized that the true human right is the victory over oneself so as to live in conformity with a correct conscience.[15]

—November 1996

## Rites for Same-Sex Unions

Question: I read reports of a book that establishes ancient liturgical rites and ceremonies to solemnize same-sex marriage. Any leads on this one?

Answer: The book in question is that of John Boswell, *Same-Sex Unions in Premodern Europe*.[16] The Editor of the *New York Times Book Review*, in the "And-Bear-in-Mind" space of that publication, described it as "[a] Yale historian's learned, knotty study of male love (whose exact nature isn't clear) and the ceremonies used to solemnize it from the 11th to 16th centuries".[17]

Two competent reviews of this work are very helpful. One by Brent Shaw in *The New Republic* is quite telling. Shaw is not only sympathetic

---

[15] *L'Osservatore Romano*, Eng. ed., (Feb. 23, 1994): 1, 8.
[16] John Boswell, *Same-Sex Unions in Premodern Europe* (New York: Villard Books, 1994).
[17] *New York Times*, Sept. 4, 1994, p. 18, sec. 6.

to the gay agenda (but apparently part of it), yet he concludes after devastating Boswell's book: "A more civil and humane modernity will not be achieved by tendentious misreadings of antiquity." [18]

Another extended review is that of Robin Young, "Gay Marriage: Reimagining Church History". Most of Boswell's book centers on some texts for a "rite of adoption" ("*adelphopoiesis*") in some Eastern churches that was extended to friends. Indeed, Young attests from her personal experience that this friendship blessing continues to this day in the Syrian Orthodox Church in Jerusalem. [19] Boswell makes no such modest claim about friendship blessings but asserts rather that these were ancient ceremonies whose cryptic and "encoded" purpose was to give ecclesiastical blessing to homosexual or lesbian unions. Young's extended and detailed review demonstrates that neither Boswell's reconstruction of history nor his argument can possibly support his strange claim.

Boswell admits that his point is "counterintuitive" since he has to admit that the early Byzantine law codes of the same time contain extremely harsh punishments for homosexual acts. Thus, he would have his readers believe that what the Church-state courts punished on one side of the street, the Church-state churches blessed on the other side of the street.

According to Young, despite the façade of scholarship, the book is studded with unwarranted assumptions, arguments from silence, dubious and in some cases "outrageously false translations of critical terms". [20] To be sure, the documents Boswell cites are real, but he uses them in a way that would make the Central Committee blush when it was their style to use citations to "prove" that some Russian invented the telephone, the light bulb, and perhaps even the Mormon Tabernacle Choir.

The central piece remains the Greek word "*adelphopoiesis*", which in English is "the making of brothers" (or "sisters" since the Greek compound could be either). The manuscripts make no mention or suggestion of any sexual relationship of any kind.

Contrary to the accepted norms of classical philology, Boswell insists that *adelphos* (brother) means "homosexual lover". After he compromises the plain meaning of the term in the great corpus of classical

---

[18] Brent D. Shaw, "A Groom of One's Own", *The New Republic* 211 (July 18 and 25, 1994): 41.

[19] Robin D. Young, "Gay Marriage: Reimagining Church History", *First Things* 47 (Nov. 1994): 43.

[20] Ibid.

literature, Boswell then turns to "constructing" the historical context—the same special pleading that predominates his prior book (*Christianity, Social Tolerance and Homosexuality* [1980]) that legal homosexual union stood side by side with legal heterosexual marriage. He needs to establish that Roman law permitted homosexual unions, so he must interpret all uses of the word "*brother*" as evidence of homosexuality and must force the reference on male friendship.

However, there is no evidence of a legal contractual same-sex marriage in Roman law or in any Byzantine code. Thus, his translation is faulty and his history is fiction. And so, Professor Young properly accuses Boswell of "*eisegesis*"—reading into a text a message that is not there.

Young properly notes that scholars of the field have known of these prayers and rituals for years; indeed, John Boswell did not discover them nor invent them, rather "he only put them to use for his own purposes". She concludes: "The author's painfully strained effort to recruit Christian history in support of the homosexual cause that he favors is not only a failure, but an embarrassing one".[21] The full review is very much worth a full read.

—March 1995

---

[21] Ibid., p. 48.

# III

# Fidelity and Dissent

# 14

# Conscience

*Cardinal John Henry Newman*

Question: I sometimes read the remark attributed to Cardinal Newman: "I shall drink,—to the Pope, if you please,—still, to Conscience
first, and to the Pope afterwards." Is this accurate?

Answer: It is true that Newman wrote that. It is the final sentence
of his famous "Letter to the Duke of Norfolk". In full it reads: "Certainly, if I am obliged to bring religion into after-dinner toasts, (which
indeed does not seem quite the thing) I shall drink,—to the Pope, if
you please,—still, to Conscience first, and to the Pope afterwards." [1]
Some seem to give more attention to this final sentence than to the
entire effort. Again, some try to convert this—in what may well be
the most profound discussion of obedience and sovereignty in the English
language—into making Newman some kind of modern dissenter. Nothing could be further from the truth. Almost all of Newman's adult
intellectual effort was to refute autonomous individualism in religion.

Indeed, in Newman's famous "Letter to the Duke of Norfolk", he
was truly prescient in repudiating in the nineteenth century a favorite
distortion of conscience that began to reign in the twentieth. Newman wrote:

> The view of conscience, I know, is very different from that ordinarily
> taken of it.... It is founded on the doctrine that conscience is the
> voice of God, whereas it is fashionable on all hands now to consider it
> one way or another a creation of man. (p. 247)

[1] John Henry Newman, *Certain Difficulties Felt by Anglicans in Catholic Teaching* (London:
Basil Montagu Pickering, 1876), p. 261.

Conscience is not a long-sighted selfishness, nor a desire to be consistent with oneself; but it is a messenger from Him, Who, both in nature and grace, speaks to us behind a veil, and teaches and rules us by His representatives. (p. 248)

Conscience has rights because it has duties; but in this age, with a large portion of the public, it is the very right and freedom of conscience, to ignore a Lawgiver and Judge, to be independent of unseen obligations. It becomes a license to take up any or no religion, to take up this or that and let it go again, to go to church, to go to chapel, to boast of being above all religions and to be an impartial critic of each of them. Conscience is a stern monitor, but in this century it has been superseded by a counterfeit, which the eighteen centuries prior to it never heard of, and could not have mistaken for it, if they had. It is the right of self will. (p. 250)

What Cardinal Newman utterly rejected in 1876—the spurious "right" of self-will: the autonomy, even infallibility, of my own self judgment—is precisely what so many dissenters have embraced as their very birthright and self-validation. No, Cardinal Newman was neither a modern, nor even a modest, dissenter.

—May 2001

## Father John J. Dietzen

Question: Our Catholic paper carries "The Question Box" by Father John J. Dietzen. A recent enclosed answer is entitled "Let Your Conscience Be Your Guide". How would you answer it?

Answer: My local Catholic paper carried the same column,[2] which I judge to be sorely incomplete and quite misleading. Father Dietzen quotes the *Catechism* regarding conscience, but so selectively as to mislead.

In our society, the expression "Let Your Conscience Be Your Guide" is an easy invitation to subjectivism: i.e., I have a "right" to do what my conscience tells me to do because my conscience tells me to do it. As John Courtney Murray taught, this is a perilous theory! The particular

---

[2] *Catholic New York* 16, no. 41 (July 17, 1997): 13.

peril is subjectivism: the notion that, in the end, it is my conscience (my decision, my choice) and not the objective truth that determines right or wrong, true or false.

The QB column does refer to the *Catechism*, but it does not accurately reflect the *Catechism's* wonderfully balanced and complete treatment of conscience (nos. 1776–802). For example, the *Catechism's* treatment of erroneous judgment of conscience (nos. 1790–94) is conveniently omitted. Also, it's a bit misleading to pull one sentence from the young theologian Father Joseph Ratzinger in 1968, while ignoring the masterful treatments of the same subject by the later Cardinal Ratzinger, Prefect of the Congregation for the Doctrine of the Faith (e.g., "Conscience and Truth", 1991). Missing from the QB column is the place, importance, and emphasis on truth in the formation and function of a *true* Catholic conscience.

The status of an *erroneous* conscience is not to be denied, but it must be seen for what it is—"erroneous". Erroneous judgment is not a desired privilege; it is an aberration in need of correction. Allowing for culpable or inculpable ignorance, one is responsible for erroneous judgments of conscience and correct judgments of conscience, but they are not morally *ex aequo*. To exalt an erroneous conscience, without necessary distinctions, is tantamount to saying we are better off ignorant of the truth, that it's just fine to be unburdened by the truth of revelation, which is exactly the distortion Cardinal Ratzinger refutes (1991).

Error needs to be corrected, as the *Catechism* teaches (nos. 1790–94), as *Veritatis Splendor* (nos. 54–64) supremely teaches. Without qualification, "Let your conscience be your guide" can mean: "Let error be your guide." That may be a media favorite, but it is not sound teaching and cannot help sound personal practice.

—January 1998

## Father Richard McBrien

Question: A parishioner sent me a quote from Catholics for a Free Choice that cites Father Richard McBrien. According to the quote, Father McBrien states that if a Catholic is convinced that his conscience is correct in spite of a conflict with the moral teaching of the

Church, that person not only may but must follow his conscience rather than the teachings of the Church. How would you respond?

**Answer:** The quote, I believe, is from Frances Kissling, president of Catholics for a Free Choice and a fanatical abortion advocate. That her group describes itself as "Catholic" is a media tactic. That group has as much to do with Catholicism as science fiction has to do with science.

Her authoritative source—Richard P. McBrien's *Catholicism*—has raised and caused many problems. This book never received an imprimatur, and some high-level Church authorities (Committee on Doctrine of NCCB) asked for but never received corrections and improvements.

The great deficit of McBrien's *Catholicism* is doctrinal minimalism— what's the least I have to accept to call myself Catholic. Doctrinal minimalism always comes with its first cousin—moral minimalism, which turns out to be moral relativism. McBrien's stated methodology and ecclesiology are so broad and fluid that the true, normative moral teaching of the Church appears as just one element among many in the formation of conscience.

For example, he writes that no one is Catholic who deliberately "excludes all reference" to official Church teaching.[3] Not a helpful reference that, since to exclude deliberately "all" reference to Church teaching really describes a genuine apostate.

On what he calls the positive side of conscience formation, McBrien suggests an antecedent "attention and respect" (N.B. "attention" not "adherence"!) toward Church teaching "without prejudice to other sources: one's associates [unnamed]; the findings of science [unnamed]; the Bible; and the writings of theologians" (p. 1005). The theologians are also unnamed but the reader can certainly presume the many he cites approvingly in his book rank higher than the moral teachings of the Church he finds so much fault with.

This method deconstructs the formation of a correct Catholic conscience, since the sacred sources (Sacred Scripture, Sacred Tradition, and the Magisterium) are relativized to the status of information or mere points of view indistinguishable from other non-sacred points of view, i.e., one's associates and other human findings and writings. This is a very attenuated ecclesiology, since it rests more on a civil-political

---

[3] Richard P. McBrien, *Catholicism* (Minneapolis: Winston Press, 1980), p. 1005.

model rather than a religious-ecclesial one. Sacred Scripture is, of course, revealed by God; Sacred Tradition is guided by the Holy Spirit; and the Church is endowed with a charism to teach in Christ's name (Lk 10:16). These are indeed "sacred sources" whose teaching is normative and directive of right conduct and necessary for the correct formation of a correct Catholic conscience.

It is true one can act on a *certain* conscience. Indeed, a conscience that is both subjectively *certain* and objectively *correct* is *per se* the only true norm for acting. But a conscience that is subjectively certain and objectively *erroneous* is only *per accidens* a norm for conduct.

An erroneous or mistaken conscience is not a true source of genuine rights because it would generate a "moral right" to do moral wrong, and that would be moral nonsense. Catholics (anyone) should be wary of expressions claiming "absolute supremacy" for autonomous or individual conscience. Any claim that does not give first place nor first mention to the *truth* about the good is bound to mislead. When the *truth* does not get mentioned first (or at all), it is hard to avoid the message that the truth does not matter (moral relativism).

A Catholic whose conscience is in conflict with authentic Catholic teaching does have a status—it is an erroneous conscience (*CCC*, no. 1790, 1791). But an erroneous conscience is an aberration. The first and most pastoral response to an erroneous conscience is to correct it, not to celebrate or absolutize it. Error celebrated can only lead to future and further errors.

Conscience, after all, does not invent the truth; at its best, conscience seeks to discern and detect the truth. Again, in the context of conscience formation, McBrien's *Catholicism* tells us the Church never claimed "to speak infallibly on a moral question" (p. 1004). Yet, the Council of Trent's absolute rejection of divorce is certainly infallible teaching on a moral question; consider as well the main principles of the Ten Commandments in view of *Ad Tuendam Fidem* (May 18, 1998)—surely many infallible teachings on moral questions. It seems to me both odd and misleading that an author wants to foster a subjectively infallible conscience while always denying any infallible moral teachings.

Sometimes too much fire and too little light is focused on the kinds and degrees of infallibility while neglecting the obvious and available moral certitude that obtains with true and certain moral teaching. Sometimes arguments about the precise degrees and grades of infallibility cause some writers to miss the moral forest while looking for an infallible twig.

No science, including moral science, should pretend a level of certitude that it often does not offer. Does that leave us bereft of true and certain moral guidance? Of course not! Consider the true teaching of Vatican II:

> In the formation of their consciences, the Christian faithful ought carefully to attend to the *sacred* and *certain* doctrine of the Church. For the Church is, by the will of Christ, the teacher of truth. It is her duty to give utterance to, and authoritatively to teach, that truth which is Christ Himself, and also to declare and to confirm by her authority those principles of the moral order which have their origins in human nature itself. (*Dignitatis Humanae*, no. 14, emphasis added)

Curiously, Father McBrien's *Catholicism* does quote (p. 1005) that passage from the Vatican Council, but the Council of course makes no mention of one's associates or the findings or writings of other non-sacred sources.

There really is a moral duty not merely to inspect or review the truth as if the true moral teaching of the Church were just "input" or mere information along with other human input and information. Rather, true teaching is to be sought and adhered to because it deserves and requires the religious assent of our soul.

Thus again, in McBrien's *Catholicism*, we are told on two particular moral matters that we are to act on an "informed conscience" (p. 1006). Notice, there is no mention nor requirement by him that our conscience be *correct* or *true*, only that it be informed.

Then in two applications we are told, regarding artificial contraception and regarding homosexual practice, to take Church teaching "seriously into account" (pp. 1027 and 1033, respectively). Nowhere is the teaching of the Church said to be true and normative for conscience formation; rather, everywhere Church teaching is said to be something to be taken "into account"—it is for the deciding subject to decide the truth while also taking into account all the usual suspects: one's associates and the findings and writings of which Father McBrien happens to approve.

Instead of that low-test ecclesiology of the civil-secular kind, much to be preferred is the religious-ecclesial framework that the Vatican

Council actually taught: "Bishops, teaching in communion with the Roman Pontiff, are to be respected by all as witnesses to divine and Catholic truth. In matters of faith and morals, the bishops speak in the name of Christ and the faithful are to accept their teaching and adhere to it with religious assent of soul" (*Lumen Gentium*, no. 25; also cf. cann. 752, 753; and *CCC* no. 892).

Notice the moral obligation is to form a correct conscience in accord with the truth and adhere to that truth with religious *assent* of soul. Divine and Catholic truth is not just mere human input you take "into account", or give a pious nod to; it is both normative and directive for living a morally sound life. Truly, error can occur in the judgment of or in the application of the truth, but error is not normative and it always misdirects.

—March 2000

## Pastoral Solutions

Question: I think you mentioned this once before, but I still run into all sorts of "pastoral solutions", which assume that principles are true in general but in concrete application (cases) need not be true.

Answer: You are correct. While conscience terminology is employed in these pastoral solutions, the result is often an erroneous conscience. Let me present an authoritative response of Pope John Paul II and then a particularly lucid examination by Professor John Finnis.

Clearly, the so-called pastoral solution is repudiated by John Paul II in *Veritatis Splendor*. He notes that such thinkers advocate giving moral truth a "double status": separating valid teaching in general from the opinion of an individual conscience, making the latter the ultimate judge of good and evil. "On this basis, an attempt is made to legitimize so-called 'pastoral' solutions contrary to the teaching of the Magisterium, and to justify a 'creative' hermeneutic according to which the moral conscience is in no way obliged, in every case, by a particular negative precept" (no. 56).

The proper function of conscience, of course, is the decision or judgment of conscience. Such decisions are using conscience not merely inspecting it. Conscience, after all, detects and discovers truth; it does not invent truth!

Professor Finnis formulates the distortion of conscience in pastoral solutions with particular clarity. In the context of seeking pastoral advice (counseling, direction, or conscience formation), one might hear this question: "May I do X?" Logically, in the context of honest direction or sincere inquiry, the question is asked in order to form a correct conscience. Thus, the question means: "Should I think I may do X?" or "Is X the right thing to do?" In response to that honest question and sincere inquiry, one might encounter the following answer posed as the pastoral solution: "If your conscience tells you, you may do 'X,' then you do no wrong in doing 'X!'"

Such advice is not so much completely false as it is illogical and misleading. Notice the following: (1) you do not answer the question asked (i.e., about the rightness or wrongness of "X") but change the subject; (2) you do answer a question that was *not* asked (i.e., what is the status of a certain but erroneous conscience?); and (3) such advice is both empty and misleading for inevitably it means that "X" may be done, except by those who think they should not do "X", which is a case of situation ethics.

It is true that situationism or situation ethics is not mentioned, but there are more ways to enter that palace of confusion than coming in the front door. This advice urges that whatever conclusion you sincerely come to is the "right" ("you do no wrong") conclusion for you—to each his own truth! Notice again, there is no mention at all of *correct* or *erroneous* conscience—the truth or objectivity of the judgment of conscience is simply finessed, unmentioned—thus, what you see as wrong is wrong, what you see as right is right. There is no place for objective morality here!

As Pope John Paul clearly teaches:

> It is never acceptable to confuse a "subjective" error about the moral good with the "objective" truth rationally proposed to man in virtue of his end, or to make the moral value of an act performed by following the judgment of an erroneous conscience. It is possible that the evil done as the result of invincible ignorance or a non-culpable error of judgment may not be imputable to the agent; but even in this case it

does not cease to be an evil, a disorder in relation to the truth about the good. (*VS*, no. 63)

The widespread use of this *false* solution, the so-called "pastoral solution", is not limited only to so-called "internal forum" solutions, or so-called "good conscience" solutions concerning divorce-remarriage-and-Eucharist. The same misuse of conscience terminology can, of course, be applied to any moral question and simply call the solution "pastoral". But, any "pastoral solution" that contradicts the Supreme Pastor of the Church simply cannot qualify as "pastoral".

—February 1996

# 15

# Church Authority

## Only One Magisterium

Question: A lecturer in theology stated that there is a "magisterium of bishops" and a "magisterium of theologians". He also insisted that this is the traditional understanding and, indeed, especially that of Saint Thomas Aquinas. Is this so?

Answer: The Magisterium of the pope and the bishops ("*doctrinae magistri*" can. 375, §1) is a "sacred source" of sacred theology, i.e., guaranteed by Jesus: "He who hears you hears me" (Lk 10:16; cf. Mt 10:40). On the other hand, the so-called magisterium of the doctors, scholars, or theologians—never known to be a univocal voice—is not a "sacred source" in any sense.

As for Saint Thomas Aquinas, his reported last words before receiving Viaticum remain a model for all believers (degreed or un-degreed): "I have taught and written much on this most Holy Body and on the other sacraments, according to my faith in Christ and in the holy Roman Church, to whose judgment I submit all my teaching." [1]

It is slightly ludicrous and anachronistic to try to recycle Saint Thomas as an early but closet "dissenter". His conviction about theology and the Church was stated with great clarity in response to the contentious question about baptizing the children of unwilling believers. In reply, he taught: "The very teaching of Catholic theologians gets its authority from the Church. Hence we

---

[1] James A. Weisheipl, *Friar Thomas D'Aquino* (Garden City, N.Y.: Doubleday, 1974), p. 326.

should stand on the authority of the Church rather than on that of Augustine or Jerome or any other divine whatsoever" (*ST*, II-II, q. 10, a. 12).

—May 1997

## *Imprimatur*

**Question:** After the Second Vatican Council, the *Index of Forbidden Books* was revoked, but was the *imprimatur* abolished? I ask because I read all sorts of Catholic books with no *imprimatur*, and, I am told, it is no longer required.

**Answer:** It is true that the *Index of Forbidden Books* was revoked by a formal notification of the Congregation for the Doctrine of the Faith (June 14, 1966).[2] The moral obligation to protect against what endangers faith and morals remains, but the legal (canonical) penalties were abrogated.

Some years later, the same Congregation issued a decree (*Ecclesiae Pastorum*, March 19, 1975) containing new norms for the censorship of books.[3] In effect, the norms of this decree became, almost verbatim, the governing canons (822–32) of the present *Code of Canon Law* (1983), which is the universal law of the Church.

More recently, the CDF issued a summary instruction, the stated purpose of which was "to give encouragement and help to the Bishops in the fulfillment of their obligations ... by calling to mind the norms of canon law, explaining their various provisions, and defining and making explicit the processes by which they are implemented".[4]

This instruction is both more reliable and more accurate than the observations that appear in the *Commentary* commissioned by the Canon Law Society of America.[5] Part 2, number 7, of *Social Communication*

---

[2] Cf. *Canon Law Digest*, vol. 6 (Milwaukee, Wis.: Bruce Publishing, 1969), pp. 814–15.

[3] *Canon Law Digest*, vol. 8 (Chicago Province S.J., 1978), pp. 991–96.

[4] CDF, *Instruction on Some Aspects of the Use of the Instruments of Social Communication in Promoting the Doctrine of the Faith* (March 30, 1992), introduction.

[5] Canon Law Society of America, *The Code of Canon Law: A Text and Commentary* (New York/Mahwah: Paulist Press, 1985), pp. 578–85.

lists the kinds of written works that require either approval or permission: "prior approval" is needed for the publication of books of the Sacred Scriptures and translations of them (can. 825, §1); for catechisms and other writings dealing with catechetical formation (cann. 775, §2; 827, §1); for textbooks dealing with those disciplines that touch on faith or morals, and on which instruction is based in elementary, middle, and also higher schools (can. 827, §2).

"Prior permission" is required for those who prepare and publish translations of Scripture in collaboration with those of other faiths (can. 825, §2); for prayer books intended for public or private use (can. 826, §3); for new editions of collections of decrees or acts issued by ecclesiastical authority (can. 828); and for what is written by clergy and religious for newspapers, magazines, or periodicals which are accustomed to attack openly the Catholic religion or good morals (can. 831, §1). Lastly, members of religious institutes need "prior permission" for the publication of writings that deal with questions of religion or morals (can. 832).

"Permission" or "approval" here does not mean *endorsement*; rather, these are essentially negative judgments that nothing objectionable is found therein.

The *Code* also "recommends" (without requiring) that books that deal with Scripture, theology, canon law, Church history, or religious or moral disciplines be submitted to the judgment of the local ordinary even if they are not employed as textbooks for teaching; and the same is true for writings in which there is special concern to religion or to good moral behavior (can. 827, §3). ("Liturgical Books" are governed by particular law; cf. cann. 838 and 826.)

Consistently, throughout this postconciliar period, the Holy See has emphasized the responsibility and vigilance of bishops—individually, and/or, in conference—to insist that writings (concerned with faith and morals) be submitted for prior approval and also the duty and right to reprobate books or writings that attack correct faith or good morals (*Ecclesiae Pastorum*, introduction, and can. 823, §1). This is little more than the correct teaching function of the Magisterium in both its positive and negative aspects.

Some few bishops have done this; most have not. Perhaps some confuse doctrine with theology. By office and ordination, all bishops are "teachers of doctrine" ("*doctrinae magistri*", can. 375, §1); whether or not individual bishops are "teachers of theology" depends on singular factors such as added training, involvement, and, apparently, personal interest.

There is no requirement that anyone in the Church has to publish a book or textbook of theology; however, it is required of the pastors of the Church that judgments be made about theological works by Catholics, at least to the extent of what is or is not in accord with correct faith or good morals. This is especially the case with so-called Catholic publishers who presumably have an "apostolate" and therefore particular obligations to the Catholic people and to the Church (cf. CDF, "*Social Communication*," pt. 3, nos. 14–15).

As most readers now know, some "imprimaturs" are not that helpful and surely not timeless. We had the embarrassment in this country, in the mid-1970s, of at least two well-publicized books—printed with an *imprimatur*—where the Vatican had to request that the archbishop who granted the *imprimatur* remove and revoke that *imprimatur*.[6]

Rescue negotiations to bring these two books back into the pale of orthodoxy failed. Paulist Press—a Catholic publisher—struck by the gospel imperative that one cannot serve both God and mammon (Mt 6:24; Lk 16:13) opted for mammon; they finessed these holdings to Harper and Row—a secular publisher—unconcerned with "imprimaturs" or orthodoxy, but concerned with what sells.

It is perhaps true that most civil and libertarian Americans (Catholics included) have been programmed from birth to consider "censorship" or "prior censorship" as some kind of unforgivable sin. It may be the only remaining journalistic dogma that is infallible and not open to reasoned discussion—there must be NO CENSORSHIP of any kind! This is a negative moral absolute not found in the Sermon on the Mount, but "sacred" to the First Amendment of our American Constitution.

The Church has an older constitutional conviction—there are such things as *bad* books; *ideas* can and do *have consequences*, and some bad ideas can and do have bad consequences. To some, this might seem quaint, even medieval, but, in fact, this stance takes thought seriously. The Church proposes truths to be believed and to be lived. She does this with utter seriousness, for these are saving doctrines with consequences for this life and the next.

---

[6] Philip S. Keane, *Sexual Morality* (New York: Paulist Press, 1977); and Anthony Wilhelm, *Christ Among Us* (New York: Paulist Press, 1975).

Is it not possible that some of the moral scandals presently afflicting the Church are simply the result of bad teaching, mixed signals, and the absence of any serious vigilance?

Some twenty years ago, two very bad books in the area of sexual ethics were oversold and under-critiqued: Donald Goergen's *The Sexual Celibate* and Anthony Kosnik's *Human Sexuality*,[7] the latter commissioned by the Catholic Theological Society in America. Both the books propose guidance that is profoundly at odds with and contradictory to Church teaching and practice.

For one season, the Goergen book seemed to be the Christmas gift of or to every religious in the country, and the Kosnik book decorated the desk or shelf of every campus minister in the country. The concern is not just academic; the concern is that ideas have consequences, especially ideas offered as teaching, guidance, and/or direction. It seems, now removed in time, that some of the teachers and counselors not only presented the "new morality" of Goergen and Kosnik, but began to act it out in life and practice. For this, the Church must now pay a heavy price morally, legally, and financially.

I cannot argue that if all teachers taught correct doctrine there would be no moral failures—for that, we would have to revoke original sin and its consequences. However, steady, positive, correct teaching together with some verifiable vigilance would seem to be a much less expensive path than learning the force of the Ten Commandments from civil and criminal lawyers.

—April 1994

## Karl Rahner Corrected

Question: In several of your columns, you often cite *Veritatis Splendor* but rarely explain it. Also, I sometimes detect a slighting tone in some of your asides regarding the great theologian Karl Rahner. Are these valid criticisms?

Answer: All criticisms of me are valid; some, but not all, are licit; and a number are quite frankly true.

---

[7] Donald Goergen, *The Sexual Celibate* (New York: Seabury Press, 1974); and Anthony Kosnik et al., *Human Sexuality* (Paramus, N.J.: Paulist Press, 1977).

I do believe the middle part of *Veritatis Splendor* (nos. 28–83) is a moral masterpiece. In saying that, I mean no slight to chapters 1 and 2, but rather that numbers 28 through 83 do respond to and critique almost every post–Vatican II moral hemorrhage and also repudiate theories and presuppositions that are contrary to the teaching of Scripture and Tradition (no. 49).

On the overall scope and contribution of Father Karl Rahner to contemporary theology, I am no expert. However, Rahner's relatively few interventions in moral theology were, in my judgment, disastrous, and their negative consequences are with us still.

While the encyclical *Veritatis Splendor* names no names, the second and central chapter does repudiate a quasi-Kantian anthropology that is rooted in and flows from positions long advocated by Karl Rahner: relation between the ethical order and the order of salvation; that authentic Church teaching is "physicalistic"; the conversion of free choice into fundamental freedom (option); the criteria of the morality of human acts; questions of historicity and historical consciousness. These five areas and what many moral theologians hold for or against Church teaching in *Veritatis Splendor* are examined in detail, with full documentation, by Professor William E. May in *Anthropotes*.

May correctly notes that many of Rahner's disciples, or alleged advocates, have gone much farther than their great mentor in separating fundamental freedom (option) from free choice,[8] but it is the quasi-Kantian anthropology of Rahner that is the real target which *Veritatis Splendor* repudiates as dualist freedom (nos. 46–53) and the fundamental option and radically revised versions of mortal and venial sin (nos. 65–70), to cite but two examples.

Perhaps the best-known Rahnerian entry in moral theology is his famous essay, "On the Question of a Formal Existential Ethics".[9] This essay and its crucial and misleading distinction have been concisely but cogently critiqued by Father Brian Mullady, O.P., in the *Newsletter—Fellowship of Catholic Scholars*.[10]

---

[8] William E. May, "Theologians and Theologies in the Encyclical *Veritatis Splendor*", *Anthropotes: Rivista di Studi su Persona e la Famiglia* 10, no. 1 (1994): 39–59, at 47.

[9] Karl Rahner, "On the Question of a Formal Existential Ethics", *Theological Investigations*, vol. 2 (Baltimore: Helicon Press, 1963), pp. 217–34.

[10] Brian Mullady, O.P., "Both a Servant and Free", *Newsletter of the Fellowship of Catholic Scholars* 17, no. 1 (Dec. 1993): 20–24.

A key insight for Rahner is that for material nature one may express the whole truth with a universal, but this can never be true for persons. Thus, Rahner posits two different sciences: (1) a science of laws, termed "Essentialist Ethics" (universal laws that can only *recommend*) and (2) another science, termed "Existential Ethics" (conscience enlivened by supernatural instinct).

This is not to suggest that universal laws (e.g., the Ten Commandments) are just a dull, mechanical set of rules that simply trump every concrete situation or specific case. But, it is to suggest that it makes no moral sense to suggest that the Holy Spirit inspires someone to perform an act (existentially) that the same Holy Spirit inspired the authors of Scripture (Ten Commandments) to prohibit (essentially).

This divorce of the universal and particular, this two-tier morality permeates the mind-set of those who deny the existence of "intrinsically evil" acts, acts which by their nature cannot be ordered to God. All dissenters and revisionists deny such acts, whereas no small part of *Veritatis Splendor* (nos. 52–53, 71–83) vigorously defends this principle, as does Catholic tradition (*VS*, nos. 81–82).

Apart from this neo-Kantian split of truths in the abstract that can recommend only but cannot bind nor authoritatively guide in concrete parameters, another Rahnerian entry that misled was an early essay in bioethics, "The Experiment with Man".[11]

Over a generation ago, the astute Protestant theologian, Paul Ramsey, perceived grave flaws and tragic consequences with Rahner's exalted esteem for man's powers of self-awareness and self-determination. He quotes Rahner's perspective: "Man is essentially a freedom-event. As established by God, and in his very nature, he is unfinished", so much so that Rahner concludes: "There is really nothing possible for man that he ought not to do." [12]

This Rahnerian notion of man as essentially "freedom-event" is actually rejected in *Veritatis Splendor*, and the terms and language rejected is almost exactly Karl Rahner's: "This ultimately means making freedom self-defining and a phenomenon creative of itself and its values. Indeed, when all is said and done man would not even have a nature;

[11] Karl Rahner, "The Experiment with Man", in *Theological Investigations*, vol. 9 (New York: Herder and Herder, 1972), pp. 205–24; cf. also, "Genetic Manipulation", in *Theological Investigations*, pp. 225–52.

[12] Paul Ramsey, *Fabricated Man: The Ethics of Genetic Control* (New Haven, Conn.: Yale University Press, 1970), pp. 139–40; see also pp. 139–43.

he would be his own personal life-project. Man would be nothing more than his own freedom" (no. 46). The Pope teaches that such doctrine is contrary to both Scripture and Tradition (no. 49).

On the publication of *Veritatis Splendor*, the London *Tablet* printed a number of ferocious articles attacking that encyclical. One of the most dyspeptic articles was that of the moralist Joseph Fuchs, S.J. Fuchs' sharpest criticism is that his reading of *Veritatis Splendor* "suggests that the Pope's theological advisors are unfamiliar with the thought-world of Karl Rahner".[13]

Perhaps, for Father Fuchs, familiarity with the "thought-world of Karl Rahner" is now a required test of Catholic orthodoxy, but his charge against and his reading of *Veritatis Splendor* is badly mistaken. The encyclical clearly does take account of the thought-world of Karl Rahner and just as clearly does not accept it; in some particular passages the encyclical formally rejects it.

This is not a slighting tone toward Rahner; it is, I believe, a correct reading of a truly important moral encyclical.

—June 1995

## Sensus Fidelium *Explained*

Question: In July 1995, a document of some eleven U.S. bishops was headlined as "Bishops/Collegiality". It says the twofold role of bishops is "to be in union with the pope and college of bishops and also to be faithful to the faith experience of our local church". Do you know any authentic source for the latter claim?

Answer: You are correct, a rather petulant and sniveling document of some eleven bishops was published in *Origins*, entitled "Issues in Restructuring the Bishops' Conference".[14] In sum, it is a document of personal complaints, strange claims about the *sensus fidelium*, and some pointed remarks: the NCCB has "too many committees" (p. 131), the Administrative Committee "appears to be much too large", and

---

[13] Joseph Fuchs, S.J., "Good Acts and Good Persons", *Tablet* 247 (Nov. 6, 1993): 1445.
[14] Archbishop Rembert Weakland et al., "Issues in Restructuring the Bishops' Conference", *Origins* 25, no. 8 (July 13, 1995): 129–34.

the Doctrinal Committee should "distinguish between doctrines and theological opinions".

The last point is introduced in a not-too-gentle slight that the NCCB Doctrinal Committee should not so much focus on the statements of other committees but work on substantive doctrinal issues for the Conference itself. This point is truly puzzling. I doubt that it really means each committee should have its own doctrine, but it does seem to be a call for more unsupervised teaching-listening and listening-teaching—the document's favored understanding of the *sensus fidelium*.

The point about distinguishing doctrine from theology is crucial, but that crucial distinction is confused throughout the document.

There is a difference between "*doctrine*" and "*theology*." All Catholic bishops, by office and ordination, are "teachers of doctrine" (*doctrinae magistri*), "priests of sacred worship" (*sacri cultus sacerdotes*), and "ministers of governance" (*gubernationis ministri*; cf. can. 375, §1). This concise canon summarizes a dogmatic principle, the concept and language of which is taken from *Lumen Gentium*, number 20, of Vatican Council II, with deep roots in the most ancient sources of Tradition (cf. note 13 of *LG*, no. 20).

The same dogmatic teaching on the episcopal office is also stated concisely in the *Catechism*: "The Teaching Office" (nos. 888–92); "The Sanctifying Office" (no. 893), and "The Governing Office" (nos. 894–96).

Notice both the Council and the *Code* (faithfully reflecting the Council) are clear: by office and ordination, bishops are "teachers of doctrine" (*doctrinae magistri*); neither says they are "teachers of theology" (*theologiae magistri*).

Of course, some bishops are by training, experience, or steadied application "teachers of theology", but that is not essential to their office, whereas it is, of course, essential that all bishops be "teachers of doctrine".

When bishops are described as articulating the "faith experience" of a local church, it is not at all clear to me how this stands as a "teacher of doctrine". The jargon-driven document of the unhappy "eleven" highlights "transformative leaders" who will "empower, convene and energize" people "to build a different world, society" (p. 134). Perhaps such language is currently in vogue among bureaucratic cheerleaders, but it is certainly not the language of doctrine or even theology. I have no idea what it means nor whether it has anything to do with the Church at all.

Listening to where people are said to be "at" seems to be the key component of the learning-listening modality of this document, but again, how this relates to being "teachers of doctrine" is unclear. Some years ago, Cardinal Ratzinger wisely cautioned bishops not to compete with professors of theology: "As bishops, their function is not that of also wanting to play an instrument in the concert of specialists."[15] Their task as "teachers of faith" (teachers of doctrine) is a different one.

The unhappy "eleven" stress greatly a simplistic notion of the *sensus fidelium*,[16] which, as good listeners at good listening sessions, they feel duty-bound to report and "brainstorm" in a "more personal, dialogical, intuitive and interactive" way.

Amazingly, they accuse Roman Documents—a polite reference perhaps to the Pope, Cardinal Ratzinger, and curial department heads—of "reinterpreting" Vatican II documents to present minority positions at the Council as the true meaning and teaching of the Council.[17] A further salvo is aimed at unnamed Roman theologians and their workings, leading us to think that authoritative Catholic teaching is not concerned with doctrinal truth but the theological agenda of those who contribute to and participate in such things.

There is a neat bit of transference here! Clearly, the heavily Americanized version of *sensus fidelium* so prominent throughout the document of the unhappy "eleven" was neither the majority nor the minority position at Vatican Council II. If anything, it is a homegrown we-are-the-church ecclesiology empowered, convened, and energized largely by a former department head of theology at Notre Dame University.

Clearly, this is not the *sensus fidelium* taught in *Lumen Gentium*, number 12, nor does it accord with the commentary of Avery Dulles. ("The fact that the faithful as a whole bear witness to the gospel does not make superfluous the teaching of the hierarchy. To them it falls to shepherd the whole flock by clear, authoritative doctrine."[18])

---

[15] Joseph Cardinal Ratzinger, *The Ratzinger Report* (San Francisco: Ignatius Press, 1985), p. 65.

[16] Weakland et al., "Restructuring the Bishops' Conference", p. 130.

[17] Ibid., p. 133.

[18] *Dogmatic Constitution on the Church* (*Lumen Gentium*), ed. Rev. Avery Dulles, S.J., in *Documents of Vatican II*, ed. Walter M. Abbott, S.J. (London: Geoffery Chapman, 1966), p. 29, n. 40.

Clearly, this is not the teaching of Pope John Paul II, speaking to the same bishops' conference (in Chicago in 1979):

> The Holy Spirit is active in enlightening the minds of the faithful with his truth, and in inflaming their hearts with his love. But these insights of faith and this *sensus fidelium* are not independent of the Magisterium of the Church, which is an instrument of the same Holy Spirit and is assisted by him. It is only when the faithful have been nourished by the word of God, faithfully transmitted in its purity and integrity, that their own charisms are fully operative and fruitful. Once the word of God is faithfully proclaimed to the community and is accepted, it brings forth fruits of justice and holiness of life in abundance. ("Address to the Bishops of the United States of America" [Oct. 5, 1979], no. 7)

The *Catechism* presents the same teaching on *sensus fidelium* as this one presented by the Holy Father (nos. 904–7).

Perhaps, the listening-sessions modality is a popular, even widespread, way of presenting the *sensus fidelium*, but the only way to advance this misunderstanding is *not to listen* to what the Church teaches on the subject.

—March 1996

# 16

# Public Dissent

## Right to Dissent

Question: What authority does the *Commentary* on the new *Code of Canon Law* have? It was commissioned by the Canon Law Society of America, has a *nihil obstat* and an *imprimatur*. My question concerns its treatment of canon 752, which calls for *obsequium religiosum* to authentic Church teaching, but the commentator continues, "Dissent is possible because the teachers mentioned in the canon can and have been mistaken." Is it not the Church's official teaching that there is no right to dissent?

Answer: In 1985, the Canon Law Society of America (CLSA) published *Text and Commentary* on the new (1983) *Code of Canon Law*. This commentary was published by the Paulist Press and is quite extensive—1152 pages. As the title indicates, it is both the "text" of and "commentary" on the 1983 *Code*. As you mentioned, it was published with a *nihil obstat* (D. B. Zimmerman) and an *imprimatur* (+ P. L. Gerety).

It is certainly the most available and accessible (English) canonical commentary in this country. There are no big problems with the text (except for some questionable CLSA translations), but, unfortunately, this massive commentary is, frankly, uneven. In some places, it is so uneven that it is not commentary at all but sheer editorial.

For example, the commentaries by the Reverend Thomas P. Doyle, O.P., on "Marriage" (cann. 1055–165), by Reverend Thomas J. Green on "Penalties" (cann. 1311–99), and Reverend (now Bishop) John J. Myers on "Temporal Goods" (cann. 1254–310) are all excellent, and they are as instructive as they are reliable.

The example you question (can. 752) is the work of the Reverend James A. Coriden from his section on "The Teaching Office of the Church" (cann. 747–833). Unfortunately, this important section of the *Code* may well be the worst and weakest entry in the entire commentary.

Your question pinpoints a clear example for this negative judgment. All agree, including the commentator Coriden (p. 548), that this canon (752) is drawn, almost verbatim, from the formal teaching of Vatican Council II (cf. *Lumen Gentium*, no. 25). Namely, it concerns the "religious submission of will and of mind"[1] to be given to the Supreme Pontiff or the college of bishops teaching authentically on faith and morals even when that teaching is not proclaimed with a definitive act.

First, Father Coriden shaves the translation to the "religious respect of intellect and will" (trans. of CLSA) to be paid to authentic magisterial teaching on faith and morals. Thus, it is not the "religious submission" of intellect and will—nor as the Abbott edition of Vatican II once translates: "religious assent of soul" (p. 48)—but merely religious "respect" for authentic magisterial teaching.

This change of words from "submission" to "respect" is a conscious watering down of Vatican II teaching to try to prop up the case for "dissent" which follows. It is here that Coriden writes: "In other words, dissent is possible" (p. 548).

This clearly is no longer commentary, for it is a comment on what is not mentioned. *Lumen Gentium*, number 25, makes no mention of "dissent" (nor does any other Vatican II document). Canon 752 makes no mention of "dissent".

Apparently, this commentator expounds perhaps what he wished the *Code* had said or the Council had taught, but they did not and do not. This is not pure commentary then but rather pure editorial. And the editorial is not canonical, for no canon in the old or new *Code* makes any mention of the point he presses. The editorial is clearly his own theological slant since it has no basis in this canon nor anywhere in the *Code*.

Furthermore, the commentator's interpretation contradicts the clear wording of the canon he is supposed to be interpreting. Canon 752

---

[1] Cf. *Documents of Vatican II*, ed. Abbott, p. 48, or *Vatican Council II: The Conciliar and Post Conciliar Documents*, ed. Austin Flannery, O.P. (Collegeville, Minn.: Liturgical Press, 1975), p. 379.

concludes: "Therefore the Christian faithful are to take care to avoid whatever is not in harmony with that teaching"; thus, the Coriden commentary advocates precisely what the canon clearly teaches all the faithful to avoid.

It is my own view that there is no such thing as a *public right to dissent*, while there could be a negative *inability* to assent to Church teaching. (A positive right to dissent and a negative inability to assent are not the same, but that requires an essay-length answer.)

In any case, the Congregation for the Doctrine of the Faith in its *"Instruction on the Ecclesial Vocation of the Theologian"* (*Donum Veritatis*, May 24, 1990) has a very nuanced treatment of "The Problem of Dissent" (cf. pt. 4B, nos. 32–41, esp. 36–38). That CDF instruction is certainly official Catholic teaching and as such would preclude giving an *imprimatur* to the Coriden editorial, for it is simply neither an adequate nor accurate explanation of canon 752.

—January 1993

## Condom Use to Prevent HIV

Question: The use of condoms to prevent or lessen the transmission of AIDS keeps returning. I sometimes read that the Vatican has changed, or a bishops' conference somewhere or any number of theologians. Has the Church changed this teaching?

Answer: The short answer is no. Clearly, the Vatican has not changed this teaching, but some dissenting theologians are all over the place on this.

In June 2001, there was a Special Session of the General Assembly of the United Nations to examine various aspects of the HIV/AIDS problem. For this purpose, Pope John Paul II wrote a formal letter (June 21, 2001) to U.N. Secretary General Kofi Annan.

On June 27, the Holy See's delegation issued (in English) a final statement addressing the U.N. document. The statement said that while the Holy See supports positive steps to address the needs of those who have been ravaged by HIV/AIDS, it has moral reservations regarding the U.N. document's use of the terms "sexual health"

and "reproductive health" when they do not refer to a holistic concept of health. Also, the U.N. statement had no mention of the
spiritual and psychological maturity needed for sexual maturity or of
the mutual love and decision-making that should characterize the
marital relationship.

The Vatican statement also said:

> The Holy See wishes to emphasize that, with regard to the use of
> condoms as a means of preventing HIV infection, it has in no way
> changed its moral position.... The Holy See also regrets that irrespon-
> sible, unsafe and high-risk behavior were not adequately discussed
> and addressed in preparing this Declaration. Finally, the Holy See
> continues to call attention to the undeniable fact that the only safe
> and completely reliable method of preventing the sexual trans-
> mission of HIV is abstinence before marriage and respect and
> mutual fidelity within marriage. The Holy See believes that this is
> and always must be the foundation of any discussion of prevention
> and support.[2]

Thus, as to the first part of your question, the Vatican has not changed
its teaching; indeed, it has reaffirmed its teaching in forums both national
and international.

As to your second question—theologians and others who claim
otherwise—there is a problem in print. A case in point is the *America*
magazine article by Jon Fuller, S.J., and James Keenan, S.J.[3] Fuller and
Keenan claimed that an article by Monsignor Jacques Suaudeau[4] of
the Pontifical Council for the Family argued that if people can't "prevent" the transmission of HIV/AIDS, they could at least "contain" it
via condoms as a so-called "lesser evil".

This allegation did not go unnoticed by the Vatican or the author.
Indeed, Father Suaudeau published a repudiation of "erroneous
interpretations" of his prior article making three points: (1) any interpretation of his article that casts doubt on the Church's official
teaching has "absolutely no foundation"; (2) the use of condoms
cannot be proposed as a solution because "it is always an intrinsic

---

[2] Quoted in *L'Osservatore Romano*, Eng. ed., July 11, 2001, p. 10.

[3] Jon D. Fuller, S.J., and James F. Keenan, S.J., "Tolerant Signals: The Vatican's New
Insights on Condoms for HIV Prevention", *America* 183, no. 8 (Sept. 23, 2000): 6–7.

[4] Msgr. Jacques Suaudeau, "Stopping the Spread of HIV/AIDS, Prophylactics or Family
Values?" *L'Osservatore Romano*, Apr. 19, 2000.

objective moral disorder"; and, (3) his use of the term "lesser evil" was strictly in the medical sense of public health and not a moral mention or moral judgment at all.[5] It is unusual, to say the least, for Vatican office-holders to publish corrections in the *L'Osservatore Romano* of misinterpretations of their own published works. But the Fuller and Keenan spin seemed to require this personal correction by the author.

For reasons that are not clear to me, Keenan, who is a professor of Christian ethics at the Weston Jesuit School of Theology, has become the point man for the advocacy and justification of condoms to prevent HIV/AIDS. In an aggressively unapologetic letter to the London *Tablet*, he argues that he has surveyed the writings of all Catholic moral theologians who have addressed HIV prevention methods in general and condom distribution and needle exchange in particular. "I found that all agreed that the promotion of these methods is morally licit" and that almost all of the same authors demonstrate no compromise with Church teaching.[6] In fact, he has coedited a book on the subject: *Catholic Ethicists on HIV/AIDS Prevention*.[7] This collection was favorably reviewed by Father Charles E. Curran of Southern Methodist University.[8]

Father Curran deftly notes that the authors (Keenan-Fuller-Cahill-Kelly) come from what he calls the "progressive" or "liberal" wing of moral theology (p. 404) since none of them defend Church teaching here. Nevertheless, Curran wonders whether Keenan et al. want "to have it both ways" (p. 405) since they maintain that Catholic moral tradition can and should contribute positively to alleviating HIV/AIDS but argue at the same time that the Catholic "tradition has to change its own sexual teaching" to do so.

Whatever the status of Father Curran's many well-publicized dissents, he is more candid than most and does not shy away from saying that the Pope is wrong or the Church is in error. The Keenan-Fuller-Cahill-Kelly school of dissent is much less candid. Up front, they are

---

[5] Msgr. Jacques Suadeau, "Response to an Erroneous Interpretation of 'Prophylactics or Family Values?'" *L'Osservatore Romano*, Sept. 27, 2000, p. 2.

[6] James F. Keenan, S.J., letter to the editor, *Tablet* 254 (July 29, 2000): 1017.

[7] *Catholic Ethicists on HIV/AIDS Prevention*, ed. James F. Keenan, S.J., Jon D. Fuller, S.J., M.D., Lisa S. Cahill, and Kevin Kelly (New York: Continuum, 2000).

[8] Charles E. Curran, "Catholic Ethicists on HIV/AIDS Prevention", *Theological Studies* 62, no. 2 (2001): 403–5.

very slow to say explicitly that Church teaching is wrong; rather they more often do not affirm Church teaching but instead quote health care workers, pastoral workers, and other dissenting voices who advocate a different and contradictory practice.

This softer dissent is then couched in terms of "listening"— listening to disparate voices; listening to prudent counsel. Then comes the suggestion that hesitant bishops, curial officials, and perhaps even the Pope should "listen" to the views and voices selectively arranged and edited by the Keenan-Fuller school. To some extent, it makes no real difference what the official Church teaches or how often that teaching is repeated.

This is close to the Frances Kissling school of advocacy by endless repetition. Ms. Kissling collects the views and voices of some Catholics who support abortion, advocate its extension, and favor its public funding. If you don't agree with her collected voices, you are *not listening*! As a personal favor to you, she will repeat her collected voices until you do listen, i.e., agree with her views and voices. Of course, if you do listen to her (i.e., agree) you cease to hold Catholic teachings.

That's why above I suggest it makes no real difference to the dissenting schools how often or how clearly the Church states and repeats her own teaching—they are simply unprepared and unwilling to accept any teaching that does not endorse their own.

—December 2001

## Keenan and Fuller Respond

We wish to respond to Monsignor William B. Smith's criticisms of us in these pages.[9] Monsignor Smith asserts that contrary to what he takes to be our position: Church teaching on the use of condoms to prevent HIV transmission has not changed. In addition, he quotes Charles Curran's review of our book (*Catholic Ethicists on HIV/AIDS Prevention*) in contending that we favor a change in Church sexual ethics in order to allow the use of condoms to prevent HIV transmission.

Father Curran states that we "argue (correctly, in my view) that the tradition has to change its own sexual teaching. The last seven

[9] Msgr. William B. Smith, "Questions Answered", HPR (Dec. 2001).

chapters definitely promote this change with the first two dealing with progress and change in Catholic moral teaching in general." [10] While it may be true that several authors in our book take the position that progress—or in some cases, "change"—in the teaching is necessary, our position is that traditional principles can allow the use of condoms to prevent death. We point out that many Church leaders around the world are turning to traditional principles to address HIV preventive measures:

> Bishops are able to take these steps because the tradition provides them with a way, as we have attempted to show, both to protect existing teachings and to simultaneously engage new problems creatively. We do not need to construct an entire new moral system, even at such a critical time as this one. Rather, the Catholic tradition is a supple and balanced legacy that we need to recognize, appreciate and utilize. [11]

As pointed out by Msgr. Smith, the Holy See's delegation to the United Nations General Assembly Special Session on AIDS ( June 2001) emphasized that, "with regard to the use of condoms as a means of preventing HIV infection, (the Holy See) has in no way changed its moral position". However, we note in the same statement an appreciation of what role condoms might have: "Responsible behavior cannot just be listed alongside condoms, but has to be prior." That is, an encouragement toward responsible moral conduct must precede any discourse about condoms.

We also note that as early as 1996, when asked in an interview with Vatican Radio whether condom distribution might qualify morally as an example of the lesser of two evils, Père Georges Cottier, O.P., Secretary General of the International Theological Commission and Theologian to the Papal Household, responded: "This is the question that moralists are asking themselves, and it is legitimate that they ask it." In addition, Cardinal Lustiger of Paris, Cardinal Simonis of the Netherlands, Archbishop (now Cardinal) Christoph Schönborn of Vienna, and other bishops, episcopal conferences, and their communities, have invoked traditional principles to recommend first responsible sexual conduct, but secondly, condom use to prevent transmission of the deadly virus.

---

[10] Curran, "Catholic Ethicists on HIV/AIDS Prevention", p. 405.
[11] Keenan et al., *Catholic Ethicists*, p. 29.

More recently, in a long-anticipated statement, the Southern African Bishops' Conference noted that in the case in which one spouse is HIV-infected, "The Church accepts that everyone has the right to defend one's life against mortal danger. This would include using the appropriate means and course of action." In a press conference further explaining the document, Cardinal Wilfred Napier of Durban indicated that this could include condoms. There was no objection by the Vatican to this judgment.

In his encyclical *Evangelium Vitae*, John Paul II notes, "Every individual, precisely by reason of the mystery of the Word of God who was made flesh (cf. Jn 1:14), is entrusted to the maternal care of the Church. Therefore every threat to human dignity and life must necessarily be felt in the Church's very heart" (no. 3). He goes on to appeal to each and every person, in the name of God, "to respect, protect, love and serve life, every human life!" (no. 5).

Our position is that the Church's fundamental interest in the protection of human life allows her to employ traditional moral principles (such as lesser evil, material cooperation, gradualism, etc.) to justify the use of condoms to prevent life-threatening HIV transmission without compromising Catholic sexual ethics. Indeed, *Humanae Vitae* itself did not rule out all therapeutic interventions that might render an individual infertile, as long as this were not one's primary intention: "... the Church does not consider at all illicit the use of those therapeutic means necessary to cure bodily diseases, even if a foreseeable impediment to procreation should result therefrom—provided such impediment is not directly intended for any motive whatsoever" (no. 15). In that light, while discussing the case of a married couple when one spouse has AIDS, Father Maurizio Faggioni, who is a physician, a professor of moral theology at Rome's Alphonsianum University, and a consultant to the Congregation for the Doctrine of the Faith, said condom use might be justified as long as the "exclusive and primary" intent was to defend the healthy partner from infection and not to prevent pregnancy. "This is a classic application" of the Catholic moral principle of "double effect", he said, in which one's good action has an unintended bad effect.[12]

---

[12] John Norton, "Theologians Say Condom Use OK in Certain Cases, Not as Policy", *Catholic News Service* (Sept. 22, 2000).

We appreciate Monsignor Smith's interest in our work. We hope by this friendly response to demonstrate that we are not dissenters. Rather, we apply centuries-old principles to a critical new question, one that UNAIDS has described as "the most devastating disease humankind has ever faced".

Jon D. Fuller, S.J., M.D.
Associate Professor of Medicine
Boston University School of Medicine

James F. Keenan, S.J., STD
. Professor of Moral Theology
Weston Jesuit School of Theology
Cambridge, Mass.

## Monsignor Smith Replies

My purpose in quoting Father Curran's review of the Keenan-Fuller-Cahill-Kelly book was that I thought the Curran comment was correct, i.e., that Keenan et al. want "to have it both ways"—to maintain Catholic moral tradition and advocate that the Church must change her moral teaching.

Perhaps, I do not read the Curran comment correctly, but I do thank the authors, Fathers Fuller and Keenan, because their response is clearer than my prior estimate of it. Here, they say they do not look for a change in Catholic moral teaching and posit that what they call "traditional principles" already allow and justify what they advocate.

In this, I take them at their printed word stated clearly, even twice, in their response: "Our position is that traditional principles can allow the use of condoms to prevent death", and again, "Our position is that ... the traditional moral principles (such as lesser evil, material cooperation, gradualism, etc.) justify the use of condoms to prevent life-threatening HIV transmission without compromising Catholic sexual ethics."

It is precisely this assertion that I thoroughly deny. Now, of course, HIV transmission is a delicate and tragic problem, but as the Holy See has pointed out in many forums, condomistic intercourse is neither the therapeutic cure nor the moral solution to this grave problem.

Since all Catholic moralists have to be attentive to first principles, indeed "traditional principles", it is crucial here that we do just that. In attending to the "principles of morality" (the traditional *fontes moralitatis* [*ST*, I-II, q. 18, aa. 2–4]), we should first examine the "moral object" (*finis operis*). What kind of an act in its moral estimation is condomistic intercourse? By its very nature, condomistic intercourse is an intrinsically disordered act of human sexuality.

Even prior to clarifying the personal intention or hoped-for result of the intending subject (*finis operantis*), the first moral determinant in the assessment of the morality of an act is to consider clearly and correctly the *moral object* of that act. This is not only the method and procedure of traditional textbooks, it is the centerpiece of the moral masterpiece of Pope John Paul II, *Veritatis Splendor* (nos. 71–83; especially nos. 74, 76–78).

Of course, the personal *intention* (*finis operantis*) of the acting subject is important—things done for the best of reasons or the worst of reasons can vary widely in moral significance. But the same moral act (condomistic intercourse) for the best of reasons (possible risk reduction) or for the worst of reasons is, by moral definition, always what it is, i.e., condomistic intercourse.

Please excuse the double negative, but the "moral object" (*finis operis*) of the act *cannot not* be intended. If done for a good reason or a bad reason, the moral act of condomistic intercourse does not cease to be the kind of act it is, unless, of course, one chooses to do something else (i.e., another, or different, moral act).

Pope John Paul II points out that a good intention is not enough, because it is the *object* of an act that determines whether or not the act can be "ordered to God" (no. 78). He details this point carefully in *Veritatis Splendor*:

> [R]eason attests that there are objects of the human act which are by their nature "incapable of being ordered" to God, because they radically contradict the good of the person made in his image. These are the acts which, in the Church's moral tradition, have been termed "intrinsically evil" (*intrinsece malum*) on account of their very object, and quite apart from the ulterior intentions of the one acting and the circumstances. (no. 80)

Indeed, the same encyclical specifically repudiates the justification of the intrinsically evil acts by appeal to the so-called lesser evil theory (the explicit claim made in the Fuller-Keenan response):

> Though it is true that sometimes it is lawful to tolerate a lesser moral evil in order to avoid a greater evil or in order to promote a greater

good, it is never lawful, even for the gravest reasons, to do evil that good may come of it (cf. Rom 3:8)—in other words, to intend directly something which of its very nature contradicts the moral order, and which therefore must be judged unworthy of man, even though the intention is to protect or promote the welfare of an individual, of a family or of society in general (*VS*, no. 80, quoting *HV*, no. 14).

If the Fuller-Keenan appeal is to "traditional principles", let us attend both to tradition and to principle. When comparing greater or lesser evils—the comparison must be an equal one, i.e., of the same species. The risk of disease is a *physical* not a *moral* evil, whereas condomistic intercourse is a *moral* evil.

Next, when invoking the so-called lesser evil, what some seem to forget is that the lesser evil is lesser only by comparison with some greater evil. When the lesser and greater evil are of the same kind (moral), the agent inevitably makes moral evil the direct object of his will. This should not be confused or lumped with "double effect", because the double effect analysis requires that moral evil not be the direct object of the will, i.e., not directly intended.

In a prior Q/A column (December 1997), I took some pains to distinguish and separate what traditional moralists do teach about counseling vs. advising the "lesser of two evils". The subtle but careful distinctions of traditional moralists differ greatly from contemporary and proportionalist usage of the "lesser evil" theory. To "advise" or "suggest" evil is to "induce" evil, and there is always scandal in that. Whereas, to "dissuade" another from part of a total evil already decided when the wrongdoer cannot be deterred from the complete wrong can be a good act. Counseling a lesser evil employs an evil act for a good end, whereas advising against part of a proposed evil can be a good act for a good end.[13]

In any case, no explanation of traditional principles holds that the so-called "lesser evil" will *justify* evil "to prevent death" or "to prevent life-threatening HIV transmission". If that were so, then the personal reason or intention of the moral agent would somehow convert (change) the moral species of an intrinsically evil act (condomistic intercourse). Such an alleged conversion would contradict the teaching of *Veritatis Splendor* in a way that is neither traditional nor principled.

[13] Cf. Fr. Ludovico Bender, O.P., *Dictionary of Moral Theology* (Westminster, Md.: Newman Press, 1962), p. 706.

Although the Fuller-Keenan response does not use the term "*proportionalism*", the methodology and logic of their response is proportionalist. The use of condoms is justified by what they presume is a proportionate reason: i.e., "to prevent death" or "to prevent life-threatening HIV transmission". This is the methodology specifically rejected by *Veritatis Splendor*, number 79.

Another attempt to justify condomistic intercourse is their appeal to Father Maurizio Faggioni's invocation of the traditional principle of "double effect". Faggioni, a physician and a moralist, argues that condom use might be justified as long as the "exclusive and primary" *intent* is to defend health and not to prevent pregnancy. This, they claim, is a classic application of the "double effect" in which "one's good *action* has an unintended bad effect" (emphasis added).

However, this as stated clearly confuses one's good intention with one's action. This first condition of the "double effect" analysis requires that the primary action (the cause that has two effects) must itself be morally good or indifferent. Since the primary act here is condomistic intercourse, it is not morally good nor indifferent; indeed, it is an intrinsically disordered act to which the "double effect" analysis cannot apply at all.

Further, mention is made of the principle of "gradualism". Just how traditional a principle that is, is open to review. As taught and explained by John Paul II in *Familiaris Consortio*, there surely is a "law of gradualness"—a step-by-step growth or advance in virtue (no. 34). That is how we all grow in virtue—gradually. But, condomistic intercourse is not virtue, indeed it is the opposite, a vice. On the other hand, in the same *Familiaris Consortio*, the Pope specifically repudiates an alleged "gradualness of law"— "as if there were different degrees or forms of precept in God's law for different individuals or situations" (no. 34). If that is what the respondents mean by "gradualism", that is not a principle at all but rather a novel form of situation ethics.

Finally, the respondents' appeal to *Humanae Vitae*, number 15, about "therapeutic interventions" strikes me as odd since one of the respondents is a physician. Surely no one in medical science or Catholic morals argues that condoms are "therapeutic"! Condoms cure no disease and certainly don't cure HIV/AIDS. The intention may well be what some call "damage control" or so-called "safer sex" with the hope of risk reduction. Even that is partly problematic and not entirely risk-free, but it is in no sense truly therapeutic.

Fathers Fuller and Keenan argue "we are not dissenters", rather they claim to apply centuries-old principles to a critical new question. As above, no moral principle, old or new, will convert (change) an intrinsically disordered act into a morally good one. No analysis—lesser evil, double effect, material cooperation, gradualism—can justify formal evil. In my judgment, the traditional principles they mention are not correctly understood nor correctly applied by them; indeed, I think they are mistaken, and if not proportionalist by name then proportionalist by logic.

As for dissenting, when authors propose as justifiable (as they clearly do regarding condoms) what the Church teaches is not justifiable, surely that is not assenting to Church teaching. I leave to our readers to decide who is dissenting.

—June 2002

# IV

# Justice and Social Order

# 17

# Crime and Punishment

## Punishment versus Revenge

Question: The local newspaper ran a story of a released sex offender out on early parole with all sorts of mandated hours of community service. He volunteered his services for all sorts of parish and social activities. I, with other parents, objected and protested. Others in the parish insist we are un-Christian, saying that love and forgiveness are unrestricted. Some say punishment is only revenge and also un-Christian. An opinion?

Answer: We live in a largely therapeutic society. Very little serious attention is given to objective right and wrong (or guilt or innocence) and their consequences.

Some feel that there are no criminals but only folks who are under-motivated, socially disadvantaged, or probably sick. Excessive fixation on individualistic rights has produced its own myth—the lone individual standing against the omnipotent state—whereas the more common reality is the prematurely free criminal making other citizens fearful.

It is true that both the love and forgiveness of the Lord Jesus was and is unrestricted, as, in a sense, every Christian perfection is. However, that does not mean that just punishment is either irrational or un-Christian. After all, justice too is a virtue with its own requirements, individual and social.

Punitive justice involves distributive and legal justice (sometimes commutative justice also) in the function of restoring the balance of equality upset by a crime.

In conventional Catholic theology, punishment in the strict sense can serve three functions—one looking back, two looking forward.[1]

[1] Cf., e.g., Austin Fagothey, *Right and Reason*, 7th ed. (St. Louis, Mo.: Mosby, 1981), pp. 365–67.

Looking back, punishment has a retributive (remedial) aspect; that is, it pays the criminal back by giving him the crime's just deserts, reestablishes the balance of justice that was upset, and reasserts the authority of the lawgiver as protector and guarantor of the common good. As for the future, punishment can have two forms: if directed to the rehabilitation or improvement of the offender, it is *corrective*; if directed to preventing similar crimes by others, it is *deterrent*.

In the ideal order, a just punishment should fulfill all three functions: retributive—restore the rights of the offended; corrective—rehabilitate the offender; deterrent—forewarn the community at large.

For the injury (crime) done to the individual, the offender is required to make restitution or compensation for the loss inflicted. But that is only part of what justice demands; it only restores things to the way they were before the offense. The state is also responsible for maintaining the order of society and for restoring that order when disrupted. This is an essential aspect of protecting and promoting the common good.

It is this state duty to the common good that is the true basis of the state's right to punish one who violates the just, legal order, together with the duty to try to reform the wayward and deter others from crime. A theistic ethic will view the evil act as a sin against God. But neither the individual offended nor the state can do much about that— true forgiveness is left to God, who is both merciful and just.

As above, our therapeutic society has no great difficulty with the corrective or deterrent aspects of punishment. But some suggest and even argue that the retributive aspect is merely another form of revenge that adds one evil to another and does not overcome evil by good as Scripture teaches.

Revenge, of course, is rightly repudiated because revenge is the emotional pleasure one takes from hurting an enemy. Retributive punishment, however, tries to secure justice, not revenge. It is not adding one moral evil to another, unless one holds that justice itself is not a good.

If punishment were merely corrective or deterrent, the government could inflict penalty on anyone, guilty or not, either to improve that person or deter others from wrongdoing. But for improving or deterring people, the state may only threaten punishment, not inflict it. Well-meant correctives can also be overdone; therapeutic tyrannies are not unheard of.

It is only when a crime has been committed and guilt established that the government can inflict punishment, that is, the use of a good and necessary means to a good end—restoring the disrupted order of society for the common good of all citizens.

Punishment may function as corrective and deterrent in addition to being retributive, but it is guilt, and nothing else, that justifies the infliction of punishment. General quotes from the Bible might sound more generous, even forgiving, but without focus these are more sentimental than rational.

Perhaps the word *retributive* sounds too harsh for our sentimental society and should be replaced by *remedial*. In any case, it is instructive that the *Catechism of the Catholic Church* repeats and presents the same conventional teaching regarding punishment:

> Punishment has the primary aim of redressing the disorder introduced by the offense. When it is willingly accepted by the guilty party, it assumes the value of expiation. Punishment then, in addition to defending public order and protecting people's safety, has a medicinal purpose; as far as possible, it must contribute to the correction of the guilty party (cf. Lk 23:40–43). (no. 2266)

—November 1997

## Restitution for Theft

Question: On two occasions, I have sought guidance on a moral question of restitution in the case of theft. Both times I was puzzled: one priest said he was surprised that I should ask such a question, and the other was more confused than I was. Has the Church changed her teaching on this?

Answer: No, but my experience with students—often graduates of Catholic schools and colleges—is not entirely different from your own. Somehow, religious instruction or catechetical formation seems to have either downplayed this or left it out entirely. Students take avid notes and ask good questions, and some admit, candidly, they are hearing about restitution (its norms, conditions, and excuses) for the first time.

Perhaps, with notable emphasis on social justice and global questions, it may be that teachers don't get around to individual questions of justice and required restitution. Perhaps also some defective moral instruction is so singularly "attitudinal" that some students seem to conclude that that's all one must do—change a bad attitude to a generous attitude. Of course, I can only guess about the cause; but there is no guessing about this teaching of the Church.

The new *Catechism of the Catholic Church* is both clear and concise about this requirement of justice: In virtue of commutative justice, the *reparation of the injustice* committed requires restitution of stolen goods to their owner. The *Catechism* passage begins with recalling Jesus' praise for Zacchaeus' promise that if he had defrauded anyone, he would "restore it fourfold" (Lk 19:8). Likewise, anyone who has, directly or indirectly, taken goods belonging to someone else must return the goods (or if that is not possible, replace them with like goods or the equivalent value in money) plus any "profit or advantages their owner would have legitimately obtained from them". This duty extends to anyone who in some way assisted or benefited from a theft: they too must "make restitution in proportion to their responsibility" (no. 2412).

It is my personal experience not to answer restitution questions off the top of my head, but to consult a reliable textbook, review the pertinent principles, and then propose a just solution to an individual case.

There is, admittedly, a shortage of reliable textbooks, but some are available in English. Karl Peschke's *Christian Ethics* treats restitution, its principles, conditions, and excusing causes.[2] Peschke's is distinctly a European view and in some areas a bit too benign. *Living a Christian Life*, by the American Germain Grisez, also treats restitution and presents the understanding, norms, and conditions with a more realistic appraisal than is found in some of the conventional manuals.[3] Some of these manuals present little more than the most minute and even mistaken minimalism.

—May 1994

---

[2] Karl H. Peschke, *Christian Ethics*, vol. 2 (Alcester, Warwickshire: C. Goodliffe Neale, 1985), pp. 557–70.
[3] Germain Grisez, *Living a Christian Life* (Quincy, Ill.: Franciscan Press, 1993), pp. 444–58.

## Pain and Suffering Settlements

Question: In million—even billion—dollar settlements for pain and suffering, is there a basic justice question here?

Answer: I believe there is, but because of some peculiarities of American law (contingency fees), there is very little written on this question that offers sound guidance.

It is a basic principle of justice that we must render to each what is his due (*cuique suum*). In the case of theft or unjust damage, there is an obligation in justice to make restitution—to restore the thing taken or repair the unjust damage done.

The approved authors then outline principles by which to judge whether the damage done is light or grave. Where there is grave harm (with moral fault), all agree there is a grave obligation to make restitution for the grave harm done. Yet, the conventional authors do state that the gravity of the damage done is measured "by the actual damage done".[4]

At first, injuries in auto accidents and medical malpractice began a trend in very high awards of damages. These have been followed by lawsuits against makers of asbestos, heartburn drugs, and tobacco, to name a few. Now sexual harassment and any kind of sexual abuse can ignite truly high-stakes litigation.

Surely, all can reasonably agree that actual damage would have to include medical bills, necessary counseling, and loss of work or pay. But there is a problem when awarding settlements for additional pain and suffering: some forms of pain are hard to prove and impossible to price.

The textbooks of European origin are not much help to our particular question since contingency fees do not exist there. What exists here is beginning to look like a legal lottery game with paid advertising and built-in incentives: if you win the case, the lawyer wins 30 percent of the prize with you; if you don't win, there's no charge.

---

[4] Cf. Peschke, *Christian Ethics*, vol. 2 (Alcester, Warwickshire: C. Goodliffe Neale, 1993), p. 695; Dominicus M. Prümmer, O.P., *Handbook of Moral Theology* (New York: P.J. Kenedy & Sons, 1949, 1958), p. 140, n. 302; H. Noldin, A. Schmitt, and G. Heinzel, *Summa Theologiae Moralis* (Rauch, 1961), p. 391, n. 431, 3; Henry Davis, S.J., *Moral and Pastoral Theology*, vol. 2, 8th ed. (London, New York: Sheed and Ward, 1959), p. 297.

The big-money lawsuits are not so much aimed at individuals; the tactic seems to be to go after corporate entities and institutions of all kinds (the deep pockets). These big organizations are not, in fact, fair game, because suing them is not free—the cost of everything rises to cover the expenses of protecting against the threat of lawsuits.

I cannot question the right to recover compensation for actual damage, but I do question whether there is a true right in justice to exaggerated awards for claims that can neither be proved nor priced. If this is what tort reform is about, its time has come.

Some states have begun to limit punitive damages; e.g., Florida limits punitive damages to $500,000 or three times the compensation award, whichever is greater. Oregon allocates 60 percent of punitive damages to a state fund for crime victims. But these limitations have driven pain-and-suffering awards even higher. In 1999, a Detroit jury awarded $21 million in a sexual harassment suit. None of that money was for punitive damages (punitive is meant to punish and deter rather than compensate); instead, $1 million was for potential lost earnings and $20 million for pain and suffering.

Mayor Bloomberg states that the annual tort judgments against New York City totaled $557.3 million in 2001. Some of these people are fully responsible for their injuries, as are those who jump in front of subway trains to attempt suicide. If that $560 million were cut in half, the city could hire 5,000 more teachers or firefighters.

Genuine restitution for real harm and actual damage is a right in justice. But it is not at all clear to me that every claim for millions on behalf of alleged pain and suffering is a justice claim; indeed, some at least seem to inflict injustice on the common good.

—December 2002

# 18

# Acting Justly

## Lying in the Catechism

Question: Is it true that in the Latin *Catechism*, the definition of the lie was corrected?

Answer: I am not sure it is so much a correction as a clarification, but it is changed.

First, the original (French) *Catechism* (1992) and the English translation (1994) state in the following in the second sentence of paragraph 2483: "To lie is to speak or act against the truth in order to lead into error someone who has the right to know the truth."

The definitive Latin *Catechism* (1997) modifies this sentence to read: "To lie is to speak or act against the truth in order to lead someone into error" (*Catechismus Catholicae Ecclesiae*, no. 2483).

In effect, this aligns the *Catechism* more completely with the classic definition of Saint Augustine—that lying is speaking against the mind (*locutio contra mentem*) with the intention to deceive (*cum intentione fallendi*).

Thus, the definitive *Catechism* simply drops the qualification of the "right to know". Over time, many Protestant theologians and some Catholic authors included in their definition of lying the violation of the right to the truth. As Karl Peschke points out, "This of course narrows the concept of the lie down in an important regard." The lie is here defined as untruthful speech where the right to the truth of the person addressed is involved. Untruthful speech that does not violate the right to truth is called "false speech" (*falsiloquium*) and not, by that definition, a lie. The *Catechism* can no longer be cited for this alternate opinion.

Peschke accepts the traditional definition of Augustine and provides a useful historical summary of this dispute.[1] Germain Grisez also

---

[1] Cf. Peschke, *Christian Ethics*, vol. 2 (1993), pp. 361–72.

negotiates the problems and challenges of this area in his *Living Christian Life*.[2] Similarly, Benedict Ashley treats the subject in his work, *Living the Truth in Love*, which anticipates this correction in the *Catechism*.[3]

—May 1998

## The Truth about Sick Days

Question: Is there any justice obligation for someone who takes time off work and is paid for sick days when in reality he is quite well? Since some employees are allowed a number of sick days each year, some say this is only lying but not an injustice.

Answer: To my mind, "only lying" never improves any situation. Consider the sober treatment of lying in the *Catechism* (nos. 2482–87). Significantly, the *Catechism* teaches that every offense "against justice and truth entails the duty of reparation" (no. 2487).

Now, it is true that some contracts and employment policies provide for a certain number of sick days; some even provide for personal days. It seems to me that when one claims a sick day when he is quite well he should convert that to a personal day as a form of reparation.

Where the personal day option does not exist, it seems to me this is still a case of fraud and not that of simple lying. Whether or not grave matter is involved would depend upon particular circumstances.

I suppose in theory all are in favor of just and fair labor relations. Their very purpose rests on and should foster just and trusted employer-employee relations. But an attitude of what's mine is mine and what's yours is negotiable will not foster or deepen just and trusted relations. Again, depending on gravity, some form of reparation (open or secret) should be applied.

Your precise question does not seem to be directly addressed in the approved authors. However, I believe that Germain Grisez is correct that legal systems typically, and reasonably, define theft narrowly but as a moral category it should be defined more broadly.[4]

---

[2] Grisez, *Living a Christian Life*, pp. 405–12.

[3] Benedict M. Ashley, O.P., *Living the Truth in Love* (Staten Island, N.Y.: Alba House, 1996), pp. 408–15, see p. 410, n. 145.

[4] Grisez, *Living a Christian Life*, p. 824.

Grisez has the courage to be concrete, arguing that many acts not usually considered theft are theft morally:

> In general, all obtaining of money, goods and services by fraud or unjust coercion involves the same injustice as theft: falsifying something's value in selling it, lying in order to obtain a more favorable contract, taking bribes or kickbacks, padding expense accounts, overstating the hours one has worked, charging for work not done. (p. 825)

Grisez also mentions what few others ever mention, namely, that many employees fail to work steadily and according to the work schedule assigned to them and to which they committed themselves:

> They begin late and quit early, take extra time off for rest periods or meals, socialize excessively during working hours, purposely work more slowly than is reasonable, shirk the work to which they have committed themselves while occupying themselves with other work, and so on. Such practices are a serious waste of time for any worker, and for employees, they are usually a serious injustice to the employer. (p. 759)

While the author notes this can admit of poverty of matter, employees should not measure themselves by a lax standard for personal performance but by a just standard by putting themselves in the employer's place and applying the Golden Rule (p. 759).

The *Catechism*, as a universal document, is less detailed, but it describes as illicit "work poorly done, tax evasion, forging checks and invoices" (no. 2409). Further, "promises must be kept and contracts strictly observed to the extent that commitments made in them are morally just.... All contracts must be agreed to and executed in good faith" (no. 2410). "Without commutative justice, no other form of justice is possible" (no. 2411).

Thus, lying within or about a good faith contract offends both truth and justice.

—March 2000


## Residency Fraud


Question: A parent asked about a public high school student who lives in our urban parish but attends a much better school in a suburban community. The student's aunt does live in that district, and she pays school taxes to that district. She is not the student's legal guardian, and he does not live with her but uses her address. Is this a justice problem and does restitution apply?

Answer: There is a justice question here since it does involve a fraud. What kind of precise civil liability is involved would depend on (1) how the relevant statute reads and (2) what the eligibility standards are.

An avid casuist might suggest that the student live with his aunt four nights of seven, but that would still not be just if the true reason for doing so is not residence but only to access what he has no legal right to obtain. One way or another, some statement or application has to be made or signed about the student's residence, and if the student lives in A, even though his aunt lives in B, a false claim is made which is a fraud.

Thus, the fraud should cease. (Some recent court decisions have come to question the justice or equity of financing public education by property taxes, but it remains for the courts, or better for the voters, to resolve that question, not fraudulent residence claims.)

The restitution question seems less clear. Per capita student costs are not per se standard. Some per capita city costs are quite high (e.g., New York City per capita costs are two or three times higher than per capita parochial school students), yet, the quality of public education offered within the same city can differ greatly even when the per capita cost is said to be the same for all.

There is little question that suburban school taxes paid directly by individual property owners are much higher than what other individuals pay. Indeed, better, or at least more responsive, school districts are often cited as a prime reason for some to move to the suburbs.

If there were a way to determine a standard per capita cost for the given urban district and the given suburban district (presumably the latter would be higher), the difference is what the city dweller is not entitled to. Strict arithmetic might not settle this adequately, since almost every state jurisdiction, and even the federal government, contribute various amounts to varying situations.

As I see it, first, stop the fraud. Next, if there is a civil penalty or a fine, the parents are not bound to report themselves to legal penalty, but neither should they profit from a fraud. They can put the difference in per capita costs in escrow and after a suitable time give it to a pious cause. If a fine or penalty does come, use the escrow to pay it.

—April 1998

## Software and Other Copyrighted Material

Question: When someone buys computer software, there is a license agreement that says when the purchaser opens the program he binds himself to use the program only on one computer at one time. Mailing or loaning the program to others, it says, is prohibited. There is a strong inclination to pass programs around and share with friends, especially those who cannot afford to purchase software for themselves. Are these agreements truly formal contracts? Are they morally binding?

Answer: The "Packard Bell License Agreement" that you sent me is, I think, both standard and typical. It says it is a "legal agreement", on which I have no informed opinion, but it does seem to fulfill what we would call a morally binding agreement, i.e., a good faith contract.

It states that "by opening this sealed disk package, you are agreeing to be bound by the terms of this agreement; if you do not agree to the terms of this agreement, promptly return the unopened disk package and the accompanying items (written materials, binders, etc.) to the place you obtained them for a full refund".

The software license is quite specific in what it grants and does not grant: (1) "Packard Bell grants to you the right to use one copy of the enclosed Microsoft program on a single terminal to a single computer. You may not network the SOFTWARE or otherwise use it on more than one computer or computer terminal at the same time." (2) "COPYRIGHT. The SOFTWARE is owned by Microsoft or its suppliers and is protected by U.S. copyright laws and international treaty provisions."

Thus, the program must be treated as copyrighted material, allowing the purchaser (as it specifically states) to make one copy for backup or archival purposes, or, transfer the SOFTWARE to a single hard disk, keeping the original solely for backup or archival purposes.

In general, copyrights exist to encourage and reward creative (or intellectual) work, and the common moral teaching of the Church is that copyrights protect a just title to ownership. Thus, Catholic teaching supports the concept of genuine work, not only its nobility but also the fruit thereof (*CCC*, no. 2428). When someone steals your car, the theft and loss are obvious, but it is no less theft to steal intellectual work only because the loss is less obvious or hard to calculate.

An available textbook (with which I do not always agree) does state this correctly: "Theft is the *appropriation* of what belongs to another. Since such an appropriation also occurs if a person does not pay his debts, if patents and copyrights are violated, if lost property is unlawfully kept, these offenses are considered equivalent to theft." [5]

Similarly, and certainly more clearly, Germain Grisez states Catholic teaching correctly: "Finally, failure to compensate fairly for the use of others' property or for damage to it also has the character of theft: infringement of patents and copyrights, purchasing goods with the intent of returning them for full credit after having used them, evading liability for accidents, and so on." [6]

It has been my experience that even generally upright people do tend to "cut corners" when money is involved. Grisez provides helpful and needed reminders that "such acts should not too quickly be regarded as light matter".[7]

—March 1995

## Fair Use

Question: Can you respond to the morality of duplicating copyrighted material (books, audio and video recordings, computer programs, etc.) for personal use? I have heard the term "fair use" but have found no solid explanation of what it means.

[5] Peschke, *Christian Ethics*, vol. 2 (1985), p. 551.
[6] Grisez, *Living a Christian Life*, p. 826.
[7] Ibid.

Answer: First, all the examples you cite are not in the same category. So, let's consider the notion of "fair use" and then attempt some applications.

What is at issue here is part of the federal copyright law—Federal Statute 17 USC §107 "Limitations on exclusive rights: Fair Use". The statute states:

> Not withstanding the provisions of sections §106 and §106A, the fair use of a copyrighted work, including such use by reproduction of copies or phono records or by other means specified by that section, for purposes such as criticism, comment, news reporting, teaching (including multiple copies for classroom use), scholarship or research, is not an infringement on copyright. In determining whether the use made of a work in any particular case is a fair use the factors to be considered shall include—(1) the purpose and character of the use, including whether such use is of a commercial nature or is for nonprofit educational purpose; (2) the nature of the copyrighted work; (3) the amount and substantiality of the portion used in relation to the copyrighted work as a whole; and (4) the effect of the use upon the potential market for or value of the copyrighted work.

Informed comment notes that although the courts have considered and ruled upon the fair use doctrine over and over again, no real definition of the concept has ever emerged. Since the doctrine is an equitable rule of reason, no genuinely applicable definition is possible, and each case raises questions that must be decided on its own facts. The courts have evolved a set of criteria which, although not definitive, provide a gauge or scale for balancing the equities.

The "multiple copies for classroom use" is a recognition that, under the proper circumstances of fairness, the doctrine can be applied to reproductions of multiple copies for the members of a class. However, the endless variety of situations and circumstances that can arise in particular cases precludes the formulation of exact rules in the statute. Beyond the broad statutory explanation of what constitutes fair use and some applicable criteria, the courts are free and bound to adapt the doctrine to particular situations on a case-by-case basis.

Your question speaks of personal use while asking about fair use. As to application, your specific mentions present different problems.

Computer programs are quite specific. The software license often comes on a sealed disk package that clearly states that by opening the sealed package you agree to be bound by the terms of agreement. If one does not agree to those terms, promptly return the unopened disk package and the accompanying items for a full refund.

Clearly, the program is treated as copyrighted material, allowing the purchaser to make one copy for backup or archival purposes, to transfer the software to a single hard disk, keeping the original solely for backup or archival purposes. What is clearly wrong is when A buys a program and allows B, C, and D to make their own copies for their personal use. That is simply theft.

Videos [or CDs] of the $19.95 commercial type may, over time, simply wear down or wear out. That's the time to buy another (if available). Some people seem to think that whatever is in their present possession, by that possession, they gain some kind of unending title to it. That is not correct; they do own the copy, but that is not a just title to copyright.

The same is true, I think, for entire musical recordings. When they wear down or wear out, buy another. When you want to record your own bit from this and bit from that for personal use on long drives, I see no wrong in that. Usually, the quality suffers, but it would be wrong to do the same so that you could give or sell copies to others. Generosity with the property of another is not a gift at all.

To duplicate an entire book is probably as impractical as it is dubious. If the book is still in print, buy another or seek out a secondhand purchase. For out-of-print books, I have found that a polite letter of request to the publisher usually elicits a reasonable response.

I offer a particular caution to Church organizations. Some seem to think that if their cause is good and holy (i.e., in the service of God), they are somehow exempt from the laws of God and of men. For complex applications of the laws of man, check with a competent lawyer. For the laws of God (the immorality of theft), no one is exempt, especially those who claim to be in the service of God.

— October 2000

# 19

# Moral Use of Money

## Church Property and Investments

Question: It is often alleged that the Church has vast holdings and that while the Church talks poverty, she and her representatives don't live that way. Are there any norms or guidance in this area?

Answer: In a highly litigious society such as ours, the "vast holdings" seem most often to be the target of opportunity for litigants energized by contingency fees. Often, in fact, "holdings" refer to Church property and buildings that cost more to maintain than they generate in income. Investments, such as they are, have their ups and downs—when down, hospital endowments and scholarships of all kinds can and do suffer.

Nonetheless, I suspect that few things alienate the faithful more quickly or more thoroughly than the twin sins of *luxuria* and *avaritia*. The Catholic faithful do not donate funds to the Church or to religious orders with the hope that the administrators of the same will always outwit the market and invest more shrewdly than investment managers.

Perhaps the administrators of dioceses and orders are themselves convinced that there is no limit to necessary security. For some, you never have enough for a rainy day even where it hardly rains at all. While airtight boundaries may not be legislated in detail, there are general norms for the whole Church to observe.

Canon 1254, section 1, of the *Code of Canon Law* establishes the right of the Church to acquire, retain, administer, and alienate temporal goods in pursuit of "its proper objectives". Section 2 of the same canon details those objectives: to regulate divine worship; support clergy and other ministers; carry out works of the apostolate and of charity, especially for the needy.

The commentary of the Canon Law Society of Great Britain and Ireland provides, I think, good guidance here. It states that canon 1254, section 2, explicates the "proper objectives" of section 1: "They must be emphasized:—the regulation of divine worship, a primary objective;—the support of those engaged in divine worship, a clear corollary;—the carrying out of apostolic works, a necessary consequence; education, care of the sick, missionary endeavors, family programs etc.;—the charitable care of the needy; ...".[1]

While that commentary notes that this list is not exhaustive, it states, I think correctly, "ecclesiastical property which is not in fact devoted to one or other of these purposes is not rightly held, and should therefore be reassigned. The Church is opposed to the accumulation of property, of whatever kind, which serves no purpose other than to provide unnecessary security".[2]

The American commentary correctly notes that this canon (1254) in the 1983 *Code* was specifically revised according to the letter and spirit of the Council (Vatican II, *GS*, no. 88) to avoid "excessive possessiveness" and to forward the conciliar teaching that "the spirit of poverty and of charity are the glory and authentication of the Church of Christ".[3]

Father Raniero Cantalamessa makes a similar point in his book, *Poverty*, that some once summarized the spirit of the old *Code* in matters of poverty as: "[p]rudent management of the economy, wise capitalization and secure bank accounts." This, he says, reduced poverty to individual dependence on superiors in the use of goods and money. The result was a poverty that was individual, not necessarily communal and collective. "Today, on the other hand, everyone would admit that it is wrong to call oneself poor when one belongs to a rich community".[4]

This applies not only to those under solemn vows, but the spirit of poverty and of charity (as virtues) apply to the whole Church. It is for me an iron rule: worldliness among the clergy guarantees disaffection among the laity.

—October 2002

[1] Canon Law Society of Great Britain and Ireland, *The Canon Law: Letter & Spirit* (Collegeville, Minn.: Liturgical Press, 1995), p. 708.

[2] Ibid.

[3] Canon Law Society of America, *New Commentary on the Code of Canon Law* (New York/Mahwah: Paulist Press, 2000), p. 1455.

[4] Fr. Raniero Cantalamessa, O.F.M., *Poverty* (New York: Alba House, 1997), pp. 32–33.

## Penal Law Theory of Taxes

Question: In discussing a tax question with my pastor, he remarked that such obligations (if any) were a matter of "purely penal law". What is this?

Answer: The so-called theory of "purely (or merely) penal law" is, I'm afraid, something more mentioned than studied. The theory is that some laws, just and proper in themselves, do not oblige in conscience to fulfill, but one is obliged in conscience to submit to the penalty imposed for their violation.

The most common argument to support the theory is that today civil legislators do not recognize the obligation of conscience as Catholics conceive it and that legislators may not intend to bind people in conscience. Its advocates do not apply this to all civil laws but most often to traffic laws, hunting and fishing laws, sanitary regulations, and above all, various forms of taxes.

Modern authors in moral theology do not advance or defend this so-called theory of purely penal law because it fails more from the nature of law than the real or imagined intentions of legislators.

It is true that many standard works of moral theology do catalogue the various opinions about penal law and versions of it,[5] but the theory itself is not really justified there. A competent article in the *Catholic Encyclopedia* simply presents the pros and cons of this position.[6]

In short, the theory that argues that a law does not bind but that there is a binding obligation for violating that non-binding law just does not make convincing sense.

1. To say a law does not bind in conscience is tantamount to say it does not bind at all. "Moral obligation" and "obligation in conscience" mean pretty much the same thing. Genuine law is an "ordinance" of reason, an ordinance directive of human activity; suggestions, proposals, advice are simply not true law.

2. So-called penal law theory makes no reasonable provision for just punishment. If there is no obligation to perform the task, refusal to do

[5] E.g., Henry Davis, S.J., *Moral and Pastoral Theology*, vol. 1 (London, New York: Sheed and Ward, 1949), pp. 142–48.

[6] "Civil Law, Moral Obligation of", *New Catholic Encyclopedia*, vol. 3 (New York: McGraw-Hill, 1967), pp. 896–97.

so cannot be sinful; where there is no sin or guilt, punishment seems arbitrary, even unjust.

3. The "intention" of the legislator is not so decisive. The obligation of law does not flow from the attitude of the lawgiver but from the agreement of the law itself with justice and right. As in so many things, an excessive voluntaristic emphasis can have unfortunate consequences.

As above, the "mention" of purely penal law is more frequent than its justification. Years ago, Bernard Haring (in his orthodox phase) argued very much against it.[7] Currently, Karl Peschke argues that the "theory" is largely "abandoned",[8] and John Finnis rather thoroughly repudiates the whole notion of "purely penal law" in his important work *Natural Law and Natural Rights*.[9]

But, as they say, not only does the "memory" linger on, but from what your pastor said, the "mention" lingers on, especially concerning the obligation to pay just taxes. This, I believe, is unfortunate because such mentions can mislead people and help construct erroneous consciences regarding what the Church does positively teach in this regard.

It is true some laws are unjust. It is also true some inequities can exist in the tax code, but rather than invoke a fallen theory to confront these anomalies, it would be better and sounder to embrace the reasoned approach of Germain Grisez in *Living a Christian Life*.[10]

First, Grisez locates the moral ground of both civil authority and civic duty (pp. 851–58). Next, he outlines our basic obligation to obey just laws (embracing the Finnis critique of purely penal law) while admitting unusual circumstances, when even a just law may not be applicable (pp. 874–83). Lastly, Grisez's *ex professo* treatment: "Citizens Ought to Pay Their Taxes" (pp. 894–97) is fully in accord with sound reason and positive Church teaching with regard to both the obligation of the individual and the social teaching of the Church.

---

[7] Cf. Bernard Haring, C.Ss.R., *The Law of Christ*, vol. 1 (Paramus, N.J.: Newman Press, 1961), pp. 270–71.

[8] Karl Peschke, *Christian Ethics*, vol. 1 (Alcester, Warwickshire: C. Goodliffe Neale, 1989), pp. 187–89.

[9] John Finnis, *Natural Law and Natural Rights* (Oxford: Oxford University Press, 1980), pp. 325–42.

[10] Germain Grisez, *Living a Christian Life* (Quincy, Ill.: Franciscan Press, 1993).

To my mind, a cogent teaching of the Second Vatican Council still pertains:

> There are those who, while possessing grand and rather noble senti-
> ments, nevertheless in reality live always as if they cared nothing for
> the needs of society. Many ... even make light of social laws and
> precepts, and do not hesitate to resort to various frauds and decep-
> tions in avoiding *just taxes* or other debts due to society. (*GS*, no. 30,
> emphasis added)

Clearly, the same positive teaching is quite specific in the new *Cat-echism*: "Submission to authority and co-responsibility for the common good make it morally obligatory to pay taxes"(no. 2240); and again, "It is unjust not to pay the social security contributions required by legitimate authority" (no. 2436).

Surely, individual points and questions remain in all of the above, but the proper discussion and resolution of them will not be helped by invoking a fallen and abandoned "theory" of so-called "purely penal law". Other and better approaches are available.

—July 1995

## Basis for Paying Taxes

Question: A prior Q/A repudiated the so-called penal law theory as little more than an excuse to avoid paying taxes. But what is the basis of the obligation to pay taxes?

Answer: It is true a prior Q/A (July 1995) focused on the so-called penal law theory. If we distinguish taxes from fees, licenses, assessments, etc., and by *tax* mean a compulsory contribution to the government imposed in the common interest for the purpose of defraying expenses incurred in carrying out public functions, there is a moral obligation to pay just taxes.

Holy Scripture affirms this obligation. The Gospels record the classic saying of Jesus regarding tribute to Caesar: "Render therefore to Caesar the things that are Caesar's, and to God the things that are God's" (Mt 22:21, with parallels: Mk 12:13–17; Lk 20:20–26). Saint

Paul is even more explicit in Romans: "Pay all of them their dues, taxes to whom taxes are due, revenue to whom revenue is due, respect to whom respect is due, honor to whom honor is due" (13:7).

The early Fathers and Doctors of the Church single out this teaching of Saint Paul and confirm it (e.g., Saint Justin Martyr, *Apologia pro Christianis*, pt. I, c. 17; and later, Saint Thomas Aquinas, *ST*, II-II, q. 87, a. 1).

The teaching of Saint Paul and the early apologists is most instructive since the state to which they were obliged was the same state that was persecuting them. Early Christians were often on the short end of the law, yet they reflected a steady tradition that it was better to suffer evil than to cause evil.

The modern pontifical Magisterium achieved great clarity in the teaching of Pope Pius XII, who clearly taught the duty and obligation of citizens to pay just taxes as their part of bearing the public expense (legal justice), while reminding state officials in promoting and protecting the common good to assess only necessary levies that are proportionate to people's means (distributive justice).

In continuity with this tradition is the explicit teaching of the Second Vatican Council, which I pointed out in my previous column. *Gaudium et Spes* makes it clear that having "grand and ... noble sentiments" is not enough, but that our actions must reflect our concern for "the needs of society". We cannot "make light of social laws and precepts" or "resort to various frauds and deceptions in avoiding *just taxes* or other debts due to society" (no. 30; emphasis added). To my knowledge, this is the first time an ecumenical council taught directly on the issue, and the relevance of that teaching still pertains, especially to those who profess "grand and noble sentiments" while avoiding or ducking true social obligations.

The same positive obligation is repeated in the *Catechism*: "Submission to authority and co-responsibility for the common good make it morally obligatory to pay taxes, to exercise the right to vote, and to defend one's country" (no. 2240).

As an obligation in legal justice, one is free to use all legal means and legal deductions, but the fundamental positive obligation to pay just taxes remains a moral one.

—February 1999

## Church Teaching on Usury Explained

Question: Why is it the *Catechism* does not mention usury? Does the Church still have a teaching on usury?

Answer: It is true that the *Catechism* does not explicitly mention the term *usury*. However, it would not be true to conclude from that non-mention that there is no teaching about or against it.

Because of a long historical controversy, this particular question needs and requires careful distinctions as to what the Church did and did not teach regarding usury. A very concise historical summary can be found in the *New Catholic Encyclopedia*, and another concise explanation is to be found in Germain Grisez's, *Living a Christian Life*.[11]

As Grisez notes that the condemnation of usury by the Church in the past can be misleading. Though looking at history on a superficial level suggests that *usury* referred to what we now call "interest", "money itself no longer is what it once was. Thus, while the Church's teaching of earlier times remains true, today it can be just to charge interest on a loan" ( p. 833).

The sin of usury is not simply the charging of interest on a loan, but charging interest without some just title, without some factor related to the loan that provides a just basis for some fair compensation. In this, the Fifth Lateran Council (1515) explained precisely what is forbidden: "For this is the proper interpretation of usury; when one seeks to acquire gain from the use of a thing which is not fruitful, with no labor, no expense, and no risk on the part of the lender" (DS 1442).

Writing almost forty years ago, in his historical study of the subject, John T. Noonan, Jr., wrote:

Nothing here meets the test of dogma except this assertion, that usury, the act of taking profit on a loan, without a just title, is sinful. Even this dogma is not specifically, formally defined by any pope or council. It is, however, taught by the Tradition of the Church ... This dogmatic teaching remains unchanged. What is a just title, what is technically to be treated as a loan, are matters of debate, positive law and

[11] Cf. T. F. Divine, "Usury", *New Catholic Encyclopedia*, vol. 14 (New York: McGraw-Hill, 1967), pp. 498–500; Grisez's, *Living a Christian Life*, pp. 833–34.

changing evaluation. The development on these points is great. But the pure and narrow dogma is the same today as in 1200.[12]

Perhaps one might have expected some mention of usury in the *Catechism* under the Seventh Commandment, especially in illicit practices mentioned in number 2409, while fair contracts at reasonable interest can be inferred in number 2410. For completion, we should recall, that the same *Catechism* insists: "The common good is always oriented towards the progress of persons: 'The order of things must be subordinate to the order of persons ...' (*GS*, no. 26, §3). This order is founded on truth, built up in justice, and animated by love" (no. 1912).

Thus, I believe it is correct and reliable to conclude with Grisez: "It can be assumed that market rates of interest are usually fair." And still, "In making personal loans to less wealthy people, however, one sometimes should lend at lower than market rates, just as one should moderate other prices, so that one's surplus wealth will be put to use satisfying genuine needs" (p. 834).

—February 1996

## Moral Investments

Question: I have some savings in a mutual fund for retirement. A friend said I should check to see whether I am supporting anti-life or immoral activities. Is there a moral question here?

Answer: There is, I think, a moral question, but a clear moral answer is not immediately obvious in this matter.

The moral question involves some form of "cooperation" (support) in evil. The direct ownership of individual stocks is a clearer target in a clearer picture. If a company is substantially or even significantly involved in immoral products or policies, it seems to me, a serious Catholic should not support nor profit from such things. Surely other options are available without any real loss.

---

[12] John T. Noonan, *The Scholastic Analysis of Usury* (Cambridge, Mass.: Harvard University Press, 1957), p. 400.

Mutual funds, however, are not direct ownership, as I understand it, but are rather shares in holding companies (mutuals) that invest in many businesses of many kinds, some funds with many turnovers. Technically, having shares in a mutual fund holding stocks in many businesses, one does not buy or own a share in any one of those businesses. It is said today that there are numerically more mutual funds than individual stock listings on the New York Stock Exchange.

The moral question of "cooperation" involves both intentionality (agreement/disagreement) and causative participation (assistance, support: how proximate, how remote?). Ownership of minor shares in mutuals holding millions of shares in multiple companies, corporations, or conglomerates does not lend itself to easy arithmetic or even meaningful causality.

The only serious treatment of this precise question that I know of can be found in Germain Grisez's *Difficult Moral Questions*.[13] Before trying to answer the question, Grisez properly reviews some prior questions that touch on the social and ethical responsibilities of wealth and investment in accord with the social teachings of the Church and, in particular, Pope John Paul II's, *Centesimus Annus* (May 1, 1991), number 35.

Grisez proposes as a form of acceptable material cooperation an investment in mutual funds when (1) there is no morally preferable way to meet reasonable needs; (2) there is some reasonable effort to investigate and exclude companies that profit from wrongdoing; (3) one resists the temptation to cooperate formally (by agreement) in any wrongdoing; and (4) one does what one can to inform (write) management to right wrongs that come to your attention. Holding stock in companies whose wrongful activities do not contribute significantly to its profits is questionable but not clearly wrong (p. 503).

Grisez notes that it is probably not feasible for every individual to find out about all the products, policies, and activities of all the businesses in various mutual funds, and where feasible, some funds often change their holdings (p. 506). He notes as well that some funds describe themselves as "socially responsible", but those labels are more often secularist—more concerned with sexual harassment, ecology, secondary smoke, and animal rights than with the destruction of innocent

---

[13] Germain Grisez, *Difficult Moral Questions* (Quincy, Ill.: Franciscan Press, 1997), pp. 502–7, q. 112.

human life or substandard wages for workers. Such "standards" tend more toward political correctness than to any standards in the Old or New Testament.

Even investments in government bonds and bills may not be entirely clean since some tiny portion of them might subsidize some activities no Christian can really approve of.

The complexity and remoteness of the mutual fund investment make it difficult to draw clear lines or truly binding obligations. Thus, the prudential norms offered by Grisez are, I think, about as clear as are available to us.

—February 1998

## Gambling

Question: Why is it that the Church never says anything about the morality of gambling?

Answer: The Church does say and teach some things about gambling. These may not be precisely what you want to hear, but it is not true to say there is no teaching on the morality of gambling.

The *Catechism of the Catholic Church* succinctly presents Catholic teaching this way:

> *Games of chance* (card games, etc.) or *wagers* are not in themselves contrary to justice. They become morally unacceptable when they deprive someone of what is necessary to provide for his needs and those of others. The passion for gambling risks becoming an enslavement. Unfair wagers and cheating at games constitute grave matter, unless the damage inflicted is so slight that the one who suffers it cannot reasonably consider it significant. (no. 2413; emphasis in original)

About one year ago, the Pennsylvania Catholic Conference (PCC) issued "Criteria for Legislation on Gambling", which are both readable and reliable.[14] Those criteria make all the appropriate distinctions: money not needed to support one's family or other just obligations,

---

[14] Cf. *Origins* 24, no. 12 (Sept. 1, 1994): 223–24.

participating freely, revenues not used for any illegal or immoral purpose, games of chance operated fairly.

Gambling itself is morally neutral, but as the PCC correctly points out, issues relating to gambling can make it morally unacceptable. This, I believe, is especially the case with state-sponsored gambling. It is a general principle of social justice that civil government should rely on equitable tax policies and not excessively on tax revenues from gambling. It is here that we may be constructing a nation of gamblers and approaching the risk of enslavement that the *Catechism* repudiates.

Today, state-sponsored gambling is a national pastime with nearly 100 million casino visitors, video gamblers, and sports bettors wagering close to $400 billion, with $40 billion going to the house. Some Native American tribes have become nations of croupiers—often in league with national gambling interests.

Much of this is under the pretense of using the profits primarily to educate children. Often state legislators advance the same fiction: look, people like to gamble anyway, so why not turn the profits into a public benefit like education. When New York first sponsored its state lottery, the presenting reason was benefits for education. This is partly true, but partly a shell game. It is true that the profits of the state lottery go into the education budget, but it's also true that the same amount of general funds is then removed from the education budget for other projects that are definitely noneducational. People were led to believe that this state-sponsored activity would enhance and increase educational funding, while in fact it increases funding for everything but education.

The result is a gambling epidemic. Thanks to the public blessing of gambling by government, the moral stigma has been removed: some high rollers now pretend to be big civic heroes. Advertisements feature overnight millionaires, but never does a loser appear in these ads— apparently it's all winners and no losers! Impossible. What we have here is a state-sanctioned redistribution of wealth—moving money from people who don't have much of it to people who have plenty.

Private, even publicly regulated, gambling is not the central misstep but rather state-sponsored gambling. Well over $30 billion dollars is consumed each year (about half at racetrack betting and the largest part in state lotteries). That is more than the gross national product of some countries. Nothing is for nothing. Crime is always only a block away from gambling, and some legislators always seem to get caught up in sweetheart deals for arranging enabling legislation to expand gambling even further.

The *Catechism* is quite correct to warn about enslavement. The budgets of several states are now at risk without gambling revenues—they are enslaved to it and by it, and so are we.

—December 1995

# 20

# Defending the Family

## Definition of Family

Question: Is there a reliable Catholic definition of *family* that has not been mugged by political correctness?

Answer: Yes, I believe there is a correct definition in the *Catechism*: "A man and woman united in marriage, together with their children, form a family. This institution is prior to any recognition by public authority, which has an obligation to recognize it. It should be considered the normal reference point by which the different forms of family relationship are to be evaluated" (no. 2202).

This classic and traditional definition is both simple and straightforward. It also has the advantage of pointing out that the family is a natural institution with natural rights that are antecedent to any political authority.

Thus, this family is not the product of the state nor should it have to seek recognition from the state as if begging for a favor. Rather the opposite is true. It is the duty, not the privilege, of public authority to promote and protect the family.

This is not just the *Catechism*; the Second Vatican Council clearly taught the same doctrine: "Public authority should regard it as a sacred duty to recognize, protect and promote their [marriage and family's] authentic nature, to shield public morality, and to favor the prosperity of home life" (*GS*, no. 52).

—April 2004

## Same-Sex Unions

Question: The Massachusetts Supreme Court has instructed the Massachusetts Legislature to draw up legislation for "same-sex marriage". Where did this come from?

Answer: It is difficult to believe that over two hundred years of American legal history and over two thousand years of Judeo-Christian moral history could, by the single vote of one unelected judge, convert a social standard into a "prejudice". Such is the editorial judgment of the *New York Times*: "The ban is simply about prejudice, the court concluded, much like the state laws barring interracial marriage, which lasted until 1967, when the Supreme Court struck them down in *Loving v. Virginia*." [1] To equate racial differences with sex differences in regards to marriage reveals a lack of understanding about the definition of marriage.

First, note the words. The *Times* editorial was titled "A Victory for Gay Marriage". I prefer the term *same-sex union*. I have the same verbal reservations about so-called gay rights. Since homosexual acts are, by definition, moral wrongs (*CCC*, no. 2357), there cannot be a moral right to do them. No one has a right to do what is wrong. But, if you keep talking about rights long enough, you might come to think a wrong is right because you call it such.

Thus far, this seems to be quibbling over words, but if we have learned anything from the past few decades of pro-life activities, we should have learned that words count. Words are tactics, and the words we use to *describe* a thing come in time to affect how we *think* about a thing and ultimately how we act about things. The movement for same-sex unions is a battle for public approval (legal sanction), and the public should not approve of nonmarital marriage. The argument is not a pedantic one about correct etymology; the point is to avoid sliding into nihilism.

The legalization of same-sex unions *seems* to have come suddenly out of nowhere—in North America: a Massachusetts court case, a Vermont statute, and legal recognition in two Canadian Provinces. In Europe, the Netherlands and Belgium now recognize same-sex unions. But, the normalization of homosexuality is the result of a long-term

---

[1] "A Victory for Gay Marriage", *New York Times*, Nov. 20, 2003, p. A30.

mass-marketing effort to frame what is discussed in the public arena and how it is discussed.[2]

One three-part strategy is to desensitize, jam, and convert the American public. Desensitizing is inundating the public with pro-homosexual advertising, articles, and shows in the least offensive fashion and talking about gayness until the issue becomes thoroughly tiresome. If you can get the straights to think homosexuality is just another choice or thing (like any other choice or thing), the battle for extra legal rights is virtually over.

Jamming is verbal terrorism meant to silence expression of or any support for dissenting opinion. This can take the form of hardball, e.g., preventing a retiring NFL player from being football commentator or Dr. Laura Schlessinger from airing a new television show.

A softer approach is to claim that famous historical figures were homosexual and put forward positive images of famous contemporary homosexuals. The negative variant of this tactic is to portray all critics as victimizers, linking them with nasty Klansmen, backwoods preachers, menacing punks, and, when all else fails, Nazi concentration camps.

It is now a media standard to lump religious opponents of homosexuality with Nazi types (who persecuted some homosexuals) and then squeeze them into making declarations of civility toward homosexuals that contribute to the fiction that they need more and extra rights than the rest of us.

All of this desensitizing and jamming ultimately aims at converting— not converting straights into gays, but converting the average American's mind, will, and emotions to acceptance and tolerance of homosexuals and associations with them in good fellowship. The conversion is a conversion of standards: i.e., there is no right and wrong here, just different strokes for different folks. And, of course, we are all different folks.

Some might think the whole culture war is overstated or nonexistent. I do not. And one reason I don't think it is overstated is the sheer numbers. How could such a small numerical minority of homosexuals possibly overturn the moral and legal standards of centuries?

The precise number or percentage of active homosexuals in the general population is not easy to come by. There is no serious scientific support for the Kinsey claims in 1948 that 10 percent of Americans are

[2] Cf. an insightful law review article by Paul E. Rondeau, "Selling Homosexuality to America", *Regent University Law Review* 14 (2002): 443–87.

homosexual. Respected studies by the National Opinion Research Center at the University of Chicago (1993) suggest that between 2 and 3 percent of the male population and 1 and 2 percent of the female population in America are homosexual.[3]

If the true figure is about 3 percent of the general population, it seems to me a near cultural impossibility that the standards and convictions of 97 percent of the population could be overturned and set aside without a massive, persistent (and successful) media and marketing campaign.

The real question is about the true nature of marriage—stable heterosexual marriage and family life that is the basic building block of every viable society, including our American society—and the reason why same-sex union is not marriage and should not be called such. The present *Code of Canon Law* correctly defines marriage as a "matrimonial covenant" by which "a man and woman" establish a partnership of their whole life which of its nature is ordered to the well-being of the spouses and to the procreation and upbringing of children (can. 1055, §1, and also *CCC*, no. 2363).

Obviously, a same-sex union has nothing to do with procreation; same-sex human procreation is a physical and human impossibility.

Similarly, a same-sex union is not truly unitive sex "ordered to the well-being of the spouses" (here, partners) because this exercise of sexuality is not a "gift of self" to the other but rather and simply masturbatory sex, a gift (if you will) of self to same self. Thus, the use of words "*love*" (love that is not marital) or "*lovers*" here is quite misleading and simply not true.

Same-sex expression—be it oral, anal, or manual—is not and cannot be marital love since the complementary, unitive dimension of human sexuality is absent. Masturbatory sex is not self-giving; it is, perhaps, self-getting and, in truth, it is self-indulgent lust. Galatians 5:24 is addressed to all Christians: "And those who belong to Christ Jesus have crucified the flesh with its passion and desires" ("*cum vitiis et concupiscentiis*" in the Vulgate).

Now, either Saint Paul, under the inspiration of the Holy Spirit, has it right or, the whole of Christian tradition has it wrong. Masturbatory

---

[3] Michael B. Flanagan, M.D., cites Census Bureau data for the Center for Disease Control with the same range: 2 to 3 percent, in "The Medical Abnormality of Homosexuality", *Linacre Quarterly* 70, no. 3 (Aug. 2003): 242.

sex is not truly unitive or procreative, and that is what the *Catechism* teaches about chastity and homosexuality (no. 2357). This fundamental teaching of the Church "is based on the inseparable connection, established by God, which man on his own initiative may not break, between the unitive significance and the procreative significance which are both inherent to the marriage act" (*HV*, no. 12; *FC*, no. 32; cf. *CCC*, no. 2366).

This unitive-procreative connection is the very meaning of human sexuality. Every misuse of human sexuality somehow tries, most often artificially, to separate and/or suppress one of these goods, allegedly for the sake of the other. Artificial reproduction removes the unitive good for the procreative, whereas contraception and sterilization chemically suppress or surgically remove the procreative good for the unitive. However, masturbation is neither unitive nor procreative and thus can never be marital. Any love that does not transcend itself is not worthy of the name *love*.

To advance legal claims, legal benefits, or arrangements to make same-sex unions supposedly stable does not change in nature or reality what this activity is. It is what it is; indeed, it cannot help but be what it is, and surely it is not marital.

Given reports of episodic or even grossly promiscuous sexual contacts between or among younger homosexual males, I find it difficult to accept that the whole homosexual community is clamoring for the legal permanence associated with exclusive, stable marriage.

Ours is a pluralist society, but we have only one civil law. Civil law in our society conveys approval or at least social sanction. Any society that sees no need to defend the worth and place of stable marriage and family life is perhaps a society not worth defending. But, it is worth it, and we must defend true marriage and resist distortions of it.

—January 2004

## Opinion on Same-sex Unions Challenged

Question: Your January column on same-sex unions borders on the hysterical, e.g., "The point is to avoid sliding into nihilism." Surely, a modest expansion of legal benefits to some is not "sliding into nihilism"?

**Answer:** On the contrary, I mean it quite literally. The real argument is not just debating points about legal benefits; rather, the core issue is the nature and reality of true marriage. Stable heterosexual marriage and family life are essential to society and its continuation. I don't give or take that as a sectarian polemic, it is, rather, a non-negotiable fact of life and of history. There is no straw man to knock down here because there is no alternate society to review or critique. It has not, does not, and cannot exist because it is unreal.

I will not repeat the points of the January Q/A column: the caution about words (call it *union* not *marriage*); the real percentage of the population pushing for this; and the amazing media achievement that homosexual union is somehow a civil rights issue.

In a legal sense, of course, homosexuals (as adult citizens) are free to marry; like other citizens they can and do enjoy the equal protection of our civil laws. However, the advocates of same-sex unions do not want what society, history, and reality offer as marriage (union between a man and a woman). Rather, they want and advocate their own invention (same-sex union) and demand that society sanction their wants in law under the banner of equal protection.

When someone does not want—indeed rejects—some social benefit, one cannot reasonably claim the unjust denial of that benefit. Equal protection is not violated when someone rejects what society does offer while demanding what society does not offer. There is no injustice in that; indeed the opposite is an unjust claim.

This is an ultimate and radical form of absolute individual autonomy. It is, if you will, absolute autonomy of individual subjective conscience. If, for the sake of discussion, you grant that this conscience claim is sincere, that does not settle or sanction the truth of the matter.

While I can respect the personal dignity of everyone who makes any conscience claim, that does not settle or guarantee the *truth* of that claim. Any erroneous conscience judgment may be sincere, but it is and remains erroneous, even if sincerely erroneous. By all means, we should concede all civil rights to erroneous persons, but that concession belongs to them as persons not because their views or judgments are erroneous or mistaken.

If rights are generated or founded merely on subjective conviction, get yourself ready for a long and strange parade of "rights". All sorts of people are subjectively convinced of all sorts of things, but mere subjective conviction does not establish a true right to do all things.

Once we separate freedom from truth or judgment from truth, we are knocking on the door of nihilism. If truth does not matter (as in true marriage), then there can be as many arrangements as creative minds can construct or invent.

Absolute autonomy has pretty much mugged what is left of medical ethics in this country. The now-famous dictum of Justice Anthony Kennedy in *Planned Parenthood v. Casey* (1992) now passes for legal wisdom in some circles: "At the heart of liberty is the right to define your own concept of existence, of meaning, of the universe arid of the mystery of life."

If the heart of liberty is the right to define your own universe, then at least that Supreme Court justice has already enshrined same-sex union as a right. A tired cheap shot at medieval theologians was their alleged pursuit of how many angels they could stack on the head of a pin. Angelic zip codes are of little interest today, but some of our leading legal lights do seem determined to see how many rights they can stack on the head of a pin.

As above, genuine rights, especially civil and human rights, are worthy of and demand the respect of all. But rights are based on real relationships, especially their relation to the truth. Erroneous persons must be respected *as persons*, but erroneous judgments or false claims that do not respect the truth (indeed, contradict it) do not generate or validate genuine rights.

In the January Q/A column, I relied primarily on the traditional definition of true marriage as found in the *Code of Canon Law* (can. 1055, §1) and the *Catechism of the Catholic Church* (no. 1601). On this precise point (i.e., civil legislation and same-sex unions), the universal Church (CDF) and the national hierarchy (USCCB) have both taught recently and relevantly.

On June 3, 2003, the CDF published "Considerations regarding Proposals to Give Legal Recognition to Unions between Homosexual Persons". This CDF document has four brief components with eleven numbered points.

As above, the primary and pervasive point is the true "Nature of Marriage" and "Its Inalienable Characteristics" (part 1). Rooted in God's revelation, it states the obvious: "In the Creator's plan, sexual complementarity and fruitfulness belong to the very nature of marriage" (no. 3).

Further, it affirms: "Marriage is holy, while homosexual acts go against the natural moral law" (no. 4). Arguments against the legal recognition of homosexual unions are then presented from right reason (no. 6), from the biological and anthropological order (no. 7), from the social order (no. 8), and from the legal order (no. 9). The last part and point addresses Catholic politicians with regard to legislation in favor of homosexual unions: "[T]he Catholic law-maker has a moral duty to express his opposition clearly and publicly and to vote against it. To vote in favour of a law so harmful to the common good is gravely immoral" (no. 10).

It concludes:

> The common good requires that laws recognize, promote and protect marriage as the basis of the family, the primary unit of society. Legal recognition of homosexual unions or placing them on the same level as marriage would mean not only the approval of deviant behavior, with the consequence of making it a model in present-day society, but would also obscure basic values which belong to the common inheritance of humanity. (no. 11)

This CDF document should not be seen as an isolated response to or an anticipation of local movements in the United States. It is rather a formal and universal teaching in response to novel and immoral legislative proposals that first came out of the European Parliament beginning in the early 1990s.

In a similar, but less formal fashion, the most recent plenary meeting of the U.S. Conference of Catholic Bishops issued a teaching document on the same subject: "Between Man and Woman: Questions and Answers about Marriage and Same-Sex Unions" (November 11, 2003).

The questions and answers are concretely instructive: (1) What is marriage? (2) What does the Faith teach about marriage? (3) Why marriage can only exist between a man and a woman? (4) Why is same-sex union not the equivalent of marriage? (5) What is the social importance of preserving the exclusive union of man and woman? (6) Is denying marriage to homosexual couples unjust discrimination? (7) Are same-sex couples entitled to the same social and economic benefits as married couples? (8) What should Catholics do?

This teaching document provides good, concrete guidance. True, it does not warn about nihilism, but if the worthwhile goods and goals it defends are lost, the sad net result is certainly social nihilism.

—May 2004

## Adoption by Homosexuals

Question: We have a local controversy in print. The pastor of one local parish has stated that the child of a same-sex couple will not be admitted to the Catholic school, whereas the pastor of another parish says it's not a problem, and children should not be punished for the faults of others. Any comment on this?

Answer: In a previous Q/A column (May 1996),[4] I proposed that an inquiring pastor should not baptize a child in his parish presented by a lesbian couple who had adopted the child, because there was no reasonable hope that the child would be raised Catholic. In response to that question I quoted the stated position of Pope John Paul II (Angelus address, [February 20, 1994]) regarding homosexual adoption.

In a more recent and formal way, the Congregation for the Doctrine of the Faith issued the doctrinal instruction "Considerations regarding Proposals to Give Legal Recognition to Unions between Homosexual Persons".

While this CDF instruction does not directly address the school question, it does address and reject the adoption question, which is at the root of the school problem. In presenting arguments from right reason against legal recognition of homosexual unions, the CDF teaches:

> As experience has shown, the absence of sexual complementarity in these unions creates obstacles to the normal development of children who would be placed in the care of such persons. They would be deprived of the experience of either fatherhood or motherhood. Allowing children to be adopted by persons living in such unions would actually mean doing violence to these children, in the sense that their condition of dependency would be used to place them in an environment that is not conducive to their full human development. This is gravely immoral and in open contradiction to the principle, recognized also in the United Nations Convention on the Rights of the Child, that the best interests of the child as the weaker and more vulnerable party, are to be the paramount consideration in every case. (no. 7)

Now, it may well be that there is a different challenge in different situations, e.g., the case of first applying for admission to parochial

4 See pp. 279–81 below.

school, as apart from a student or students already admitted (knowingly or unknowingly).

Some might try and frame this question in terms of permissible or impermissible cooperation in homosexual adoption or homosexual parenting. I would not frame this in terms of moral cooperation but rather in terms of theological scandal and contradictory witness.

Catholic education rests on and is rooted in parental rights. It is not accidental but essential to insist on and cultivate parental involvement in Catholic education. Parent-teacher association is both desirable and necessary. Parental involvement in sacramental preparation is now a universal feature in Catholic education.

I doubt that any pastor or Catholic school principal wants to be confronted with an immoral arrangement of which neither that school nor the Church can approve. It seems to me most unwise to admit a child or children to a Catholic school with the droll requirement that the couple that sends the child may not and should not attend (as a couple) any parental meetings, groups, or sacramental preparation programs. It seems to me that couple could and would cause scandal. If same-sex couples were afforded the same status as true parents, would not the Catholic school and parish be sending a message of counter-witness?

Some might argue that not all the parents of all our Catholic school children are truly married. Of course, this is true of those who are canonically in irregular situations. But, most of these situations remain private. And even when they are known publically, they are, at least potentially, open to some canonical resolution when and if some circumstance or obstacle changes. Same-sex unions can hardly be hidden, and objectively such unions will never be open to canonical or moral acceptance no matter what the circumstances.

Unlike the doctrine of unanticipated consequences, I suppose these unfortunate consequences could have been anticipated but were not. As little as ten years ago, same-sex unions were not a pressing issue. Now they are. Then came same-sex adoption and now difficulties in schools and parishes.

Personally, I would not like to see any Catholic child deprived of a Catholic education, especially in a Catholic school. I remain convinced that when the school, the home, and the parish all teach and witness the same true values, there exists the best possibility for sound moral education. However, when what is taught in church and school is contradicted in life and the home environment by objectively immoral circumstances, that does not support consistent witness but rather counter-witness. Thus, if I were the pastor of the parish school, I would first avoid this situation by preventing it and restrict it as much as possible where I found it in place ahead of me.

—March 2005

## Gender Equity in the Military

Question: I read in the *Washington Times* and the *Washington Post* that you think male and female officers should not work together lest it constitute an occasion of sin. Isn't that a bit dated?

Answer: Everything I write is dated. I don't know what the *Washington Times* or *Post* reported, but I did offer an opinion not on the generalities of the workplace but on a highly specific and most unusual situation.

My part in this was quite modest and limited. But the points at issue are shared by seasoned veterans of military service: Archbishop Edwin F. O'Brien of the Archdiocese for Military Services and John Cardinal O'Connor, Archbishop of New York and former chief of chaplains.[5] To the amazement of many, the U.S. Air Force seems unwilling to make a reasonable accommodation within their long and rich tradition of reasonable religious accommodations.

The facts are these, as I understand them. Lieutenant Ryan Berry, a recent West Point graduate, is a married Catholic officer with one child. He serves now with the Air Force in Minot, North Dakota.

Part of this involves service in a missile crew in a small underground capsule (bunker) in shifts of 24 or 48 continuous hours. The bunker is small—about the size of a yellow school bus, and when you subtract the space for controls, machines, and computers, the remaining open space is about the size of an aisle in a school bus. These are tight quarters by any definition.

[5] Cf. "Lt. Berry's Moral Integrity", *Catholic New York* 18, no. 44 (July 29, 1999): 5.

During these 24- or 48-hour continuous shifts, only one crew member is needed to work the controls, so a work-sleep schedule is made with a single bed and bath separated by a privacy curtain.

When first assigned, Lieutenant Berry sought religious counsel and support that he not be assigned with a female officer in such close quarters sharing one bed and bath. This was not a refusal to serve in the field or fly with female officers, nor was it a refusal of any other professional assignment: it was only this peculiar, single-quarters, common-bed-and-bath reality he declined.

At first, the Air Force honored his request, but in time someone decided that this accommodation offended gender-integrated activity and gender equity, which seems to be a value so high up in the military code that no accommodations can be permitted.

It was when Lieutenant Berry's accommodation was revoked that a mutual friend asked me to offer some points of Catholic morality since some stated that Lieutenant Berry's position was based perhaps on some "private" biblical understandings and not based on Catholic doctrine.

The points I offered then (April 1999), I offer here. At least two points of Catholic moral teaching converge here: one is the generic question of "scandal" (cf. *CCC*, nos. 2284–87) with particular focus on occasions of sin; and the second a well-formed Catholic conscience (*CCC*, nos. 1776–802).

A contemporary Catholic moralist correctly teaches—to overcome sin, its occasions must be avoided:

> Occasions of sin are situations or actions which in some way conduce to a temptation to sin and which can be avoided or modified so that the temptation will be less likely and/or more easily resisted. Charity toward God, whom sin offends, as well as toward oneself and one's neighbor, whom sin harms, requires avoiding sin, and so requires the use of appropriate means to avoid it.[6]

The same author states: "Work on occasions of sin is a strict and grave moral obligation."[7]

Now, every conscience claim does not automatically validate itself simply because it is so claimed. Rather, that judgment of conscience has to be made in accord with some true standard of true teaching.

---

[6] Germain Grisez, *Living a Christian Life* (Quincy, Ill.: Franciscan Press, 1993), p. 221.
[7] Ibid., p. 775.

When this is so, a Catholic can be said to have a correct Catholic conscience.

It seems to me the crux of the question is *not* working with a female soldier, nor flying with one, nor any other field or office assignment. Rather, the difficulty is almost living with (albeit temporarily) a female soldier. I presume neither enlisted personnel nor officers in the Armed Services share sleeping and bathroom quarters in such intimate proximity, i.e., the same room at the same time.

I would be surprised if an observant Orthodox Jew or a devout Muslim did not raise the same objection.

Concerning "occasions of sin" in the Catholic understanding, especially "proximate occasions"—that we are bound to avoid—there can be some range in judgment since occasions can be "absolute" or "relative" (from the point of view of the person) as they can be "voluntary" or "necessary" (from the point of view of the cause).

It does seem to me that a situation with such intimately proximate bed-and-bath facilities is closer to the absolute occasion rather than a relative one. Such arrangements for 24 or 48 continuous hours seem to me to offend common sense—and basic Christian standards of scandal—not only what is evil but has the appearance of evil and is likely to be a stumbling block for others.

It seems to me a serious and sober Catholic, after thoughtful prayer and religious counsel, could reasonably and rightly claim that his well-formed conscience does not permit knowing participation in such unusual, if not unique, circumstances.

To me, it is not scrupulous but rather prudent that an observant Catholic would choose conscientiously not to be placed in such a strange circumstance.

— November 1999

# 21

# Catholic Civics

## *Principle of Subsidiarity*

Question: Is the principle of subsidiarity still a part of the Church's social and moral teaching? I ask because whenever an elected official calls for program reform or spending cuts, some Church official (often from the USCC) announces that society has taken on a nasty and brutish tone, is canonizing Social Darwinism, and that is contrary to Church teaching.

Answer: It is neither my place nor competence to endorse or oppose "reforms" without qualification. It seems to me that each proposal should be examined on its merits as to justice, fairness, and reasonableness. But surely, some part of that reasonable examination must include the principle of subsidiarity.

Yes, "subsidiarity" is, and has long been, a part of authentic Church teaching. The new *Catechism* states its nature and importance concisely. It begins by asserting that socialization includes certain dangers, namely, threats to "personal freedom and initiative" if state intervention becomes "excessive". Then it quotes John Paul II's explanation of the Church's principle of *subsidiarity*: "[A] community of a higher order should not interfere in the internal life of a community of a lower order, depriving the latter of its functions, but rather should support it in case of need and help to co-ordinate its activity with the activities of the rest of society, always with a view to the common good" (*Centesimus Annus*, no. 48, §4).

The *Catechism* description of subsidiarity continues:

> God has not willed to reserve to himself all exercise of power. He entrusts to every creature the functions it is capable of performing, according to

the capacities of its own nature. This mode of governance ought to be followed in social life. The way God acts in governing the world, which bears witness to such great regard for human freedom, should inspire the wisdom of those who govern human communities. They should behave as ministers of divine providence.

The principle of subsidiarity is opposed to all forms of collectivism. It sets limits for state intervention. It aims at harmonizing the relationships between individuals and societies. It tends toward the establishment of true international order. (*CCC*, nos. 1883–85)

You will note in the above that the definition of "*subsidiarity*" is from number 48 of the encyclical *Centesimus Annus* of Pope John Paul II. The rest of the same paragraph from the same encyclical is most instructive not only for officials of the state but also of the Church:

By intervening directly and depriving society of its responsibility, the Social Assistance State leads to a loss of human energies and an inordinate increase of public agencies, which are dominated more by bureaucratic ways of thinking than by concern for serving their clients, and which are accompanied by an enormous increase in spending. In fact, it would appear that needs are best understood and satisfied by the people who are closest to them and who act as neighbors to those in need. (no. 48)

There is, at least, a double insight here: inordinate growth of agencies with their bureaucratic thinking and enormous spending. However pertinent to the state, the same insights could well apply to some in our own Church, which could be why bureaucrats of Church-OR-State so often use the same code words: "nasty", "brutish", "Social Darwinism". Why? Because some are dominated more by bureaucratic ways of thinking than by concern for serving their clients (their parishioners—if any).

I was ordained (1966) shortly after the completion of Vatican Council II, which ended in December 1965. At that time, there was an explosion, more properly a construction, a veritable pentagon of committees and commissions to implement the Council in every diocese and on the national level as well.

Surely, now, almost thirty years after the Council, most of the Council has been implemented: all seven sacraments have been reformed; the Church's universal law has been re-codified, and the true teaching of the Council has been faithfully conveyed in the *Catechism of the Catholic Church*.

Yet, the committees and commissions of implementation never come to closure but seem only to expand, as do their mailings, meetings, directives, conferences, directors, coordinators, and associations of the same—often in triplicate—on the diocesan, regional, and national level. "Renew" itself has become a permanent growth industry. Surely, no one questions the basic priorities and necessity of worship, education, and charity. But has not the time come, indeed long past, when the inordinate increase of ecclesiastical agencies, "dominated ... by bureaucratic ways of thinking" and "accompanied by an enormous increases in spending", be examined precisely in light of the principle of subsidiarity?

Consider, for example, the greatly expanded national agencies and associations of the Church in this country. The Kenedy Directory of 1966 lists the National Catholic Welfare Council—its board, departments, committees, and associations on three and a quarter pages (pp. 11–14). The same Kenedy Directory for 1994 lists "National Organizations" over thirteen pages of much smaller print (pp. lxxxii–xciv).

Nor is this simply an American phenomenon. Cardinal Ratzinger has stated:

> Just think, in the Munich archbishopric we had 400 staff members and employees, all regularly paid. Now, it is known that because of its nature every office must justify its existence by producing documents, organizing meetings, planning new structures. To be sure, all had the best intentions. But it has often enough happened that the parish priests have felt more burdened than sustained by the quantity of "auxiliaries".[1]

The same Cardinal Prefect notes that while he had a staff of four hundred in Munich, the "doctrinal section" of the Congregation in Rome "does not number more than about 10 persons".[2]

Perhaps one reason we hear so little about subsidiarity from certain voices in the Church is that it is so little practiced in the Church. *Pro dolor!*

—May 1995

---

[1] Joseph Cardinal Ratzinger, *The Ratzinger Report* (San Francisco: Ignatius Press, 1985), p. 66.
[2] Ibid., p. 68.

## Less-than-Perfect Legislation

Question: Is it not true that your predecessor, Father Joseph Farraher, S.J., once wrote a Q/A column that argued the possibility that
a conscientious legislator could support less-than-perfect legislation that
did restrict abortion while not eliminating it entirely?

Answer: Yes, Father Farraher did write a carefully constructed and
correct column to that effect (November 1990). His column provoked
some scorn from a few and one most unfair accusation of his being a
schismatic dissenter.

At the request of the editor, Father Kenneth Baker, S.J., I wrote a
letter to *HPR* in support of Father Farraher's position, citing the published teaching of Cardinal Édouard Gagnon, Cardinal John O'Connor,
and Bishop John Myers.[3]

To that distinguished line of fine Catholic churchmen, I am pleased
now to add the welcome teaching of Pope John Paul II in his latest
encyclical, *Evangelium Vitae*, both as tribute to Father Farraher and
as of interest to the readers of *HPR*. First the Holy Father makes it
clear that one can never licitly obey "an intrinsically unjust law, such
as a law permitting abortion or euthanasia" or, quoting the Congregation for the Doctrine of the Faith, to "take part in a propaganda
campaign in favor of such a law, or vote for it" (*Declaration on Procured Abortion*, no. 22). However, a legislator may vote for a "more
restrictive law", such as one "aimed at limiting the number of authorized abortions":

> [W]hen it is not possible to overturn or completely abrogate a pro-
> abortion law, an elected official, whose absolute personal opposition
> to procured abortion was well known, could licitly support proposals
> aimed at *limiting the harm* done by such a law and at lessening its
> negative consequences at the level of general opinion and public moral-
> ity. This does not in fact represent an illicit cooperation with an unjust

[3] Cardinal Édouard Gagnon, Letter to Paul Weyrich, *Origins* 17, no. 9 (July 30, 1987):
148; Cardinal John O'Connor, "Abortion: Questions and Answers", [*Catholic New York*,
June 14, 1990], *Origins* 20, no. 7 (June 28, 1990): 107; and Bishop John Myers, "The
Obligations of Catholics and the Rights of Unborn Children", *Origins* 70, no. 20 (June
14, 1990): 69 [also available at the Roman Catholic Archdiocese of Newark website:
http://www.rcan.org/archbish/jjm_letters/rightsunborn6-90.htm].

law, but rather a legitimate and proper attempt to limit its evil aspects. (no. 73)

—August 1995

## Pro-abortion Catholic Lawmakers

Question: Some Catholics in Congress have supported abortion and its financing. Have they excommunicated themselves from the Church? If not, why not? Can a Catholic constituent do anything to join the issue canonically?

Answer: Certainly, many Catholic politicians have hidden behind the deceit of "I am personally opposed to abortion, but ..." By now, all pro-lifers and political observers know that this is not personal opposition at all, because their actual voting record never opposes but always proposes and expands the financing and practice of abortion, even to the point of safeguarding legal late-term abortion.

To me, this is a scandal to the faith and is radically inconsistent with being a practicing Catholic. It is not, however, an automatic excommunication.

Scandal, of course, is sinful and in some cases gravely sinful. However, the canonical penalty of excommunication is carefully delineated in Church law and purposely limited in application. In fact, it is a general principle of canon law that penalties of law and the restriction of rights are to be interpreted strictly (can. 18), that is, narrowly. It is a traditional rule: favorable understandings are amplified (*favorabilia amplianda*); harmful ones narrowed (*odiosa restringenda*).

Now, it is true that one of the few automatic excommunications in the new *Code* is the abortion canon: "[O]ne who actually procures an abortion, where the effect follows, incurs a *latae sententiae* excommunication" (can. 1398). *Latae sententiae* means "automatic"—you do it, you got it.

By extension, the same penalty of excommunication applies to *necessary* cooperators in actual abortions—that is, those without whose help (*sine eorum opera*) the crime (abortion) would not have been committed (can. 1329, §2). Cooperators include those who help, assist, promote, encourage, even praise abortion, but the only cooperators penalized by this canon are those "without whose assistance" the abortion would not be done.

The Congress did not legalize abortion; the Supreme Court did that (January 22, 1973) by evacuating all the states' criminal laws against abortion. In fact, the Congress rarely votes up-or-down on abortion per se, although there have been recent up-or-down votes to criminalize partial-birth abortion. More often, the Congress votes to fund (subsidize) abortion or expand its practice (e.g., military base hospitals, District of Columbia, government insurance policies). It also grants large sums to national and international Planned Parenthood.

Now, some argue and have argued that a number of abortions would not have occurred without federal or state funding. This *may* well be so. But since it "may be" so and is not patently clear, causal participation in an actual abortion, then it seems to me this is outside the scope of canon 1329, section 2, and does not engage the penalty of excommunication.

We need both caution and perspective here. To say that voting for abortion funding does not involve automatic excommunication is not to say it's okay, nor is it to say Catholic representatives are off the hook for their share in the responsibility.

Recall, this penalizing canon is narrowly drawn on purpose and strictly applies only to cases where it clearly applies. Some have the impression that there are automatic excommunications all over the place. That is not true. Curiously, our Latin Western *Code of Canon Law* has no canonical penalty for first-degree murder; whereas the Eastern *Code of Canon Law* (1990) does (can. 1450, §1). In a sane society, we should be able to assume that the criminal code would prohibit and punish crimes against human life.

Nevertheless, whatever civil or canon law omits or narrows, we must never forget that abortion is the direct killing of a moral innocent (i.e., morally, it's murder). By every moral standard, every direct and deliberate act of that kind (murder) is an objective offense against the natural law and divine positive law, from which no one on this planet is exempt. By definition, this is grave scandal and incompatible with being a practicing Catholic.

Those who promote, sustain, and expand abortion cannot disentangle themselves completely from this grave sin and objective injustice.

The gravity of this crime against life and supporting cooperation in it is significantly highlighted by the explicit teaching of two recent universal documents. The *Catechism of the Catholic Church* formally proscribes direct abortion (nos. 2270–71) and "formal cooperation" in the same (no. 2272). It is most unusual for a catechism—any catechism—to go into the specifics of canonical penalties, but the 1992 *Catechism* does.

Also, Pope John Paul II's encyclical *Evangelium Vitae* (on the "Gospel of Life") specifically details the canonical discipline on abortion and cooperation in it (no. 62). Again, it is most unusual for a papal encyclical to delve in canonical details, but *Evangelium Vitae* does.

Thus, it is not wise to judge maximum moral teaching or its seriousness by the presence or absence of one canonical penalty. The canon law of the Church has its own rationale and worthy purposes; it is not a shadow government to monitor or censor everything that is morally wrong in every society.

On the other hand, any elected representative who can talk away or talk around the direct killing of the innocent is a walking, talking inconsistency. It is my personal conviction that this verbal dodge and inconsistency cannot be confined to one subject area. It will show up elsewhere and undermine other important values; after all, if you can't trust them with life, just what can you trust them with?

—August 2000


## Separation of Church and State

Question: While a Supreme Court decision regarding school vouchers was welcome, did it not open the "wall of separation" for unwelcome consequences?

Answer: First, let's attend to facts. The "wall of separation" (i.e., the separation of church and state) is not mentioned in the Constitution at all. It is not in the Constitution proper nor the first ten amendments of the Constitution—the Bill of Rights.

It is the First Amendment that addresses and guarantees freedom of religion: "Congress shall make no law respecting an establishment of religion, or prohibiting the free exercise thereof." (That amendment continues with freedom of speech, of the press, of people to assemble peaceably, and to petition the government for a "redress of grievances".)

The part that concerns us (religion) is stated with the Constitution's notable brevity and looseness; there shall be no law that establishes a state or official religion, nor any law prohibiting the free exercise of religion. Note that there is no "wall" or even "separation", and, a fortiori, no "wall of separation". That expression simply does not appear in our founding document or fundamental law.

Where does the "wall of separation" come from? The first popular use of note comes from Thomas Jefferson in an 1802 letter to the Baptists of Danbury, Connecticut The words are not original with Jefferson; Roger Williams urged a "wall of separation" in a 1644 treatise. Jefferson and Williams did not share religious beliefs. No one could have been a purer Puritan than Roger Williams. (Consider his statements about Quakers, the Church of England, and Catholicism.) Jefferson's religious convictions, if any, were so unorthodox (or idiosyncratic) that he chose not to make them public in his own lifetime.

In time, Jefferson became the American patron saint of Enlightenment thinking. But there is no recorded protest by Jefferson against chaplains in the army, religion in the schools, or even religious schools. He held to the basic separation—which we can and should hold—i.e., separation between the institutions of the state and the institutions of the churches: that is to say, the state should not be controlling the churches any more than the churches should be controlling the state. But that separation of institutions need not and should not be the separation of religion from life. The proper separation of institutions can and should allow for a wide variety of accommodation of religious belief and practice.

Indeed, all sorts of reasoned and reasonable accommodations between church and state existed at the time of Jefferson and throughout the entire nineteenth century and the first half of the twentieth. But then began the construction of another "wall of separation", what I would call a "wall of hostility" toward religion. This was not Jefferson's "wall"; rather the architects of the "wall of hostility" were justices William Douglas and William Brennan of the U.S. Supreme Court and the on-site foreman, who more often than not was attorney Leo Pfeffer, of the American Jewish Congress, who guided a stream of test cases and friend of the court briefs on crucial church–state cases.

The gradual elimination of prayer in public schools (1962) and Bible reading (1963) eventually led to the Lemon decision (1971) with its three-prong test that became the high point in the wall of hostility and the high watermark of militant, absolute secularism—with absurd contradictions to follow. Children could not use the school (public property) for an after-hours Bible study, but they could to read and discuss the *Little Red Book* of Mao Tse-Tung.

It was no longer a "wall of separation" but a wall of aggressive hostility toward religion. As a result, any vote, voice, or voucher that was rooted in, inspired by, or even connected with any religious conviction was declared invalid, inimical to the American way of life, and contrary to basic comity.

Father Richard J. Neuhaus had it quite right in his book *The Naked Public Square* (1984). The truth was, and is, the naked public square was not entirely naked—militantly secular clothing was permitted, but any and every religious insight or association was simply prohibited from public life, public discourse, or even serious public discussion.

This particular "wall of hostility" was so high that it should not stand. Thus, the 2002 Supreme Court decision regarding school vouchers (*Zelman v. Simmons-Harris*) is, to me, a welcome decision. I have no real understanding of the complexities or workability of varied vouchers in different and differing situations. But this is surely a step in the right direction; indeed, a step in the direction of equal justice for all.

But even more welcome to me is that the Supreme Court has taken a small but decisive step away from and against the "wall of hostility" toward religion, and this can allow rational discussion of reasoned and reasonable accommodations between church and state—a situation that prevailed for our nation's first one hundred and fifty years.

—November 2002

## Sinful Voting

Question: Some have said it's a sin to vote for a particular candidate. Is it morally correct to speak in those terms?

Answer: In a prior Q/A column, I admitted difficulty in answering this question when formulated in that precise way. Then as now, I don't try to duck the question, because my hesitation concerns whether the question itself is properly formed.

Manuals of moral theology that predate the Second Vatican Council are not a great help in this question. Those manuals regarded voting as a privilege, which citizens were free to exercise or not. When not seen as a positive duty, there was not much mention of moral obligation. But, with some prior teaching of Pius XII, the Second Vatican Council did enhance the obligation of voting both as a right and as a duty.

That Council taught explicitly: "Hence, let all citizens be mindful of their simultaneous right and duty to vote freely in the interest of advancing the common good" (GS, no. 755). The Catechism simply repeats this teaching, stating that it is "morally obligatory to pay taxes, to exercise the right to vote and to defend one's country" (no. 2240). As a positive duty it can admit of excusing causes or legitimate omissions.

Some current textbooks of moral theology do state a moral obligation that binds in conscience, at least whenever a good candidate has an unworthy opponent. They also say it's wrong to vote for a regime completely hostile to religion or against freedom of conscience. The same would be true of completely immoral laws or programs. The common good can involve grave consequences for great numbers of people, and that certainly involves grave matter.

Most textbooks, however, do not address the specific question of the rightness or wrongness (indeed—sinfulness) of voting for or against an individual candidate for a specific office.

Thus, I wrote previously that it was more a question of stupidity than sin to vote for someone who significantly contradicted true moral principles. Now in the short space of seven years, aspects of this question have received much focus, wide discussion, and an amount of formal Church teaching.

Given our American location, some might think that much recent discussion here has been about hot-button topics related to particular candidates. One can't ignore that some discussion of these was highlighted and reported in the election process. But, it is also true that several moral issues far transcend the American scene with profound consequences for the common good. It is not a single issue but several: direct killing of the innocent (abortion, euthanasia), deliberate embryonic destruction, human cloning, same-sex unions, parental choice in education. These are not just local issues but fundamental moral principles of universal import with grave consequences for the common good.

As above, some media reports tried to dumb this down as the "interference" of some (conservative) bishops in the election cycle. That would be the standard posture of the *New York Times* and other mainstream media. Any cleric who sees things their way is a responsible citizen; any cleric who sees otherwise is obviously trying to undermine their version of the separation of church and state.

On the other hand, my own reading is quite different. It seems to me that a formal teaching document of the Congregation for the Doctrine of the Faith, "Doctrinal Note on Some Questions regarding the Participation of Catholics in Political Life" (November 24, 2002), contributed an original and important focus on a kind of "ethical pluralism which sanctions the decadence and disintegration of reason and the principles of the natural moral law", especially through legislation (no. 2).

It was precisely in the context of democracies and voting that some concrete moral problems were addressed—anti-life legislation (abortion and euthanasia), embryonic destruction, same-sex unions. This was not in response to American politics and the debates of 2004, since it was about two years before it.

One purpose of this formal doctrinal note was to refute the slogan "I'm personally opposed, but ..." What is at issue here, according to the CDF, is the very coherence between faith and life, gospel and culture, one of the central aspects of Christian life.

This is not just an American challenge. Indeed, a rabid form of "intolerant secularism" that seeks to deny any engagement of Catholicism in public or political life is far more advanced in the European Parliament than it is there.

It is, I think, with the background of the 2002 doctrinal note that a number of U.S. bishops have properly addressed "moral voting". Without being partisan, i.e., without formally endorsing any particular candidate for any particular office, some have published teaching documents that present relevant moral principles for the formation of a correct Catholic conscience.

Among the best that I have seen is "On Our Civic Responsibility for the Common Good" by Archbishop Raymond Burke of St. Louis, Missouri (October 1, 2004). Recalling the basic teachings of the Council and the *Catechism* on correct conscience, Archbishop Burke addresses the priority and urgency of the right to life and the sanctity of marriage and especially those activities that are intrinsically evil. To give practical priority to killing the innocent along with heterosexual marriage is not to neglect other moral issues but to underline the "foundational" nature of the right to life and stable marriage both for individuals and society. When the first and "foundational" right is at risk—or worse, destroyed—all other rights are moot and empty.

The Archbishop repeats what has been conventional teaching—i.e., we have an obligation in justice to vote, and we are obliged to vote for worthy candidates. Also, it would be wrong to vote for one whom you judge would do grave public harm.

Somewhat novel, but now needed, he offers some principles to consider voting as formal or material cooperation in another's sin (nos. 36–40). It is never right to vote for someone in order to promote the immoral practices he endorses and supports. In that, one would share the same evil intention as the candidate, and that, morally, would be "formal cooperation" in evil, which is not permissible.

Often life, and especially politics, does not offer such stark choices. Sometimes it is practically impossible to avoid all cooperation in evil. Thus, it could, in a given case, be moral to vote for someone who supports some immoral practices, while opposing other immoral practices.

This is what moralists call "material cooperation", which can be justified when certain conditions are present: (1) there is no viable candidate who supports morality fully; (2) the voter opposes the immoral practices espoused and supports only the good practices; and (3) the voter avoids scandal by telling anyone who asks or knows his vote that it was to advance the good practices and not the immoral ones the candidate endorses and promotes.

The Archbishop wisely adds that no amount of distinctions would justify voting for those who endorse and support the deliberate killing of the innocent or same-sex unions as legal marriage. These goods are so fundamental to the common good that they cannot be subordinated to other causes, however good (no. 39). Surely, this is not the final word on this delicate question of responsible voting. It is, however, a welcome and principled contribution to a question that deserves and demands our most serious attention.

—December 2004

## The Civic Virtue of Tolerance

Question: It seems that the only operative virtue in American civic life is the virtue of tolerance. Where does this stand in Catholic tradition?

Answer: Webster's *Dictionary*[4] defines "*tolerance*" as: "being tolerant of other's views, beliefs, practices", with the politically correct addition: "freedom from bigotry or prejudice".

In the conventional *Dictionary of Moral Theology*, Pietro Palazzini writes that *tolerance* indicates a stance that permits, for a proportionately good reason, an evil or improper situation of a person. In the practical order, the evil is some vice; in the intellectual order, it is an error that is allowed to exist without positive approval.[5] To refrain from opposing any doctrine, on the basis that all doctrines are equally good, is called *dogmatic* tolerance; whereas a passive attitude concerning erroneous opinions, without approving the error, is called *practical* tolerance. For Palazzini, *dogmatic tolerance* is not licit since it is and flows from dogmatic or moral relativism. *Practical tolerance* can be permitted for good and serious reasons. It is still true that error or evil have no objective right to be promoted or pursued, but the failure to impede error, by law or coercion, can be justified in the interest of a higher and greater good.

As your question notes, the modern rhetoric and advocates of tolerance present it as the central social virtue, if not the only virtue, of contemporary life. The conventional Catholic understanding is more modest, more nuanced, and greatly limited.

Saint Thomas Aquinas, for example, who presents the whole of his moral teaching within the framework of the virtues (e.g., the second part of his *Summa Theologiae*), does not list tolerance as a special or central virtue at all. His singular treatment of it is within the general categories of the consequences of the virtue of faith—the specific question being: "Are the rites of infidels to be tolerated?" (*ST*, II-II, q. 10, a. 11).

The *Catechism of the Catholic Church* is rather careful in its four mentions of tolerance (nos. 1737, 2279, 2338, 2383), and none of these

---

[4] Webster's *Dictionary*, 2nd ed. (New York: Simon and Schuster, 1979).
[5] See *Dictionary of Moral Theology*, ed. Pietro Palazzini (London: Burns and Oates, 1962), pp. 1236–37.

refers to tolerating freely and deliberately chosen immoral behavior. Clearly, the traditional Catholic understanding of tolerance is not the panacea and all-inclusive trump card so favored by contemporary advocates of evil and aberrant behavior. Strangely, some who are the most absolute about the relativism of all morals have invented their own revelation—the new gospel of tolerance. Questioning or critiquing the behavior of anyone else immediately makes someone a prejudiced bigot. G. K. Chesterton's quip is not far off the moral mark: "Tolerance is the favorite virtue of those who don't believe in anything."

It remains, of course, true that the real Christian gospel directs us to speak "the truth in love" (Eph 4:15) and not to "be overcome by evil, but overcome evil with good" (Rom 12:21).

Nevertheless, the secular gospel of tolerance is not just an elite media sound bite but a serious obstacle to rebuilding a culture of life, as Pope John Paul II carefully analyzes and explains in his encyclical *Evangelium Vitae*.

In chapter 3 of *Evangelium Vitae* (nos. 68–74), when detailing the correct relationship between civil law and the moral law, the Pope notes carefully:

> At the basis of all these tendencies lies the *ethical relativism* which characterizes much of present-day culture. There are those who consider such relativism an essential condition of democracy, inasmuch as it alone is held to guarantee *tolerance*, mutual respect between people and acceptance of the decisions of the majority, whereas moral norms considered to be objective and binding are held to be authoritarianism and intolerance.
>
> But it is precisely the issue of respect for life which shows what misunderstandings and contradictions, accompanied by terrible practical consequences, are concealed in this position. (no. 70; emphasis added)

The Pope honestly admits that some crimes have been committed in the name of truth.

> But equally grave crimes and radical denials of freedom have also been committed and are still being committed in the name of "ethical relativism". When a parliamentary or social majority decrees that it is legal, at least under certain conditions, to kill unborn human life, is it not really making a tyrannical decision with regard to the weakest and most defenseless of human beings? Everyone's conscience rightly rejects those crimes against humanity of which our century has had such sad

experience. But would these crimes cease to be crimes if, instead of being committed by unscrupulous tyrants, they were legitimated by popular consensus? (no. 70)

Democracy, the Pope teaches, is not a substitute for morality or a panacea for immorality. Fundamentally, democracy is a means not an end, and "the value of democracy stands or falls with the values which it embodies or promotes" (*Centesimus Annus*, no. 46; also *EV*, no. 70).

The basis of sound values cannot be provisional, temporary, ad hoc, and changeable majority opinions. There must be some objective moral law (natural law), some obligatory point of reference for the civil law itself. Otherwise, given contemporary skepticism about truth and objective morality, in the name of democracy we will undermine democracy itself by relativizing the most fundamental, even inalienable, human rights.

"First and fundamental among these is the inviolable right to life of every innocent human being." Public authority can never presume to legitimize as a "right" what is, in fact, an offense and crime against another person. "The legal *toleration* of abortion or of euthanasia can in no way claim to be based on respect for the consciences of others, precisely because society has the right and the duty to protect itself against the abuses which can occur in the name of conscience and under the pretext of freedom" (*EV*, no. 71).

As ever, a constant teaching of John Paul II is not to separate freedom from truth (cf. *VS*, nos. 28–34; Freedom and Law, nos. 35–53; Conscience and Truth, nos. 54–64). "Truth and freedom either go hand in hand or together they perish in misery" (*Fides et Ratio*, no. 89). This is a constant teaching from his first encyclical, *Redemptor Hominis* (1979), no. 12, to his latest encyclical, *Fides et Ratio* (1998), no. 89.

Uncritical tolerance is not the essence of democracy; it may well be the destruction of it.

—August 1999

# V

# Sacraments and Priesthood

# 22

# Baptism

## Profession of Faith at Baptism

Question: A baptized Christian received into full communion is required to profess: "I believe and profess all that the holy Catholic Church believes, teaches, and proclaims to be revealed by God." Does this suggest that new converts need only believe strictly infallible doctrines? Does not this formula omit infallible teaching not formally revealed by God?

Answer: The Profession of Faith for those cases required by law (can. 833) is, since 1989, more specific in precise content than what is required of all the faithful or the Profession used in the Liturgy.

Commonly, the Nicene-Constantinople Creed is used at Sunday Mass; the Apostles' Creed is used to renew baptismal promises on Easter Sunday and can be used at Children's Masses. The *Rite of the Christian Initiation of Adults* requires a Profession of Faith (no. 219) and, depending on which creed was used "in the presentation" (no. 186), either the Nicene or Apostles' Creed can be used.

You are correct that in the *Rite of Reception of Baptized Christians into Full Communion with the Catholic Church* (January 6, 1972), when the reception is within Mass, "the one to be received then recites the Nicene Creed with the faithful" (no. 15). After this, the one to be received adds: "I believe and profess all that the Holy Catholic Church believes, teaches, and proclaims to be revealed by God" (no. 15).

In my opinion, "believe and profess all that the Holy Catholic Church believes, teaches, and proclaims" means just that—*all* that the Church believes and *all* that the Church teaches. I do not think that the beginning of that formula makes or requires distinctions about the precise level of infallible teaching. Thus, I do not read the end of the formula ("to be revealed by God") as a qualification of inclusion or exclusion referring to precise theological notes.

In fact, this expression—"all that the Holy Catholic Church believes, teaches, and proclaims"—resembles very much the Act of Faith: "I believe these and all the truths which the Holy Catholic Church teaches, because Thou hast revealed them, who canst neither deceive nor be deceived." That traditional Act of Faith is rooted in the definition of Vatican Council I (DS 3008) and is reflected again in the *Catechism* (nos. 156, 168–71).

Perhaps all do not read it my way; but it is arguable. Perhaps as well, should the question actually arise, we could follow the practice of the Roman Congregations and provide more specificity when such specificity is asked for or about.

A canonical Profession of Faith was once published in the front of the 1917 *Code of Canon Law*. Another and extensive profession of faith and abjuration of error was published (March 28, 1942) and can be found in *Canon Law Digest*.[1] A shorter formula was published by the same Holy Office (June 13, 1956).[2]

The 1983 *Code* did not publish a formula for the Profession of Faith but did specify who had to take it (can. 833). After the Council, the Congregation for the Doctrine of the Faith published (December 20, 1967) a new Profession of Faith that replaced the anti-Modernist Oath and reduced the former Profession to the *symbolum fidei* and a very condensed form of acceptance of the Magisterium.[3]

The same CDF updated its 1967 text with two documents published March 1, 1989: a Profession of Faith and an Oath of Fidelity. Clearly, what was much (too much?) condensed in the 1967 text is made explicit and detailed in the 1989 Profession. Apparently, the CDF saw a genuine need to make explicit the kinds and levels of Church teaching, reflecting as it does, Vatican II's *Lumen Gentium*, number 25.

If a prospective convert were to raise the kinds of questions your letter raises, it seems to me, the best thing to do is to review with and

---

[1] *Canon Law Digest*, vol. 2 (Milwaukee: Bruce Publishing, 1943), pp. 182–84.

[2] Cf. *Canon Law Digest*, vol. 5 (Milwaukee: Bruce Publishing, 1963), pp. 407–8.

[3] *Code of Canon Law Annotated*, ed. Ernest Caparros, et al. (Montreal: Wilson and Lafleur, 1993), pp. 540–41.

explain to that convert the Profession of 1989. Otherwise, either Creed, with the added statement for full communion, seems adequate and appropriate for the Liturgy and ceremonial reception.

—August 1997

## Child Adopted by Homosexuals

Question: I am the pastor of a large suburban parish. A year ago, a lesbian couple asked about having or adopting a child. The conversation went nowhere, and they went away. Now they are back with an adopted child from China and have asked to have the child baptized. Should I baptize the child?

Answer: My answer here would not only be to go slowly, but don't proceed in that direction at all. Rather, for the good of the child another direction should be urged entirely.

First, let's state the obvious. Church law requires that there must be a realistic hope that a child presented for baptism will be brought up in the Catholic religion. If that hope is truly lacking, the baptism is to be deferred (cf. can. 868, §1, no. 2).

It is my hope that no part of this answer will be misunderstood or distorted into some kind of statement against infant baptism. That is not my purpose; indeed, the opposite is my purpose—I accept fully the Church's teaching. (See CDF, *Instruction on Infant Baptism*, October 20, 1980.)

Baptism is necessary for salvation and is not lightly nor quickly deferred, much less refused. Transmitting the faith and administering baptism are closely linked to the express command of the Lord Jesus (Mt 28:19). Further, the Council of Trent clearly teaches that baptism is not just a sign of faith but also a cause of faith. Children are, of course, baptized "in the faith of the Church" not merely in the faith of parents, relatives, or surroundings.

But assurance that the child will be raised Catholic must be given before administering baptism. "As a rule, these assurances are to be given by the parents or close relatives, although *various substitutions* are possible within the Christian community" (CDF, *Instruction on Infant*

*Baptism*, no. 28, emphasis added). I would argue that the two lesbians are not and cannot be one of the "various substitutions".

Sadly, the highest court (court of appeals) in my home state of New York decided on November 2, 1995, by a 4-to-3 vote, that a couple does not have to be married to adopt a child in New York, opening the way for homosexuals to adopt children. The court took note of "fundamental changes" in the American family to position and justify its decision. I would submit that the decision is wrong, the agenda that fuels it is misguided, and the social consequences it unleashes, especially for the children involved, will be worse. An unmarried couple is not a family, and two homosexuals are not a family.

In response to a similar resolution approved by the European Parliament, Pope John Paul II said in his Angelus address on February 20, 1994:

> Forgetting Christ's words, "the truth will set you free" (John 8:32), the attempt has been made to tell the inhabitants of this continent that moral evil, deviation, a kind of slavery, is the way to liberation, thus distorting the true meaning of family. *The relationship of two men or two women cannot constitute a true family*; still less can one grant such a union *the right to adopt children who lack a family*. These children suffer great danger, grave harm, because in these "substitute families" they do not have a father and mother, but "two fathers" and "two mothers". And this is dangerous.[4]

A few months later, the same Pope taught clearly that human sexuality and the human family are both God's plan and God's creation: "It actually has its own unique psychological and biological structure, aimed at both communion between man and woman and at the birth of new persons. Respecting this structure and this unbreakable connection is not 'biologism' or 'moralism' but concern for the truth of what it means to be human, to be a person."[5]

Relying on the same principles, Father Gino Concetti, O.F.M., argues that the "child has a right to be born in a real family"—the right to be born in a regular family, born in a natural way, the right to be welcomed into a regular family that wanted him and raised by both

---

[4]John Paul II, Angelus, February 20, 1994, *L'Osservatore Romano*, Eng. ed. (Feb. 23, 1994): 8, emphasis in the original.

[5]John Paul II, Angelus, June 26, 1994, *L'Osservatore Romano*, Eng. ed. (June 29, 1994): 1, 2.

parents. "Those who in the name of progress legitimize homosexual unions neglect these truths, whether deliberately or not. They say that two women who live together can guarantee a child the same rights as a regular, stable heterosexual couple. But this position not only distorts nature, it falsifies it." [6]

The existence of single-parent or adoptive families does not legitimize this aberrant situation. As Francisco Elizari writes: "The 'accidental' existence of such families (e.g., resulting from the death or separation of one partner) does not legitimate the intentional, planned creation of a situation which, in the opinion of numerous child psychologists and psychiatrists, will not help this child to grow up in a balanced way." [7]

The motivation of nonmarried couples to adopt should also be examined with some care. Is the child seen more as a thing or an accomplishment to satisfy some subjective desire for motherhood or to avoid loneliness? Is the child seen as a token, even a trophy, to advance some social agenda against nature? These, no one can answer at a distance, but as the CDF instruction *Donum Vitae* reminds us, a child is *not a thing* but a person: "The child is not an object to which one has a right, nor can he be considered as an object of ownership; rather, a child is a gift, 'the supreme gift' and the most gratuitous gift of marriage, and is living testimony of the mutual giving of his parents" (pt. 2, no. 8).

It seems then to me that the best interests of this adopted child from China will be served by suggesting and offering to help seek adoption by a real family. If the new adopters are Catholics, then there will be no obstacle to the child's proper baptism.

It seems to me both unwise and improper to accept and honor the present request. Since they are presumably your parishioners, it is surely inevitable that one or the other of these parties will announce, perhaps even publicize, the fact the Catholic pastor baptized the child. Whatever your personal hesitation or reservation, that result guarantees misunderstanding, even scandal, since it will be assumed that the Church does not object to what she really does object to, i.e., adoption by homosexuals.

—May 1996

[6] Fr. Gino Concetti, O.F.M., *L'Osservatore Romano*, Eng. ed. (July 20, 1994): 2.
[7] Francisco J. Elizari, *Bioethics* (Collegeville, Minn.: Liturgical Press, 1994), p. 76.

# 23

# Confession

## The Necessity of Integral Confession

Question: My question concerns a practice in using Form II of the sacrament of Reconciliation. In helping a nearby pastor, we priests were lined up across the sanctuary. Then the instruction was given to the penitents to single out one particular sin (to save time), approach one priest, and confess only that one sin. Absolution was given individually. Is this acceptable practice?

Answer: I do not know how extensive this arrangement is, but your question is not a singular one. The procedure is an abuse of the sacrament of Penance in the first place because it is an open invitation to violate the integrity of integral confession and certainly so in the case of serious sins.

Both the *Code of Canon Law* (can. 960) and the *Catechism of the Catholic Church* (no. 1456) teach the need and norm of "individual and integral confession and absolution" for those aware of serious sin to be reconciled with God and with the Church.

Further, the *Code* directs the priest-confessor "to adhere faithfully to the doctrine and the norms enacted by competent authority" in the administration of this sacrament (can. 978, §2).

Whether the teaching of the Council of Trent falls on open ears or deaf ones, it remains the defined doctrine of the faith. The Congregation for the Doctrine of the Faith repeated this very doctrine in *Pastoral Norms for the Administration of General Sacramental Absolution* (*Sacramentum Paenitentiae*, June 16, 1972), summarizing the formal teaching of the Council of Trent: "It [Trent] also taught that absolution is given by the priest, who acts as judge, and that it is necessary by divine law to confess to a priest each and every mortal sin and the circumstances that alter the species of sins that are remembered after a careful examination of conscience."[1]

Form II (or "B") is the Rite of Reconciliation of several penitents with individual confession and absolution. Thus, this is not "general absolution", but individual confession with individual absolution (*Rite of Penance*, no. 55). The same defined doctrine is repeated throughout the *Rite of Penance*.[2]

Thus, in every case, the doctrine is clear, but in the case given, it depends on the acts of the penitent. If indeed there are no serious sins, the absolution would be valid (DS 1680). But, if there is serious sin—which is known but not mentioned—or, multiple grave sins known but only one mentioned, what is known and not mentioned is not validly absolved.

The fault here is more with the priest than the penitent since it is bad pastoral practice to so arrange and instruct people in such a way that you invite them to violate the necessary completeness of integral confession. It may be that a penitent never heard the terms "integral confession", but there is no excuse for the priest-confessor being ignorant of this, and priests should neither construct nor encourage arrangements (allegedly for "saving time") that open to and basically invite the abuse of a sacrament.

—August/September 1993

## General Absolution

Question: It has been my experience in talking to penitents who have received general absolution that they were not instructed to confess in due time grave sins that could not be confessed at the time general absolution was given. One penitent told me he was instructed that, apart from mortal sin, just being present was enough for valid general absolution. Is this so?

---

[1] The CDF cites canons 4 and 6 to 9 of Session XIV of Trent; DS 1704, 1706–9. Cf. also DS 1680.

[2] Cf. *Rite of Penance*, no. 6b, "Sacrament of Penance and Its Parts", fn. 32, and no. 7b, "Necessity and Benefit of the Sacrament", fn. 36.

Answer: The focus of concern and study here is canon 962. A review of available commentaries in English did not address this novel instruction, e.g., *Text and Commentary*, the more reliable *Code of Canon Law Annotated*, nor *The Canon Law* (respectively, the American, the Navarra, and the English-Irish commentaries).[3]

As with the colleague who sent me the question, I consulted with several reliable priests who also could not find an authentic source that would provide a good answer.

Facing the same lacuna of sources, one colleague submitted the question as a *dubium* (regarding can. 962, §1) to the Pontifical Council for the Interpretation of Legislative Texts. The official response of that Pontifical Council (PN #5043/96) was that the precise question does not refer to a "true *dubium iuris*" requiring an authentic interpretation from that Council. Rather, it is less a matter of the interpretation of law than its correct application, and for that reason the request was forwarded to the Congregation for Divine Worship and Sacraments.

The Congregation for Divine Worship and Sacraments also responded (PN #1313/96/L) that the question is more related to catechesis than to the interpretation of the *Code of Canon Law*.

This Congregation then responded:

> The mere fact of being present in the assembly when General Absolution is given does not mean that absolution is automatically received. Canon 962, §1 states the requirements explicitly:
> ... validly to receive sacramental absolution given to many at one time, it is required that (the individual) not only *be suitably disposed* but also at the same time *intend to confess individually* the serious sins which at present cannot be confessed.
> The requirement to be "suitably disposed" also applies to one who may not have any serious sins to confess.

This authentic response corrects, and correctly answers I believe, the faulty and misleading "instruction" given in the instance of those in venial sin only.

[3] *The Code of Canon Law: A Text and Commentary*, ed. James A. Coriden, Thomas J. Green, and Donald E. Heintschel (New York: Paulist Press, 1985), pp. 679–80; *Code of Canon Law Annotated*, ed. Ernest Caparros, et al. (Montreal: Wilson and Lafleur, 1993), pp. 612–13; and Canon Law Society of Great Britain and Ireland, *The Canon Law: Letter & Spirit* (Collegeville, Minn.: Liturgical Press, 1995), pp. 526–27.

My experience is limited, but my experience is that where general absolution is abused, it is the requirements for validity (cf. can. 962) that are often not mentioned at all, especially the intention of making an individual confession of grave sin not yet submitted to the power of the keys of the Church (can. 988).

—February 1997

## Valid Absolution

Question: Once, in confession, the priest used the formula: "It is my privilege to absolve you, and I do it in the name of the Father, and of the Son and of the Holy Spirit" for absolution. Another time he said, "I forgive your sins" instead of "I absolve". Are these valid?

Answer: The teaching and practice of the Church require close attention and exact observance when exercising the valid form of sacramental absolution. The new *Rite of Penance* (December 2, 1973) clearly states the essential formula in large letters: "*Et ego te absolvo a peccatis tuis in nomine Patris, et Filii, + et Spiritus Sancti.*" To which the penitent responds: "Amen" (*Ordo Paenitentiae*, no. 46).

The formula has undergone changes in the course of the Church's history. The direct indicative form now employed in the Latin Rite is, of course, obligatory. The prayer that accompanies the "form" ("*Deus, Pater misericordiarum . . .*") is not required for validity.

Session 14 of the Council of Trent (November 25, 1551) taught that the form of the sacrament chiefly lies in the words of the minister: "*Ego te absolvo. . . .*", to which words by a praiseworthy custom of Holy Church some prayers are added that do not affect the essence of the form (DS 1673).

The classic textbooks of moral theology ("approved authors") address this point in some detail. All the "approved authors" admit the validity of "*Absolvo te a peccatis tuis*" ("I absolve you from your sins"). The same authors are in near-agreement on what is probably valid but insist (1) it is not lawful to use other forms and (2) there is no reasonable excuse for permitting forms that are no more than probably valid.[4]

In your second example, to use the word "*forgive*" instead of "*absolve*"—the rest being proper—Marcellino Zalba argues these are materially equivalent words (his examples: *remitto* or *condono*) and are valid.[5]

However, of your first example, I am not so sure: "It is my privilege to absolve you and I do it.". . . Hieronymus Noldin and Albert Schmitt give careful attention to what constitutes the essence of valid absolution. Their conclusion is threefold; it must include the following: (1) the one absolving (*absolvo*); (2) the one absolved (*te*); and (3) what's absolved (*a peccatis*).[6] The strange formula you report does mention the first two, but it does not mention the third—what's absolved. Some might judge this probably valid; in my opinion, it's probably invalid. We are not free to invoke "Probabilism" where the validity of a sacrament is at stake.

The sadness in all of this is that it is so unnecessary. Also, when we focus exclusively on validity, we tend to forget that what is illicit or highly illicit is, in fact, sinful disobedience (on the part of the confessor). If we all did faithfully what the Church provides and proposes, such sorry abuses would not even exist. If novelties continue, seek another priest: sometimes those who play fast and loose with solemn laws are the source of fast and loose advice.

—August/September 2000

## Telephone Confession

Question: Are confession and absolution possible by telephone?

Answer: To my knowledge, the Church has never formally answered this question directly. On July 1, 1884, when the Penitentiary in Rome

---

[4] Cf. Dominicus M. Prümmer, O.P., *Handbook of Moral Theology* (New York: P. J. Kenedy & Sons, 1957), p. 294, n. 648.

[5] Marcellino Zalba, *Theologiae Moralis Compendium*, vol. 2 (Madrid, 1958), n. 830, 1, p. 462.

[6] H. Noldin, A. Schmitt, and G. Heinzel, *Summa Theologiae Moralis*, vol. 3 (Rauch, 1962), p. 205, n. 234.

was asked, "whether in the case of extraordinary· necessity, is it possible to give absolution by telephone?" The response was "no answer need be given" (*nihil est respondendum*, more below).

The "approved authors" have traditionally taught that for *valid* absolution there must be a "mutual presence" of priest and penitent. Clearly, this is true in genuine physical presence, but all those authors allow for a "moral" presence as well. "Moral" has to do with the degree of nearness wherein people can and are accustomed to converse. Most put this at twenty paces, beyond which they suggest "conditional absolution".

Similarly, in cases of grave necessity—shipwreck, street, rail, or air accidents and those in mines—conditional absolution may be given.

The same "approved authors" argue that speaking by telephone cannot be said to be "mutually present", and some observe that the voice on the telephone is not a direct human voice but a substitute as in a broadcast. Thus, they consider this invalid.[7] Still, Davis argues: "Nevertheless, in real necessity conditional absolution might thus be given, for the reverence for the Sacrament is then safeguarded."[8]

Noldin, Schmitt, and Heinzel argue that absolution by telephone seems (*videtur*) invalid because sacraments should be administered and received in a human and natural way, requiring mutual presence.[9] In a footnote, Noldin-Schmitt cite both Merkelbach and Lehmkuhl on the non-answer of the Penitentiary above—that the answer is not in the province of the Penitentiary but of the (then) Holy Office, today the Congregation of the Doctrine of the Faith.[10]

Zalba argues that since some kind of direct reciprocal communication cannot be denied through telephone conversation, he reasons in practice "in extreme necessity it is possible to give conditional absolution."[11]

Aertnys, Damen, and Visser argue that absolution by telephone is invalid since bodily presence is entirely lacking; for them, the telephone is a means of communicating with one who is absent, not present. Nevertheless, they teach that because very serious authors do not hold

---

[7] Cf. Henry Davis, S.J., *Moral and Pastoral Theology*, vol. 3, 8th ed. (London, New York: Sheed and Ward, 1959), p. 255.

[8] Ibid.

[9] Cf. Noldin-Schmitt-Heinzel, *Summa Theologiae Moralis*, p. 209, n. 238, 2, e.

[10] Ibid.

[11] Zalba, *Theologiae Moralis Compendium*, p. 463, n. 830, 1, ad-d.

the opposite opinion to be entirely improbable, they think that "in extreme necessity" conditional absolution can be given by telephone.[12]

In effect, the approved authors are in agreement—in extreme necessity (basically danger of death), conditional absolution by telephone may be valid. It is still true that very grave problems and dangers remain. From the priest's point of view, you don't know to whom you are speaking; you don't know if it is recorded; and there are dangers to the seal of confession.

It is not superfluous to recall that the Congregation for the Doctrine of the Faith promulgated a decree that established a penalty of *latae sententiae* excommunication for those who divulge the content of a sacramental confession through means of social communication or who record it in any way on some device (*Decree regarding the Excommunication of Those Who Divulge Confessions*, September 23, 1988).

Given that tasteless TV knows no bounds and acknowledges no limits, there is reason for more caution with advanced technology today. Not long ago (December 1996), the phone conversation of an Ohio Representative with the Speaker of the U.S. House was scanned and recorded without the knowledge or permission of either. Technology can bring some great benefits, but that kind of invasion is not one of them.

—December 1998

## The Seal of Confession

Question: An American lecturer, while here in Australia, told an assembly of religious women that in the Archdiocese of New York that the seal of confession does not apply to sexual abuse cases—that confessors hearing such were obliged to report them. Would you comment?

Answer: This is false; it is not true because it can't be true. If some professional said that, he is simply and totally wrong.

[12] Joseph Aertnys, Cornelius Damen, and Jan Visser, C.Ss.R., *Theologia Moralis*, vol. 3, 18th ed. (Rome: Marietti, 1968), p. 329, n. 339, 4.

I am myself a priest of the Archdiocese of New York and am fully familiar with the policy and practice of my diocese. We are not "exempt" from the universal law of the Church in this or any other discipline.

Canon 983, section 1, of the *Code of Canon Law* is clear: "The sacramental seal is inviolate. Accordingly, it is absolutely wrong for a confessor in any way to betray the penitent, for any reason whatsoever, whether by word or in any other fashion."

That canon concerns the violation of the seal, and the next concerns "prohibited use of knowledge" from confession: "The confessor is wholly forbidden to use knowledge acquired in confession to the detriment of the penitent even when all danger of disclosure is excluded" (can. 984, §1).

The penalty mentioned in the universal law clearly governs our diocese and every other diocese: "A confessor who directly violates the sacramental seal, incurs a *latae sententiae* excommunication reserved to the Apostolic See; he who does so only indirectly is to be punished according to the gravity of the offense" (can. 1388, §1).

The CDF established a penalty of excommunication for those who divulge the content of a sacramental confession through means of social communication or who record it in any way on some device. The penalty applies whether the confession is true or fictitious (*Decree regarding the Excommunication of Those Who Divulge Confessions*).

Our New York diocese published in June 1993 formal policy and procedures for sexual misconduct cases. These procedures are in accord with the national guidelines published by the NCCB.[13] None of these policies, national or local, ever mention or even suggest any violation of the seal because they cannot. It is simply out of the question.

I, of course, am not the spokesman for my diocese. However, I know of and am involved in teaching this subject area in our seminary. No such thing has ever been taught or suggested here; indeed, we clearly teach the opposite.

—August/September 1997

---

[13] Cf. *Origins* 25, no. 20 (Nov. 12, 1995): 337; 339–43.

# 24

# Eucharist

## Sunday Mass Obligation

Question: Your predecessor in this column once proposed that the reasoning of Pope Paul VI regarding fast and abstinence ("substantial observance") could be applied to the Sunday Mass obligation. Do you teach that?

Answer: In a word, no. My respect for the late Father Joseph Farraher was great, but in the instance you mention, I believe his proposal was mistaken and his cited authorities were badly mistaken.

It is true that in his *HPR* columns of May 1981 (pp. 68–69) and October 1981 (p. 70), Father Farraher correctly stated the norm of Pope Paul VI's *Paenitemini* regarding fast and abstinence, i.e., its substantial observance binds gravely.

Citing and following Karl Peschke, he asks: Could not the same norm be proposed regarding the gravity of the Sunday Mass obligation?

Peschke begins with the traditional statement: "According to universal interpretation the obligation to Mass attendance on Sundays and obligatory holidays is by its nature grave." [1] But, within three more paragraphs, by the "substantial observance" rule, Peschke sees that fulfilled by making more Sunday Masses than you miss. Thus Peschke concludes: "A grave matter on the other hand would be had if a person misses Mass more often than he attends it." [2] By this standard, one could miss Mass for the summer months (June, July, August) and still have "substantial observance"? I think that is an erroneous and unjustified interpretation.

[1] Karl H. Peschke, *Christian Ethics*, vol. 2 (Alcester, Warwickshire: C. Goodliffe Neale, 1985), pp. 141–42.
[2] Ibid., p. 143.

I would like to consider Father Farraher's proposal just that—a proposal for consideration. Peschke's reasoning does not convincingly support or uphold that proposal. Indeed, no authoritative teaching of the Holy See has ever suggested or proposed this transfer of norms from fast and abstinence to Mass attendance. (One might even consider how successful the proposal was regarding the actual penitential discipline of fast and abstinence in actual practice today.)

In any case, the opinion of Germain Grisez in *Living a Christian Life* is a better explanation of the gravity of this obligation and a reliable guide for practice.[3]

Lastly, the 1992 *Catechism* is, I believe, an authoritative confirmation of the traditional teaching in this regard and quite clearly precludes the transfer of the "substantial observance" to this point of practice. The *Catechism* teaches:

> The Sunday Eucharist is the foundation and confirmation of all Christian practice. For this reason the faithful are obliged to participate in the Eucharist on days of obligation, unless excused for a serious reason (for example, illness, the care of infants) or dispensed by their own pastor (can. 1245). Those who deliberately fail in this obligation *commit a grave sin.* (no. 2181, emphasis added)

—January 1995

## Work on Holy Days

Question: One of my parishioners is a public school teacher who objects to working ("servile work") on holy days of obligation. She has petitioned the local school board and asked me to testify that our Catholic religion requires this. Any guidance?

Answer: While I am immediately sympathetic with any Catholic trying to live and live out conscientious convictions, I could not say, in conscience, that our Catholic religion requires this in our country.

Let me summarize what I take to be pertinent here. Surely, for a professional teacher, teaching is their chosen "work" for which they are rightly compensated by right and by contract.

---

[3] Germain Grisez, *Living a Christian Life* (Quincy, Ill.: Franciscan Press, 1993), p. 148.

I would, however, be careful about the use of the term "servile work". It is a traditional term and can be found in canon laws and moral theology since the thirteenth century right up to the *Code of* 1917 (*"abstinendum ab operibus servilibus"*, can. 1248). Significantly, the term "servile work" does not appear in the new *Code of Canon Law* (1983), though the substance of the law (can. 1247) is the same: participation in the Mass and rest, but the new wording is different.

Thus, on Sundays and holy days of obligation the faithful are positively obliged to participate in the Mass, but the negative prohibition now urges the faithful "to abstain from such work or business that would inhibit the worship to be given to God, the joy proper to the Lord's Day, or the due relaxation of mind and body" (can. 1247).

No doubt, it will take some time and settled practice before a universally accepted interpretation of that new wording pervades the Catholic community. The real difficulty of interpreting "servile work" fairly in modern circumstances may have been one of the reasons for not including that term in the new *Code*. Further, one aspect of the present wording explicitly mentions the "Lord's Day", which Sundays are and holy days are not. This might suggest that the "rest" aspect more properly is addressed to Sundays than holy days.

Still, it is also true that the *Catechism* (no. 2187) states: "Sanctifying Sundays and holy days requires a common effort. Every Christian should avoid making unnecessary demands on others that would hinder them from observing the Lord's Day." Again, one notes that the first sentence mentions holy days, while the second sentence does not.

Practically, in the United States, Christmas Day and New Year's Day are already holidays for everyone. Apart from summer school, August 15 would not seem to be an issue for teachers, so the holy days in question would be Ascension Thursday, All Saints (November 1), and Immaculate Conception (December 8).

Now, in the Latin Rite in the USA, there is an unusual and uneven observance—many dioceses have 5/7ths of a holy day, in that if those days land on a Monday or Saturday, they are not observed as holy days in most places. Such an uneven application makes it more and more difficult to assert that our religion requires a particular abstention from work.

Apart from that and long before it, the question of proper interpretation remains. Canon 27 tells us that custom is the best interpreter of law; indeed, a number of canons detail a proper understanding of custom (cann. 23–28).

The fact that for over one hundred years in the USA, we have observed only six of the ten universal holy days on the Church's calendar is itself instructive. Since ours is not and never was a Catholic country, holy days of obligation were not civil holidays (except for Christmas and January 1). The positive obligation of Mass attendance was always urged, but abstention from work on those days was never required.

Even today, a number of Catholic educational institutions—especially higher education—in their pursuit of adapting to the civil calendar (or the challenges of bus schedules in primary and secondary education) themselves do not observe holy days of obligation by closing school.

Thus, while I would decline the opportunity to testify against any conscientious Catholic, I would point out personally to that parishioner that I would not be her best witness. If asked directly: Does the Catholic religion require a Catholic teacher not to teach (work) on a holy day of obligation? My answer would be no! I know of no such obligation as it is understood and interpreted for over one hundred years in this country. I doubt that that answer would or could help her case.

—April 2000

## Travelers and Holy Days

Question: Does the precept of holy days of obligation bind travelers?

Answer: It can. According to the *Code of Canon Law*, universal (or general) laws are binding everywhere on all those for whom they were enacted (can. 12, §1).

The universal law (can. 1246, §1) stipulates ten feast days as holy days of obligation. Of these ten universal holy days, we in the United States have long observed, by indult in 1885 and again in 1983, only six: we do not observe Epiphany, Corpus Christi, Saint Joseph, or Saints Peter and Paul as feasts of obligation.

On the other hand, if a particular conference of bishops were to designate, by *particular* law, the national patron saint's feast as a holy day of obligation, travelers (*peregrini*) would not be bound by that particular law (can. 13, §2).

It seems to me that this has to be reasonably interpreted. If some U.S. traveler just happens to land in some airport, or just arrives or is just leaving such a place where Corpus Christi is a holy day (observed there but not where he is from), serious inconvenience would excuse (cf. *CCC*, no. 2181). If travelers are well settled in for some days, then they should observe a universal feast that is observed there.

—March 1996

## Unworthy Reception of Communion

Question: Does a person in the habit of practicing contraception or masturbation (both grave) commit at least a venial sin when he receives Holy Communion without sacramental absolution, if he doesn't know the action to be sinful (without full knowledge) or is not totally free, e.g., pressure from a spouse or habit (without complete consent)?

Answer: Several different points intersect here so it might be best to try to sort them out individually. To the basic question, as posed, it seems to me at least a venial sin to receive Holy Communion with an unrepentant practice of contraception or masturbation. Indeed, it is surely unworthy reception of the Eucharist and probably more grave than venial (more on that below).

First, I don't think anyone questions that sacrilegious reception of Holy Communion is itself grave matter (*CCC*, no. 2120). The traditional citation from Scripture is 1 Corinthians 11:27–28: "Whoever, therefore, eats the bread or drinks the cup of the Lord in an unworthy manner will be guilty of profaning the body and blood of the Lord. Let a man examine himself, and so eat of the bread and drink the cup." While that text can admit of a specific imperative to unity, it has generally and traditionally been accepted as a biblical standard for the worthy reception of the Eucharist.

Next, it is the received and normative teaching of the Church that both contraception (*CCC*, nos. 2368–72, esp. 2370) and masturbation (*CCC*, no. 2352) do involve grave matter. Individual factors can lessen or diminish subjective responsibility (cf. the same 2352, second paragraph) but "grave matter" remains what it essentially is—*grave*.

There have been emphases, even moral theories, that so maximize subjective mitigating circumstances that the truth of the objective moral order functionally disappears or becomes practically unobtainable. One of the clarifying points of John Paul II's *Veritatis Splendor* clearly repudiates this drift:

> If acts are intrinsically evil, a good intention or particular circumstances can diminish their evil, but they cannot remove it. They remain "irremediably" evil acts; *per se* and in themselves they are not capable of being ordered to God and to the good of the person.... Consequently, circumstances or intentions can never transform an act intrinsically evil by virtue of its object into an act "subjectively" good or defensible as a choice. (no. 81)

Now, the language of the *Catechism* deserves some close attention here. It states that venial sin is described in terms of "less serious matter" or "a grave matter, but without full knowledge [*sine plena cognitione*] or without complete consent [*sine pleno consensus*]" (no. 1862). These adjectives (full or complete: *plenus-a-um*) are consistent with the prior description of mortal sin: "Mortal sin requires *full knowledge* [*plenam cognitionem*] and *complete consent* [*plenumque consensum*]". But that prior reference adds the important standard: "It also implies a consent sufficiently deliberate to be a personal choice" (no. 1859).

"Personal choice" is what moral theology calls a *human act*—i.e., an act that proceeds from the will with a knowledge of the end (no. 1732). The qualifiers "*full*" and "*complete*" when used of knowledge and consent can admit, I suppose, of a maximal or minimal interpretation. I take the correct meaning to be one of sufficiency—sufficient knowledge and sufficient consent to qualify as a truly human act. Thus, sufficient knowing and sufficient willing that the act is of *your doing*— for "praise or blame, merit or reproach" (no. 1732).

Thus, in your specific example "without full knowledge" seems to translate, "They don't know these actions to be sinful." If this is so, and I find it hard to believe it is so, this person certainly has an erroneous conscience.

Again, your question equates "not totally free"—because of pressure from a spouse or habit—as "without complete consent". Many factors can lessen or lower human responsibility but "complete consent" does not mean 100 percent complete, otherwise every evil act out of or with pressure from another or habit would become venial.

There surely is a range of responsibility, but knowledge does not have to be 100 percent "full", nor consent 100 percent "complete"— the meaning and standard is one of *sufficiency* rather than 100 percent perfection. This standard is one of human reasonableness. If the bar of responsibility is raised too high—to the level of near perfection—we might eliminate most blame and fault, but we remove most praise and merit as well. Most of us do not operate anywhere near perfection level most of the time. Any theory that explains away most fault also explains away most virtue and that is not a standard of human reasonableness.

It is my personal opinion that no one can keep doing what is objectively wrong (knowingly or unknowingly) without real consequences in his life. Single evil acts are not hermetically sealed off from the rest of life. The first casualty is a correct conscience; indeed, the opposite is the result—an erroneous conscience. The moral sense and search is then dulled; true virtue is not pursued; and the truth about the good is first neglected, then irrelevant. This is not a program for spiritual growth; it is rather a spiritual illness that needs serious and immediate correction.

My presumption, in view of this, is that unworthy reception of the Eucharist is itself a sacrilege and gravely wrong. By exception, there may be cases where knowledge is so lacking and consent so absent that formal grave sin is not engaged. But in these one might begin to wonder what kind of knowledge and consent is engaged in the personal reception of Holy Communion as well.

It may well be that some overemphases on mortal sin have the unintended result of reducing venial sin to a nonentity or nonevent. The same *Catechism*, cited above, rightly presents the great Doctor of Grace, Saint Augustine, for his helpful and needed reminder:

> While he is in the flesh, man cannot help but have at least some light sins. But do not despise these sins which we call "light" if you take them for light when you weigh them, tremble when you count them. A number of light objects makes a great mass; a number of drops fills a river; a number of grains makes a heap. What then is our hope? Above all, confession. (*In ep. Jo.* 1, 6: PL 35 [1982], quoted in *CCC*, no. 1863).

—May 2001

## Consecration Intention

Question: I am a seminarian working as a sacristan in a parish. One of my tasks is to purify communion plates and instruments after Mass. The pastor has rebuked me for being overly scrupulous about this. He said his intention at the consecration is "not to consecrate particles", therefore they do not contain the Body of Christ, and there is no need to be fastidious. Is this intention licit?

Answer: Is it licit? No. Is it even possible? I don't think so. This "intention" is so novel that I cannot find a reference to it in any of the conventional textbooks of moral theology.

All the approved authors have some treatment of the essential matter and the essential form of the sacrament of the Holy Eucharist. The essential matter here of bread (i.e., bread made from wheat, mixed with water, baked with the application of heat, and substantially uncorrupted [cf. can. 924, §2]) is not at issue here.

Also, the correct form, i.e., the words of institution or consecration, seems not to be at issue here. Rather, it is the intention of this individual priest who confects the Eucharist with this novel, if not bizarre, intention.

Now, it is standard teaching and practice that to confect a sacrament an "actual intention" is best, but a "virtual intention" is sufficient. The intention must be to consecrate the material or at least do what the Church does. The extent to which the celebrant understands material to be included in his intention is specified by the word *this* in "This is my body."

Altar breads are to be clean and unbroken. The word *this* in the words of consecration refers to and is addressed to the host held in hand and the hosts in a ciborium or a pyx on the corporal. The whole host is consecrated intact; particles of it do not become unconsecrated if they fragment or when the consecrated host it broken (*fractio*). "Small particles remaining in the ciborium or pyx or on the corporal are considered to be consecrated." [4]

Since the whole intact host is consecrated, and, since it is impossible to know beforehand what, if any part, might fragment, it seems

---

[4] Nicholas Halligan, O.P., *The Sacraments and Their Celebration* (New York: Alba House, 1986), p. 69.

to me that this novel intention is simply empty if not impossible. It's like intending a "future condition", which is not an actual intention at all.

The Latin textbooks speak of three kinds of intention in their treatment of "the voluntary" or "human acts". These are acts that proceed from the will with a knowledge of the end. The first two (actual and virtual intentions) are sufficient to confer or confect a sacrament, whereas a "habitual intention" is sufficient to receive something (a sacrament) passively but not to confer or confect a sacrament. Some textbooks refer to an "interpretative" intention, which is not an intention but a hypothetical and not a voluntary act—there is no reality to it. Perhaps it is this last hypothetical that best describes the so called "intention" that your letter reports.

From another point of view, the practice of the Church is neither silent nor forgetful about eucharistic fragments and what to do about them.

*The General Instruction of the Roman Missal* (1970) presents directive rubrics on "Purifications":

> If a fragment of the host adheres to his fingers, especially after the breaking of the bread or the communion of the people, the priest cleanses his fingers over the paten and, if necessary, washes them. He also gathers any fragments, which may fall outside the paten. (no. 237)
>
> The vessels are washed by the priest or deacon or acolyte after the communion or after Mass, if possible at a side table. The chalice is washed with wine and water, or with water only, which is then drunk by the priest or deacon. The paten is ordinarily wiped with the purificator. (no. 238)

The new *General Instruction of the Roman Missal* (2001; published in English 2003) has the same normative directives (cf. nos. 278, 279).

Since the Church has a remote and recent teaching and practice to solve this question, it seems to me that a novel and unnecessary "intention" might create a problem rather than solve it. Scrupulosity is to be avoided, but intentions that can't be intended surely deserve sober and scrupulous review and recall.

—November 2003

# 25

# Other Sacraments

## Anointing before Execution

Question: The media reported that Timothy McVeigh received the "last rites of the Church" from a priest chaplain before his execution. Would not Penance be the appropriate sacrament and not anointing of the sick?

Answer: I have no more facts available to me than the same media reports that puzzled me also when I read them. I believe you are correct. As I understand the case, this is confused sacramental practice and contrary to received teaching and practice.

The *Rite of Anointing* (in universal use since January 1, 1974) has a section in the introduction on "The Subject of Anointing of the Sick" (nos. 8–15). Number 8 of the *Rite* specifies: "Those who are dangerously ill (*periculose aegro-tant*) due to sickness (*propter infirmitatem*) or old age (*senium*) receive this sacrament." The *Rite* here reflects precisely the teaching of Vatican Council II (*Sacrosanctam Concilium*, no. 73).

The present *Code of Canon Law* legislates the same point: "... who, having reached the age of reason, begins to be in danger by reason of illness or old age" (can. 1004, §1; cf. as well, the *Catechism of the Catholic Church*, no. 1514). If this sacrament is to take effect, the intention to receive it is already clearly required (can. 1006), whereas it is not to be conferred on those who obstinately persist in a manifestly grave sin (can. 1007).

The article in the *New Catholic Encyclopedia* on the "anointing of the sick" explains well what is required of the recipient of this sacrament:

> The subject of this sacrament must, of course, be baptized, have attained the use of reason, and be here and now sick. These conditions are all

necessary for the validity of the sacrament.... Illness, not danger of death, is an intrinsically necessary requirement in the subject of this Sacrament for its valid reception. Danger, even certainty, of death from a cause other than sickness or old age does not entitle one to receive this Sacrament.[1]

The commentary of the Canon Law Society of Great Britain and Ireland, *The Canon Law*, is clear and specific about this case. Among the conditions listed for administering this sacrament is the following: "(c) he or she must be in danger of death by reason of illness or old age. In danger of death from other reasons, e.g., before execution or battle, the sacrament is not to be administered."[2] The revised commentary of the Canon Law Society of America is silent on this point.[3]

The "approved authors" are unanimous and most often quite explicit that the "danger of death" has to be *internal* not *external*. For example, Marcellino Zalba writes that it is certainly required for validity that the subject of this sacrament be (a) baptized; (b) have or had the use of reason; (c) in danger of death *ex cause interna*—from which he explicitly excludes any *causa extrinseca*, namely, an execution of capital punishment or soldiers going into a dangerous battle.[4]

Hieronymus Noldin and Albert Schmitt make the same point that the illness or danger must be internal (*in ipso organismo exsistens*), but it is not valid to administer to soldiers before battle or *qui capitis damnatus est*.[5]

Joseph Aertnys, Cornelius Damen, and Jan Visser state the same teaching that the danger must be from illness, so this sacrament is not for the healthy (*sano corpore*) in face of external danger, specifically capital punishment (*capite mox plectendi*).[6] Henry Davis repeats the same traditional teaching: "Those who are not sick cannot validly receive this Sacrament. Therefore, it may not be administered to soldiers going

---

[1] "Anointing of the Sick", *New Catholic Encyclopedia*, vol. 1 (New York: McGraw-Hill, 1967), p. 573.

[2] *The Canon Law: Letter & Spirit* (Collegeville, Minn.: Liturgical Press, 1995), p. 546.

[3] Cf. *New Commentary on the Code of Canon Law* (New York/Mahwah: Paulist Press, 2000), pp. 1187–91.

[4] Marcellino Zalba, *Theologiae Moralis Compendium*, vol. 2 (Madrid, 1958), pp. 692–93, n. 1203, 1.

[5] H. Noldin, A. Schmitt, and G. Heinzel, *Summa Theologiae Moralis*, vol. 3, 33rd ed. (Rauch, 1962), p. 382, n. 444.

[6] Joseph Aertnys, Cornelius Damen, and Jan Visser, C.Ss.R., *Theologia Moralis*, vol. 4 (Rome: Marietti, 1968), p. 17, n. 12.

into battle, condemned criminals, travellers on a dangerous journey, etc." [7]

In a comprehensive and closely reasoned canonical dissertation, "The Recipient of Extreme Unction", Charles G. Renati presents the conventional points cited above. Renati summarizes:

> Bodily illness is, without doubt, a requirement *de necessitate sacramenti* in the recipient of Extreme Unction. Remove this condition and it is difficult to find a distinctive purpose for this sacrament. One who is healthy and in serious sin has the Sacrament of Penance, as does also a sick person as long as he can manifest his sinfulness and sorrow.
>
> For the Christian in danger of death there is the "last and indispensable" sacrament, Viaticum, which is the consummation of the whole Christian life, the sacrament that prepares man for his journey to Christ and the vision of God. The sacrament for those in danger of death is not the anointing, but Viaticum, as the I Council of Nicea (325) taught over sixteen hundred years ago. [8]

Renati continues:

> The particular contingency in the Christian life for which Extreme Unction was instituted is not primarily dying or of death. If it were, one would rightly expect it to be conferred on all who are in danger of death, no matter what the cause, whereas in fact it is refused to those who are in danger of death if they are not sick. Sickness is an indispensable condition for the anointing. (pp. 8–9)

To the very case at issue, Renati correctly notes:

> Convicts about to be executed, soldiers ready to plunge into an odds-against-survival battle, passengers on sinking ships, people trapped in a burning building, or persons about to risk their lives in an effort to save someone else from certain death—none of these can be anointed because they are not sick, and thus they do not fit into the class described by St. James as the beneficiaries of this sacrament—"Is any among you sick?" (p. 12)

Since Renati's dissertation was written before Vatican Council II (1962–1965), he uses the then-correct terminology "extreme

---

[7] Henry Davis, S.J., *Moral and Pastoral Theology*, vol. 4, 8th ed. (London, New York: Sheed and Ward, 1959), p. 7.

[8] Charles G. Renati, *The Recipient of Extreme Unction* (Washington, D.C.: Catholic University of America, 1961), pp. 7–8. For canon 13 of Nicea, cf. *Decrees of the Ecumenical Councils*, vol. 1: *Nicaea I–Lateran*, ed. Norman P. Tanner (London, Washington, D.C.: Sheed & Ward and Georgetown University Press, 1990), p. 12.

unction", but if you substitute the current correct description "anointing", his theological reasoning is quite correct and accords perfectly with what the Council taught (*Sacrosanctum Concilium*, no. 73), what the new *Rite of Anointing* (no. 8) prescribes, what the *Code* (can. 1004, §1) legislates, and what the *Catechism* (no. 1514) teaches.

Many, indeed all, of the final moments and intentions of Timothy McVeigh are completely unknown to me. If, in fact, he "made his peace with God", that would be through the worthy reception of the sacrament of Penance—a sacrament apparently made available to him by the prison chaplain. However, if as the press reported it—he received the "last rites of the Church"—that suggests to me that both McVeigh and the chaplain caused confusion to the very end.

As I understand it, he was not a proper recipient of the anointing of the sick, and, the wide media coverage (if accurate) distorts the teaching of the Council, the Rite, the *Code*, and the *Catechism*. Surely, God wishes all men to be saved, but none will be saved against their will, and no one will be helped by confusing and confounding the sacramental order of the Church.

—October 2001

## Catholic Freemason Funeral

Question: A prominent parishioner was also a prominent Mason. Because of some scandal and publicity, the pastor did ask this parishioner to cease being an extraordinary minister of the Eucharist. Yet, at the same man's Catholic funeral, Masons in some of their regalia were pallbearers and took part in the Mass. When asked, one of the priests said that all "the old rules have changed" and that even some bishops were Masons. What gives?

Answer: Some "old rules" have changed, but some "new rules" have replaced them. The old 1917 *Code of Canon Law* did specifically mention Masonic membership and penalized membership in groups that "plot against the Church" ("*contra Ecclesiam ... machinatur*", can. 2335).

As a matter of style and procedure, the present 1983 *Code* did not specifically name groups, sects, or associations that plot against the Church (*"contra Ecclesiam machinatur"*, can. 1374).

The present *Code* became effective on November 27, 1983, but the very day before the new *Code* went into effect, the Congregation for the Doctrine of the Faith issued a declaration which said in part:

> Therefore the Church's negative position on Masonic associations remains unchanged since their principles have always been regarded as irreconcilable with the doctrine of the Church and therefore membership in them remains forbidden. The faithful who enroll in Masonic associations are in a state of grave sin and may not receive Holy Communion. (*Declaration on Masonic Associations*, November 26, 1983)

Furthermore, the CDF declaration states that local ecclesiastical authorities do not have the faculty to pronounce a judgment that diminishes or lessens this declaration.

Thus, as to specifics, no bishop, priest, or deacon can be a Mason without penalty. Such was the case under the old *Code*, and the same is true of the new *Code*.

Next, given the notoriety you describe, it seems to me that the pastor's first action was eminently correct. When he asked that parishioner to cease being an extraordinary minister of the Eucharist, this makes perfect sense. Certainly, ministers of the Church, even extraordinary ones, should be people whose integrity of life conforms clearly with the authentic life of the Church they serve.

Lastly, I find the funeral service in the same parish with Masonic pallbearers and Masonic regalia completely unaccountable, even unbelievable. This simply makes no sense in a Catholic service in a Catholic church and should *never* be permitted. Since it is a public service, and given that regalia are public signs, this must be considered a form of scandal.

Oddly, Masonic Lodges are pretty clear on this. After a religious service, if any, the Lodge takes charge of graveside ceremonies. All the pallbearers must be Masons, who typically wear their lambskin aprons, white gloves, and high hats. Neither the Church nor any other organization may participate in the Masonic service. If this is so, and since it is so, our insistence on only Catholic rites in a Catholic service is a simple matter of reciprocity and consistency.

An excellent resource concerning all things Masonic and Catholic is William J. Whalen's updated *Christianity and American Freemasonry* recently published by Ignatius Press.[9] This book is a remarkable source of sober information and balanced judgment.

—May 1999

## Cremation and Burial of a Fetus or Bodily Member

Question: Is it permissible to cremate a fetus or bodily member? I do not find any directive on this in the new *Ethical and Religious Directives*.

Answer: Among a number of ambiguities and omissions in the new NCCB *Ethical and Religious Directives*, there is no mention of burying and/or cremation of a fetus or bodily member. Why this was omitted, I do not know.

However, there was such a directive in the NCCB 1971 *Ethical and Religious Directives*. It read: "If there is reasonable cause present for not burying a fetus or member of the human body, these may be cremated in a manner consonant with the dignity of the deceased human body" (no. 43). Probably the best commentary on this old directive is that of Monsignor Orville Griese in his book, *Catholic Identity in Health Care*.[10]

The Church prefers that her faithful members including fetuses and amputated limbs be buried in a Catholic cemetery or other suitable place. Provided that the reason for cremation is not an anti-religious one, the Church is not opposed to cremation.[11]

As Griese points out, the Church has always insisted on the dignity of every human individual from the moment of conception—most recently and emphatically in John Paul II's *Evangelium Vitae*, number 60.

If at all possible, stillborns and dead fetuses should be buried in a Catholic cemetery, especially if they have been baptized. The parents

---

[9] William J. Whalen, *Christianity and American Freemasonry*, 3rd ed. (San Francisco: Ignatius Press, 1998).

[10] Msgr. Orville N. Griese, *Catholic Identity in Health Care* (Braintree, Mass.: Pope John Center, 1987), pp. 149–51.

[11] CDF, "Letter to the Bishop of Cleveland regarding the Questions Proposed on the Cremation of Foetuses and Members of the Human Body" (Mar. 7, 1967).

and pastor can make the arrangements with a minimum of expense and ceremony. In the case of a stillborn or newborn infant who dies shortly after birth, the *Order of Christian Funerals* (1989), number 318, suggests that the "Rite of Final Commendation for an Infant" may be used in those cases.

Cremation, however, is allowed in earlier cases if circumstances are such that a burial would place a heavy burden on the family, or if some danger of contagion or health hazard is present. Where civil law allows it and parents give permission, a fetus may be retained for autopsy or even research or teaching purposes—quite apart from the experimentation or exploitation condemned in *Evangelium Vitae*, number 63. In these cases, cremation of the remains would be the more hygienic procedure. The ashes should be buried in a Catholic cemetery, and most cemeteries have special plots for such burials.

With regard to major body parts, i.e., parts that retain human characteristics after amputation (e.g., arms, legs, feet, hands, etc.) cremation is most often the only reasonable solution. Large hospitals usually have refrigerated storage facilities so that a preferred option for a mass burial from time to time can be scheduled. If the option is for cremation, it should be done as a separate cremation for human remains *only*. It would be an offense to human dignity to cremate such remains along with the usual cargo of hospital refuse (bandages, equipment, pathology tissues, etc.). The ashes of such special cremations should also be buried in a reserved cemetery plot.[12]

—April 1996

---

[12] Griese, *Catholic Identity in Health Care*, p. 150.

# 26

# Priestly Life

## Obligation to Recite the Divine Office

Question: Several younger priests tell me that the Liturgy of the Hours is a "monastic" prayer. Further, they say they were taught in the seminary that the Office is highly "appropriate" when priests are gathered in common at or near the actual liturgical hour. Is there no more obligation than appropriateness in common?

Answer: This question combines several and oft-repeated questions. I know what is taught in my own seminary—we do *not* teach that the Divine Office is "monastic" or that it is only "appropriate", i.e., merely a collective option (cf. *CCC*, nos. 1174–78).

For a correct and scholarly history and development of the Liturgy of the Hours, one should confer the magisterial work, *The Church at Prayer*, especially the third section, "The Liturgy of the Hours", by Aimé Martimort.[1]

It was my unscientific view that this masterly work of Martimort served pretty much as a textbook in most seminaries. Clearly, your question and many others indicate that this is not the case; and if it is required reading, it is also clear that some do not understand and/or remember what they read.

To say that the Office is monastic is to presume that the Church had no regular prayer patterns before the invention of monasteries. Such an assertion indicates an ignorance of the time of Christ, the life of Christ, the apostolic community, and Church life up to and through

---

[1] Aimé G. Martimort, Irénée H. Dalmais, O.P., and Pierre Jounel, *Liturgy and Time*, vol. 4 of *The Church at Prayer* (Collegeville, Minn.: Liturgical Press, 1986), esp. sect. 3, "The Liturgy of the Hours", pp. 151–275.

the third century. Communal hours of prayer in the fourth and fifth centuries were not the beginning of Christian prayer patterns, but one notable form of it. Martimort describes well the richness and diversity of Christian prayer life and the goal of the Second Vatican Council: "truth of the hours".[2]

Confining this answer to the question of obligation, it is true to say that there is an obligation for clerics who so promise, but that obligation is nuanced since November 1, 1970 (Pope Paul VI, *Laudis Canticum*) in a way different from previous authentic instruction and interpretation.

The precise nature and bearing of the "mandate" of the Liturgy of the Hours is detailed in number 29 of the *General Instruction on the Liturgy of the Hours* by the Congregation for Divine Worship.[3]

Remotely, the virtue of fidelity—fidelity to our promised word—is at stake. In the ordination of deacons, after the instruction by the bishop and the commitment to celibacy, there follows an examination. The fourth question of this asks: "Are you resolved ... to fulfill faithfully the Liturgy of the Hours for the Church and for the whole world?" The candidate answers: "I am." Thus, this is a promise that every deacon aspiring to priesthood makes in the Latin Rite.

Next, in the context of required practices in the pursuit of holiness, the *Code of Canon Law* states the universal norm. Canon 276, section 2, number 3, states that priests and deacons aspiring to the priesthood "are obliged [*obligatione tenentur*] to fulfill the Liturgy of the Hours daily [*cotidie*] in accord with the proper and approved liturgical books". This obligation is repeated in canon 1174, section 1.

This "mandate" or "commission" to bishops, priests, and deacons aspiring to the priesthood is specified in the *General Instruction of the Liturgy of the Hours*, numbers 28 to 32, in particular number 29.

We are told that first importance is given to Morning and Evening Prayer, which should not be omitted "except for a *serious* reason". Next, that the Office of Readings is truly a celebration of the Word of God, and there is a daily duty of receiving the word of God into our lives. And lastly, "to celebrate the whole day more

[2] Ibid., pp. 157–78.

[3] For the text of this instruction, cf. vol. 1 (blue) of *Liturgy of the Hours*, the effective date of which for the USA was November 27, 1977.

perfectly" recite the Daytime Hour and Night Prayer to round off the whole "Work of God". It is clear from the "mandate" that there is an obligation "to recite the whole sequence of Hours each day", but it is also clear that there is a relative weighing of the parts (Hours), rather than a grave-light matter scale measured in arithmetical times and parts.

Clearly, Lauds and Vespers are not omitted except for a "serious reason". And a lesser reason would justify the omission of the Office of Readings, the Daytime Hour, or Night Prayer. John Lynch notes, I think correctly, in his commentary: "The Instruction leaves to the discretion of the minister the judgment of justifying reasons." [4]

There is, of course, the danger of self-deception in this kind of decision, but there are as well reasons and causes that excuse from other positive precepts of Church law. Priests experienced in pastoral practice are often asked their opinion about excusing causes; they might compare properly the standard they ask of others with the standard they live themselves. Nevertheless, calling this "monastic", or insisting on group presence, or some narrow correspondence with true sun time are not, objectively, serious reasons.

Two recent documents of the Holy See continue the reform of Vatican Council II about the place and necessity of the "truth of the hours" in the life of every priest. Pope John Paul II in his post-synodal exhortation, *Pastores Dabo Vobis* (March 25, 1992) details an essential element of priestly formation—a prayerful and meditated reading of the Word of God (no. 47). If the priest is to be a "teacher of prayer", he must be trained in the school of prayer and continue in it. The highpoint of Christian prayer is the Eucharist and the Liturgy of the Hours, necessary for the formation of every Christian, and in particular every priest (no. 48).

The common sense warning of Saint Charles Borromeo needs to be observed not excused: Are you in the care of souls? Then don't neglect your own. "My brothers, do not forget that there is nothing so necessary to all churchmen than the meditation which precedes, accompanies and follows all our actions: I will sing, says the prophet, and I will meditate (cf. Ps 100:1)" (*Pastores Dabo Vobis*, no. 72).

---

[4] Fr. John E. Lynch, "The Obligations and Rights of Clerics", in *The Code of Canon Law: A Text and Commentary*, ed. James A. Coriden, Thomas J. Green, and Donald E. Heintschel (New York: Paulist Press, 1985), p. 208.

Lastly, the *Directory on the Ministry and Life of Priests* (January 31, 1994) of the Congregation for the Clergy mentions that the priest must program his life to include prayer, including "the complete and fervent celebration of the liturgy of the hours on a daily basis" (no. 39).

The mind of the Church is clear in this regard. Unfortunately those who dismiss or wrongly self-excuse from this obligation are not thinking with the Church, reading with the Church, or, most importantly, praying with the Church.

—October 1994

## Enneagram in Spiritual Direction

Question: I have read of many books, conferences, and workshops about the use of the Enneagram. Now, it seems to be the rage in spiritual direction for some. Is this really compatible with Catholic doctrine and practice?

Answer: I suspect that I have seen the same ads and notices; indeed, a visit to any bookstore, with a quick look at the religion section, would indicate that the Enneagram movement has gone big time.

First, what is the Enneagram? The term *"Enneagram"* is a compound of the Greek word *"ennea,"* meaning "nine", and the suffix *"gram"*, meaning "a drawing". It is a geometric figure of lines that touch or cross. The Enneagram is a circular diagram on which nine personality types are systematically represented at nine equidistant points on the circumference. Lines connect various points to each other.

It is this diagram itself which is the Enneagram, and it is used as a psychological tool of self-discovery. Each of the nine personality types (numbered 1 through 9) is described negatively by some compulsion, fixation, or basic driving force to avoid something unpleasant. This compulsion is seen as one's basic psychological orientation. To discover your number, you have to realize what you seek to avoid, what your compulsion is.

Most Enneagram books have many circular charts, with the "avoidance chart" as usually the most significant, but there are also charts to depict time consciousness, or dominant passions. There are even symbolic animal charts—"totems" as they are called. Here, one's compulsion is given pictorial representation: ones, who are perfectionists, are like terriers "who snap at people's heels"; twos, who are helpers, are like cats, "affectionate but with an air of independence"; eights and nines do not fare so well—they are like rhinos and elephants, respectively; some take the animal pictorials quite seriously; others never mention them.

The origins of the Enneagram are admitted by all—it comes from the oral tradition of Sufi masters. Sufism is the mysticism of Islam. If you want to check it out in your library, look first under "Occult Sciences".

Consider personality typologies first. Most people can probably have fun with an Enneagram because most of us enjoy getting a little quick glance at ourselves.

Personality typing is not new. Some of the ancients theorized about the four temperaments of mankind; contemporary Myers-Briggs typology posits at least eight (maybe 16) personality types; various systems all have their advocates in some schools of clinical psychology: MMPI (mental health categories); Taylor-Johnson (interpersonal interaction), and Hall-Tonna Inventory (values perspective). The basic premise of the Enneagram is that there are nine and only nine personality types; this is simply given as true, it is nowhere demonstrated as proven.

To my knowledge, there are no scientific studies to determine whether Enneagram theory can be integrated with other typologies, but that would not really bother some advocates one way or the other. In most cases, much more is claimed than just sorting out psychological understanding. For example, on the cover of the book *What's My Type?* readers are enticed to "use the Enneagram" in order to "identify the secret promise of your personality type; break out of your self-defeating patterns; and transform your weaknesses into unimagined strengths".[5] The more you read about it, the more it begins to resemble a college-educated horoscope, and that is not compatible with Catholic doctrine or practice.

---

[5] Kathleen Hurley and Theodore Dobson, *What's My Type?* (San Francisco: Harper Collins, 1991).

Delving into Sufi sources is well beyond this question-answer format, but the more one runs into claims of an "upward spiral of self-transformation", the further we seem to be *away* from Christianity and the more we get involved *in* Neoplatonism and Gnosticism.

As a tool for spiritual direction, it seems to me most deficient, even dangerous. The Enneagram is really built on a theology(?)—perhaps ideology—of self-renewal and self-regeneration that is a far cry from (perhaps contradiction of) the Gospel teaching: "Truly, truly, I say to you, unless a grain of wheat falls into the earth and dies, it remains alone; but if it dies, it bears much fruit" (Jn 12:24).

Dorothy G. Ranaghan, in an extended pamphlet, "A Closer Look at the Enneagram", makes these points among others: philosophically and logically the Enneagram remains tied to Sufism; has differing views of holiness and morality; and the goals of Christian life and prayer life are already rooted in the immensely diverse riches of the Christian heritage.[6] It's somewhat like the transplant problem: medicine is capable of stitching almost any organ from anybody in almost any other body, but the stitching or patch-on is not the real problem—immunological rejection is always present and relentless.

Further, on October 15, 1989, the Congregation for the Doctrine of the Faith issued a letter to Catholic bishops, "On Some Aspects of Christian Meditation". As the first footnote of that letter explains, the "eastern methods" to which it refers are those "inspired by Hinduism and Buddhism, such as 'Zen', 'Transcendental Meditation' or 'Yoga'". But, the footnote continues that the document is "intended to serve as a reference point not just for this problem, but also, in a more general way, for the different forms of prayer practiced nowadays in ecclesial organizations, particularly in associations, movements and groups."

The same document, "On Christian Meditation", number 12, cites a standard taught by Pope John Paul II (Homily, November 1, 1982) that pertains here: "Any method of prayer is valid insofar as it is inspired by Christ and leads to Christ who is the Way, the Truth and the Life" (cf. Jn 14:6). The Enneagram is not The Way, nor is it The Truth and on those bases not truly compatible with—much less essential to—The Life in Christ.

—March 1993

[6] Dorothy G. Ranaghan, "A Closer Look at the Enneagram" (South Bend, Ind.: Greenlawn Press, 1989).

## Priestly Recreation

Question: Isn't it a scandal that so many priests play so much golf?

Answer: Yes, if they play poorly; no, if they play well. I have no idea how many play or how much. However, golf is very much like moral theology—the ball goes where you hit it. You can cry conscience, or impediments (ignorance, force, fear, concupiscence), but the ball still goes where you hit it.

Unlike a society drowning in moral relativism, when you hit the ball out of bounds, you are out of bounds and must pay penalty. Your fundamental option may be the middle of the fairway or the middle of the green, but even the most convinced fundamental opticians must hit it there not just wish it there.

You must also pay close attention to nature and reality. Measured yardage is always numerically the same—but an uphill green and a downhill one don't play the same way. You must also figure out which way the wind is blowing; it can help you or hurt you. Figuring out which way the wind is blowing is unfortunately a highly perfected skill for ambitious Church bureaucrats.

Social justice advocates will be glad to know that the handicap system was really the first and oldest affirmative action system. Unsteady golfers love it; steady golfers grin and bear it because they have to. Actually, a priest's handicap may answer your question. If his handicap is in the mid- or upper 20s, he does not play enough; if the handicap is single digit (under 10), he plays too much golf. Traditionalists will also be glad to know that *par* is a Latin word.

—February 1997

## Required Psychiatric Treatment

Question: This is a composite question. Some priests have written or contacted me for canonical advice about their rights when, apart from any criminal or immoral behavior, they are required by their bishop or religious superior to undergo inappropriate testing and even mandated residence in a psychiatric institute or hospital. Is this moral?

Answer: I am not a canon lawyer and possess no expertise in that subject except what is available to all, i.e., reading the *Code of Canon Law* and reliable commentaries on it.

Sadly, we all know of some high-profile cases where individual priests and religious have broken their promised vows, broken the commandments of God, and have caused great harm to victims and to the Church. Some think that the media exaggerate these immoralities, but when you offer up sad and juicy ammunition in the public forum, it is not unreasonable to expect their torrid publication.

I presume every adult has learned to make distinctions. The failure of *some* is not the condemnation of all; the moral failures of *some* are no reason to say there are no moral standards for all. These are, after all, *moral failures*.

However, apart from immoral and criminal acts (which should be reported to appropriate civil authorities), another type of squeeze play is now questioned. Some priests who find themselves in disfavor by a superior are required, under threat of loss of faculties or non-assignment, to enter some treatment program or institute to be re-wired with politically correct thinking. This, I believe, is wrong and only a few steps from a clerical "gulag".

The Catholic Medical Association has published a "Position Paper" concerning psychiatric care of the clergy.[7] The "Position Paper" makes eight valid and common sense points, I wish to highlight just a few.

Psychiatry is a medical specialty dedicated to the treatment of individuals with mental disorders. It should not be used as a means to punish or isolate a priest (or anyone) in disfavor by someone else (no. 1).

Optimal treatment of a patient requires a confidential relationship between the physician and patient. A priest deserves the same dignity and respect as a lay patient. Only generic data should be provided to an employer, information confined to fitness to work, date of return, restrictions at work, and whether follow-up care is advised (no. 2).

Privileged communication excludes criminal behavior such as sexual battery, molesting, or other acts. This should be reported to appropriate civil authorities as soon as practical (no. 3).

The final point (no. 8) of the "Position Paper" deserves careful attention:

---

[7] Cf. Catholic Medical Association, "Position Paper", *Linacre Quarterly* 67, no. 1 (Feb. 2000): 56–58.

Catholic psychiatric hospitals should operate in accordance with the philosophy of the teachings of the Church. The Church teaches that homosexuality is morally wrong and the desire for homosexual acts is a disorder. We agree with this teaching. Priests who are patients that agree with this Church teaching should not be treated adversely and labeled as homophobic. We dispute the opinion of the American Psychiatric Association (APA) and similar groups that, on the basis of an opinion poll of some of their members, no longer see homosexuality as a disorder. Although the APA view may appear popular, as it has been promoted by the entertainment industry and the media, it has no scientific validity. The APA view has been detrimental and confusing to adults and youth, and contributed significantly to the degradation of the moral values of our culture. We choose to support groups called *Courage* and *Encourage* that help homosexuals lead chaste lives and offer help to their families. The groups were developed by the Reverend John F. Harvey, O.S.F.S., enlightened author of the book *The Truth about Homosexuality* (1996).

—June 2000

## Professional Secrecy

**Question:** *Time* magazine ran the article "New Rules for Keeping Secrets", alleging that priests and lawyers have made it easier to speak out. A priest in the story revealed in court what someone had told him in confidence. Is a priest free to do this?

**Answer:** My first response is simply "No!" Very often, I attribute confusion to confused reporting, but in this instance it is what the priest himself reported of himself that caused confusion, and I suspect some scandal.

In capsule form, the case was this: Some thirteen years ago, a Bronx resident asked a priest friend to visit him at home—he told the priest he felt terrible because two of his friends were tried and convicted for the 1987 murder of José Antonio Rivera, which they did not do. Allegedly, he told the priest in 1989 that he himself had murdered Rivera. The priest told him then to turn himself in, which he began to do by saying the same to his Legal Aid lawyer, who gave different advice.

Now, in July 2001 federal court testimony, the priest revealed in court what Jesus Fornes (since deceased) had first revealed to him.

To outline an adequate response, two canonical realities must be acknowledged and observed. *First*, canon 983, section 1, states clearly that the sacramental seal of confession is inviolable—it is a crime for the confessor to betray that trust by word or any other way for any reason. *Second*, canon 984, section 1, concerns what is called "prohibited use of knowledge", i.e., a confessor is absolutely forbidden to use knowledge acquired from confession when it might harm the penitent. These are the settled law and the certain moral practice of the Church.

At first, some media reports raised a related but not identical question. Namely, what are the limits and/or limited exceptions not of "confessional" secrecy but of "professional" secrecy? Thus, the question is not the status of natural or promised secrets, but rather what is called the "professional secret" one that rests on the *condition* one will keep it secret. The "professional secret" is the most binding (apart from the confessional secret that admits of no exceptions) as the *Catechism* points out and explains (no. 2491).

In modern society, the most important type of "professional secret" involves physicians, lawyers, psychiatrists, social workers, and priests counseling *extra tribunal*, i.e., priest counselor or confidant, apart from or outside the tribunal of Penance.

The moral textbooks do note that professional secrets can admit of disclosure but only by exception, and then, only under the most stringent conditions, (e.g., to avert *grave* danger to the common good; to avert serious and unjust harm to innocent third parties; or to avert *grave* danger to the one who reveals); thus, not just some personal danger but only grave danger. Note as well, the *Catechism* refers to cases only of "very grave harm" (no. 2491).

Apart from the professional codes and requirements of the other professions, the priest outside of confession raises some peculiar and exquisite problems that demand careful adherence. An older but thoroughly reliable treatment of this subject can be found in Robert Regan's Catholic University dissertation: *The Moral Principles Governing Professional Secrecy*.

Father Regan correctly notes, "that the priest, entirely apart from the sacrament of Penance, is the recipient of confidences which must be rigorously guarded, ... the obligation of extra-sacramental secrecy pertains to those confidential matters entrusted to him *by reason of his sacred ministry (ratione sacri ministerii)*".[8]

The author continues:

> The priest has the serious moral obligation to preserve inviolate the secrets of those persons who confide in him by reason of his sacred ministry. This duty of secrecy is owed by the priest both to the person who confides in him (in commutative justice) and to society (in legal justice).
>
> The duty to the person seeking help takes the form of an onerous contract, or at least that of a quasi-contract, implicitly entered upon by the assumption of the confidential relationship. The revelation or other use of such secret knowledge by the priest contrary to the reasonable will of the client is a sin, grave or light, depending on the nature of the matter revealed or used, against both commutative and legal justice.[9]

It seems to me a fair statement that the basic assumption, among our Catholic people, is that what you tell a priest in confidence goes no further. Whether people are at all aware of the difference between confessional secrecy and professional secrecy or aware of some text-book limits and possible exceptions to professional secrecy does not strike me as all that relevant. Our people presume that what they say in confidence to a priest goes no further—period!

Thus, I teach seminarians that they are not free to reveal these extra-sacramental secrets. In a given case of very serious or very grave harm to the common good, they must find some way or pressure to move the person to take it out of this privileged forum and tell someone else who is free to act on it or with it.

In the case at hand, it seems to me that that was the first proper response of the priest involved who told the man to tell his Legal Aid lawyer who, in turn, approached the sentencing judge apparently to no avail. Lawyers, by license and profession, are all officers of the court and have detailed responsibilities in this regard. In my judgment, what the priest first did thirteen years ago was correct; what he did recently was not correct, and he should have done and said no more.

Unfortunately and catastrophically, first media reports of the priest's recent appearance in federal court have the priest saying that after the

[8] Robert E. Regan, *The Moral Principles Governing Professional Secrecy* (Washington, D.C.: Catholic University of America, 1941), p. 172.

[9] Ibid., p. 173.

long, heart-to-heart conversation, "Father Towle said, he granted Mr.
Fornes absolution for his sins at the end of their meeting." [10] Sub-
sequently, the same priest describes his courtroom testimony as "I was
repeating—not revealing—what Jesus Fornes had stated." [11]

Whatever the distinction between professional and confessional secrecy,
the mention and the fact of *sacramental absolution* here changes everything and complicates things both morally and canonically.

I suspect that almost every priest has, at one time, had a long conversation with someone which was concluded with absolution. In that
case, the whole prior conversation is privileged and under the seal of
confession. It is then no longer a debatable possible exception of professional secrecy but instead a violation of confessional secrecy—a violation that is morally wrong and carries a canonical penalty.

The *Time Magazine* byline is, I think, misleading—there are no "New
Rules for Keeping Secrets"; [12] there is, rather, the old rule, the good
old rule: if you want to keep a secret don't tell anyone.

There are pressures, sometimes great personal and civic pressures, to
reveal professional secrets. Priests, I think, should decline to do that
and always find some other way to move someone to disclose to someone else what the common good might demand where actual conditions truly require that. Confessional secrets simply and strictly admit
of no revelation: "by word or any other way for any reason".

—November 2001

## Ordaining Homosexuals

Question: I enclose an editorial from *America* magazine on ordaining homosexuals. Do you have an opinion?

Answer: I do, and my opinion is the opposite. For the fall semester
2003, *America* magazine has offered a continuing course on "Ordination and Same Sex Attraction".

[10] Jim Dwyer, "In Court, a Priest Reveals a Secret He Carried for 12 Years", *New York
Times*, July 17, 2001, p. B-4.
[11] Jim Dwyer, "Testimony of Priest and Lawyer Frees Man Jailed for '87 Murder", *New
York Times*, July 25, 2001, p. B-3.
[12] Adam Cohen, "New Rules for Keeping Secrets", Aug. 12, 2001.

The opening lecture was two basic opposites. Arguing that the best and safest course is not to ordain homosexuals was the Reverend Andrew R. Baker of the Congregation of Bishops in Rome. Arguing "Yes, Gay Men Should be Ordained" was Bishop Thomas J. Gumbleton, Auxiliary Bishop of Detroit.[13] A weekly series of ferocious "letters to the editor" against the Baker position followed.[14] Name-calling was not kept to a minimum: "homophobic", "fear-ridden", "unscientific", etc. Perhaps the neatest oversimplification was that of Francis DeBernardo: "While Fr. Baker argues from law, theory and church documents, Bishop Gumbleton's evidence comes from the lived experience of people with whom he has met and spoken."[15] Thus, the sources of sound theology are simply trumped by "lived experience". Very experiential no doubt! Just how you establish a doctrinal or moral norm on that basis simply eludes me. Sociology, yes! Theology, no!

Next, the editors of *America* published their own editorial, "Ordaining Gay Men" concluding: "Preventing the ordination of gay men would deprive the church of many productive, hard-working and dedicated ministers and would, moreover, ignore the promptings of the Holy Spirit, who has called these men to holy orders."[16] No sacred source is cited to help us see that the Holy Spirit calls this "call"; we are simply told by the editors that this is so.

More ferocious "letters to the editor" continue from November 11 through December 9, with two notable exceptions: Kevin L. Flannery, S.J. (Nov. 18) and John M. McDermott, S.J. (Dec. 2). Next, two articles by faculty members of Weston Jesuit School of Theology, both of whom argue for accepting gays into the priesthood.[17] More "letters to the editor" follow from December 23, 2002, up to February 17, 2003.

In sum, the *America* short-course is a gay advocacy seminar cast largely in the terms and rhetoric of alleged "victimhood" and

---

[13] Cf. Andrew R. Baker, "Ordination and Same Sex Attraction", and Thomas J. Gumbleton, "Yes, Gay Men Should be Ordained", *America*, Sept. 30, 2002, pp. 7–13.

[14] See issues Oct. 7; Oct. 14; Oct. 21; Oct. 28; and Nov. 4, 2002.

[15] Francis DeBernardo, letter to the editor, *America*, Oct. 21, 2002, p. 29.

[16] The Editors, "Ordaining Gay Men", *America*, Nov. 11, 2002, p. 3.

[17] Jon Fuller, S.J., "On 'Straightening Out' Catholic Seminaries", and Edward Vacek, S.J., "Acting More Humanely: Accepting Gays into the Priesthood", *America*, Dec. 16, 2002, pp. 7–14.

"discrimination"—the usual special pleading of the gay civil rights movement.

But, we must attend to some realities of life and fact. First, no man has a "right" to be ordained. There is neither moral right nor any civil right to ordination. There are indeed standards in place, and these standards for suitability are to be judged by the proper bishop or competent major superior, which, among other things, include: "a good reputation", "moral probity", "proven virtue", and "other physical and psychological qualities appropriate to the order to be received" (can. 1029). The tests of moral probity and proven virtue have to be determined person by person, as do the tests of psychological qualities—a subject on which authoritative sources have not been silent.

Next, the *Catechism of the Catholic Church* clearly teaches that homosexual acts are a "grave depravity" and are "intrinsically disordered" (no. 2357). Moreover, the homosexual tendency or inclination is itself "objectively disordered" (no. 2358). It is a contradiction to assert that an "objective disorder" is somehow a "gift" of God. If an objective disorder is a gift from God, the word *gift* has lost its meaning.

The context and background of the *America* seminar is the grave national scandal of clerical sexual abuse. In truth, the number of child molesters (pedophilia) is small, indeed tiny, in men of any orientation. But, the majority, indeed the superabundant majority, of clerical sexual abuses has involved young teenage boys (ephebophilia), and that properly points to homosexuality.

It is only factual common sense, not supposed intolerance nor alleged scapegoating, that suggests and requires that we not ordain men with that disordered inclination. Simple prudence demands that we not put at risk those with the highest risk inclination.

In judging the suitability of candidates for ordination to priesthood, the bishop or major superior should have moral certitude about the capability and suitability of a given candidate. All positive doubts should be resolved in favor of the Church, thus, not ordain candidates of doubtful suitability.

Real judgments involve real people and real circumstances, and it would thus be positively imprudent to ignore or to deny the presence of aggressive lobbies and advocacy groups that simply did not exist two or three decades ago. The pervasive fact of moral and cultural relativism actively promotes as "alternate" or "alternative" lifestyles what are not moral alternatives but indeed contradictions and denials of true Christian standards.

"Moral probity" and "proven virtue" are not singular qualities limited only to sexuality. Almost always, those who promote, tolerate, or minimize objective disorders are already partial dissenters, who came with built-in personal difficulty defending or proclaiming true moral doctrine with integrity and genuine conviction.

As above, authoritative Church sources have not been silent about psychological qualities. Back in 1961, the Congregation for Religious in a document specifically on the selection and training of candidates for Holy Orders stated: "Advancement to religious vows and ordination should be barred to those who are afflicted with evil tendencies to homosexuality or pederasty, since for them the common life and the priestly ministry would constitute serious dangers." [18]

Next, the Congregation for Catholic Education in its *Guide to Formation in Priestly Celibacy* (1974) directs: "In order to talk about a person as mature, his sexual instinct must have overcome two immature tendencies, narcissism and homosexuality, and must have arrived at heterosexuality. This is the first step in sexual development, but a second step is also necessary, namely, 'love' must be seen as a gift and not a form of selfishness." [19]

Again, the Congregation for Religious (now renamed) issued "Directives on Formation in Religious Institutes" (*Potissimum Institution*, February 2, 1990), which says those who are unable to overcome homosexual tendencies should be dismissed from religious life (no. 39).

In his magisterial exhortation, *Pastores Dabo Vobis*, specifically on the formation of priests in the present day, Pope John Paul II stresses human, spiritual, intellectual, and pastoral formation (nos. 43–59). Human formation is presented as the basis of all priestly formation (nos. 43–44). Over and over, the Pope insists on "affective maturity" that is the result of true and responsible love. This includes the "nuptial meaning" of the human body and the truth about human love and the sincere gift of self.

---

[18] Congregation for Religious, *Careful Selection and Training of Candidates for the States of Perfection and Sacred Orders*, in *Canon Law Digest*, vol. 5 (Milwaukee: Bruce Publishing, 1963), p. 471.

[19] Congregation for Catholic Education, *Guide to Formation in Priestly Celibacy* (Apr. 11, 1974), no. 2, in NCCB *Norms for Priestly Formation* (Jan. 21, 1994).

This "affective maturity" is essential for living celibacy (no. 43). While it is true that there is no explicit mention of homosexuality or homosexual tendency in *Pastores Dabo Vobis*, it is transparently obvious that an "objective disorder" is no part of "affective maturity".

And this is what the same Pope did recently teach to some Brazilian bishops on their *ad limina* visit: "It would be deplorable that, by a mistaken act of tolerance, he [the bishop] would ordain young men who are immature or who exhibit clear signs of affective disorders, who, as is sadly known, could cause serious confusion in the consciousness of the faithful with obvious harm for the whole Church."[20] The date (September 2002) of that statement clearly addresses the current scandals that afflict the contemporary Church.

One remark above might strike some as slightly gratuitous. That is, my assertion of a connection between the advocacy of the ordination of homosexuals and the likelihood of dissent from authentic Catholic moral teaching.

Here I cite not *America* magazine but *Theological Studies*, a quarterly published for the Society of Jesus in the U.S. In particular, confer a very extensive, "bibliographical overview" by the Reverend James Keenan, "The Open Debate: Moral Theology and the Lives of Gay and Lesbian Persons".[21] Clearly, a twenty-three-page review is a substantive contribution to that or any other journal. It presents what the author calls "critical reactions" to authentic Catholic teaching (i.e., dissenting authors), some specific moral investigations, and the experience of people whose lives or advocacy think the Church is wrong about the immorality of homosexual practice.

The author describes this as an "Open Debate", which, I suspect, it truly is in print. However, I would caution, theologically, that this is not an "open question", i.e., it is not theologically "freely disputed" in the sense that one can take either position and in correct conscience act upon either.

The lived experience and/or advocacy of all sorts of people, properly recorded, may well be genuine, but it is not for that reason normative, nor is it, properly, a theological source. The objective immorality of homosexual acts is clearly rooted in the sacred sources of sacred

[20] Pope John Paul II, "Address to the Bishops of Brazil's Eastern Region on Their 'Ad Limina' Visit", Sept. 5, 2002, no. 5.

[21] James F. Keenan, S.J., "The Open Debate: Moral Theology and the Lives of Gay and Lesbian Persons", *Theological Studies* 64, no. 1 (Mar. 2003): 127–50.

theology: the teaching of Holy Scripture is certain; the teaching of Sacred Tradition is unanimous; and the teaching of the Magisterium is both certain and perfectly consistent.

This moral teaching of the Church is both unchanged and unchangeable. It is not, theologically speaking, merely a freely disputed question.

—May 2003